"No other guid[...]
a pleasure to re[...]

". . . Excellently organized for the casual traveler who is looking for a mix of recreation and cultural insight."
Washington Post

★ ★ ★ ★ ★ (5-star rating) "Crisply written and remarkably personable. Cleverly organized so you can pluck out the minutest fact in a moment. Satisfyingly thorough."
Réalités

"The information they offer is up-to-date, crisply presented but far from exhaustive, the judgments knowledgeable but not opinionated."
New York Times

"The individual volumes are compact, the prose succinct, and the coverage up-to-date and knowledgeable . . . The format is portable and the index admirably detailed."
John Barkham Syndicate

". . . An abundance of excellent directions, diversions, and facts, including perspectives and getting-ready-to-go advice — succinct, detailed, and well organized in an easy-to-follow style."
Los Angeles Times

"They contain an amount of information that is truly staggering, besides being surprisingly current."
Detroit News

"These guides address themselves to the needs of the modern traveler demanding precise, qualitative information . . . Upbeat, slick, and well put together."
Dallas Morning News

". . . Attractive to look at, refreshingly easy to read, and generously packed with information." *Miami Herald*

"These guides are as good as any published, and much better than most." *Louisville* (Kentucky) *Times*

Stephen Birnbaum Travel Guides

Acapulco
Bahamas, and Turks & Caicos
Barcelona
Bermuda
Boston
Canada
Cancun, Cozumel & Isla Mujeres
Caribbean
Chicago
Disneyland
Eastern Europe
Europe
Europe for Business Travelers
Florence
France
Great Britain
Hawaii
Honolulu
Ireland
Italy
Ixtapa & Zihuatanejo
Las Vegas
London
Los Angeles
Mexico
Miami & Ft. Lauderdale
Montreal & Quebec City
New Orleans
New York
Paris
Portugal
Puerto Vallarta
Rome
San Francisco
South America
Spain
Toronto
United States
USA for Business Travelers
Vancouver
Venice
Walt Disney World
Washington, DC
Western Europe

CONTRIBUTING EDITORS

Elizabeth Carroll
Larry O'Conner

SYMBOLS
Gloria McKeown

MAPS
Mark Stein Studios

A Stephen Birnbaum Travel Guide

Birnbaum's VANCOUVER 1993

Alexandra Mayes Birnbaum
EDITOR

Lois Spritzer
EXECUTIVE EDITOR

Laura L. Brengelman
Managing Editor

Mary Callahan
Jill Kadetsky
Susan McClung
Beth Schlau
Dana Margaret Schwartz
Associate Editors

Gene Gold
Assistant Editor

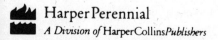

HarperPerennial
A Division of HarperCollins*Publishers*

To Stephen, who merely made all this possible.

BIRNBAUM'S VANCOUVER 1993. Copyright © 1993 by HarperCollins Publishers. All rights reserved. Printed in the United States of America. No part of this book may be used or reproduced in any manner whatsoever without written permission except in the case of brief quotations embodied in critical articles and reviews. For information address HarperCollins*Publishers,* 10 East 53rd Street, New York, NY 10022.

FIRST EDITION

ISSN 0749-2561 (Stephen Birnbaum Travel Guides)
ISSN 1061-5407 (Vancouver)
ISBN 0-06-278061-1 (pbk.)

93 94 95 96 97 CWI 10 9 8 7 6 5 4 3 2

Contents

GETTING READY TO GO

All the practical travel data you need to plan your vacation down to the final detail.

When and How to Go

Preparing

On the Road

THE CITY

A thorough, qualitative guide to Vancouver. Each section offers a comprehensive report on the city's most compelling attractions and amenities, designed to be used on the spot.

DIVERSIONS

A selective guide to more than a dozen active and/or cerebral vacation themes, including the best places to pursue them.

DIRECTIONS

Six of the most delightful walks through Vancouver.

A Word from the Editor

Quick, name a city whose gardens are among the most beautiful on the planet, where an offshore island is as English as the British Isles, and where you can down the most delicious dim sum this side of Hong Kong. Give up? It's Vancouver.

On more than one occasion, my husband Steve Birnbaum and I would arrange our trips to the Far East so that we could spend several days in Vancouver, just strolling through its lovely streets, stopping to sample the ample rewards of the city's restaurant boom. (Steve once set a record for consuming the greatest number of steamed dumplings west — and north — of the Mississippi at a Sunday brunch in the city's Chinatown. Even though I was busily occupied with sucking the remaining morsels out of my crab legs, I kept count.) We marveled at the richest of rhododendron groves, hyper blue and pink hydrangeas, and Beverly Hills–scale homes, many of them now owned by Hong Kong Chinese who've gotten a jump on "who knows what might happen in 1997." The aforementioned flora does, however, come at a price: old jokes that accurately reflect existing weather conditions.

"It only rains twice a year in Vancouver; for six months at a time."

"That's not a tan on my face, it's rust."

You get the drift. Yes, it rains a lot in Vancouver, normally followed by drizzle, downpour, and damp. Then there's fog and overcast. All this moisture has its salutary side: The brightness and size of the flowers and blooming shrubs in even the most modest front yard look as though they couldn't possibly be real. But when the sun does shine, it dazzles. A walk along Vancouver's frenetic and fabulous harbor on a clear day should dispel any doubts. So pack up a folding umbrella and get set to enjoy a combination of much of what is quintessentially Canadian: a hearty spirit and courtesy.

Vancouver offers visitors the civility of London seasoned with the salt of the Pacific Northwest. Totems and afternoon tea happily coexist. That this city satisfies cosmopolitan cravings with generous helpings of Upstairs/Downstairs country living and yet manages to offer a mixture of modern, manicured Canada with just the right touch of the Dominion's rugged past only adds to its charm.

My own evolution as a traveler (which happily continues) is mirrored by the evolution of our guidebook series. When we began our series of modern travel guides, we logically began with "area" books, attempting to publish guides that would include the widest possible number of attractive destinations. When the public seemed to accept our new way of delivering travel data, we added titles covering only a single country, and when these became popular we began our newest expansion phase, which centers on a group of books that deal with only a single city. Now we can not only highlight our favorite urban destinations, but really describe how to get the very most out of a visit.

Such treatment of travel information only mirrors an increasingly pervasive trend among travelers — the frequent return to a treasured travel spot. Once upon a time, even the most dedicated travelers would visit distant parts of the world no more than once in a lifetime — usually as part of that fabled Grand Tour. But greater numbers of would-be sojourners are now availing themselves of the opportunity to visit a favored part of the world over and over again.

So where once it was routine to say you'd "seen" a particular city or country after a very superficial, once-over-lightly encounter, the more perceptive travelers of today recognize that it's entirely possible to have only skimmed the surface of a specific travel destination even after having visited that place more than a dozen times. Similarly, repeated visits to a single site permit true exploration of special interests, whether they be sporting, artistic, or intellectual.

For those of us who now have spent the last several years working out the special system under which we present information in this series, the luxury of being able to devote nearly as much space as we'd like to just a single city is as close to paradise for guide writers and editors as any of us expects to come. But clearly this is not the first guide to the glories of Vancouver — one suspects that guides of one sort or another have existed since the day when English navigator and explorer Captain George Vancouver started charting the waters on the northwest coast of the continent — so a traveler might logically ask why a new one is suddenly necessary.

Our answer is that the nature of travel to Vancouver — and even of the travelers who now routinely make the trip — has changed dramatically of late. For the past 200 years or so, travel to even a town within our own country was considered an elaborate undertaking, one that required extensive advance planning. But with the advent of jet air travel in the late 1950s and of increased-capacity, wide-body aircraft during the late 1960s, travel to and around once distant destinations became extremely common. Attitudes as well as costs have changed significantly in the last couple of decades.

Obviously, any new guidebook to Vancouver must keep pace with and answer the real needs of today's travelers. That's why we've tried to create a guide that's specifically organized, written, and edited for the more demanding modern traveler, one for whom qualitative information is infinitely more desirable than mere quantities of unappraised data. We think that this book, along with all the other guides in our series, represents a new generation of travel guides — one that is especially responsive to modern needs and interests.

But I should, I think, apologize for at least one indulgence in this text that is baldly chauvinistic, and that is our reference to citizens of the US as "Americans." Strictly speaking, Canadian citizens are just as much residents of the North American continent as US citizens, and we apoligize for any slight our Canadian readers may feel about our having appropriated this terminology. It was done strictly in an effort to simplify the narrative, rather than an attempt to appropriate a common continental distinction.

For years, dating back as far as Herr Baedeker, travel guides have tended to be encyclopedic, seemingly much more concerned with demonstrating expertise in geography and history than with a real analysis of the sorts of things that actually concern a typical modern tourist. But today, when it is hardly necessary to tell a traveler where Vancouver is (in many cases, the traveler has been there nearly as often as the guidebook editors), it becomes the responsibility of those editors to provide new perspectives and to suggest new directions in order to make the guide genuinely valuable.

That's exactly what we've tried to do in this series. I think you'll notice a different, more contemporary tone to the text, as well as an organization and focus that are distinctive and more functional. And even a random reading of what follows will demonstrate a substantial departure from the standard guidebook orientation, for we've not only attempted to provide information of a more compelling sort, but we also have tried to present the data in a format that makes it particularly accessible.

Needless to say, it's difficult to decide just what to include in a guidebook of this size — and what to omit. Early on, we realized that giving up the encyclopedic approach precluded our listing every single route and restaurant, a realization that helped define our overall editorial focus. Similarly, when we discussed the possibility of presenting certain information in other than strict geographic order, we found that the new format enabled us to arrange data in a way that we feel best answers the questions travelers typically ask.

Large numbers of specific questions have provided the real editorial skeleton for this book. The volume of mail we regularly receive emphasizes that modern travelers want very precise information, so we've tried to organize our material in the most responsive way possible. Readers who want to know the best restaurants or the best place to buy Eskimo art in Vancouver will have no trouble extracting that data from this guide.

Travel guides are, understandably, reflections of personal taste, and putting one's name on a title page obviously puts one's preferences on the line. But I think I ought to amplify just what "personal" means. Like Steve, I don't believe in the sort of personal guidebook that's a palpable misrepresentation on its face. It is, for example, hardly possible for any single travel writer to visit thousands of restaurants (and nearly as many hotels) in any given year and provide accurate appraisals of each. And even if it were physically possible for one human being to survive such an itinerary, it would of necessity have to be done at a dead sprint, and the perceptions derived therefrom would probably be less valid than those of any other intelligent individual visiting the same establishments. It is, therefore, impossible (especially in a large, annually revised and updated guidebook *series* such as we offer) to have only one person provide all the data on the entire world.

I also happen to think that such individual orientation is of substantially less value to readers. Visiting a single hotel for just one night or eating one hasty meal in a random restaurant hardly equips anyone to provide appraisals that are of more than passing interest. No amount of doggedly alliterative or oppressively onomatopoeic text can camouflage a technique that is essentially specious. We have, therefore, chosen what I like to describe as the "thee and me" approach to restaurant and hotel evaluation and, to a somewhat more limited degree, to the sites and sights we have included in the other sections of our text. What this really reflects is a personal sampling tempered by intelligent counsel from informed local sources, and these additional friends-of-the-editor are almost always residents of the city and/or area about which they are consulted.

Despite the presence of several editors, writers, researchers, and local contributors, very precise editing and tailoring keep our text fiercely subjective. So what follows is the gospel according to Birnbaum, and it represents as much of our own taste and instincts as we can manage. It is probable, therefore, that if you like your cities stylish and prefer small hotels with personality to huge high-rise anonymities, we're likely to have a long and meaningful relationship. Readers with dissimilar tastes may be less enraptured.

I also should point out something about the person to whom this guidebook is directed. Above all, he or she is a "visitor." This means that such elements as restaurants have been specifically picked to provide the visitor with a representative, enlightening, stimulating, and above all pleasant experience. Since so many extraneous considerations can affect the reception and service accorded a regular restaurant patron, our choices can in no way be construed as an exhaustive guide to resident dining. We think we've listed all the best places, in various price ranges, but they were chosen with a visitor's enjoyment in mind.

Other evidence of how we've tried to tailor our text to reflect modern travel habits is most apparent in the section we call DIVERSIONS. Where once it was common for travelers to spend an urban visit in a determinedly passive state, the emphasis is far more active today. So we've organized every activity we could reasonably evaluate and arranged the material in a way that is especially accessible to activists of either athletic or cerebral bent. It is no longer necessary, therefore, to wade through a pound or two of superfluous prose just to find the very best salmon or dim sum in Vancouver or the best place to buy 19th-century English antiques in Victoria.

If there is a single thing that best characterizes the revolution in and evolution of current holiday habits, it is that most travelers now consider travel a right rather than a privilege. No longer is a family trip to the far corners of the world necessarily a once-in-a-lifetime thing; nor is the idea of visiting exotic, faraway places in the least worrisome. Travel today translates as the enthusiastic desire to sample all of the world's opportunities, to find that elusive quality of experience that is not only enriching but comfortable. For that reason, we've tried to make what follows not only helpful and enlightening, but the sort of welcome companion of which every traveler dreams.

Finally, I also should point out that every good travel guide is a living enterprise; that is, no part of this text is carved in stone. In our annual revisions, we refine, expand, and further hone all our material to serve your travel needs better. To this end, no contribution is of greater value to us than your personal reaction to what we have written, as well as information reflecting your own experiences while using the book. We earnestly and enthusiastically solicit your comments about this guide *and* your opinions and perceptions about places you have recently visited. In this way, we will be able to provide the most current information — including the actual experiences of recent travelers — and to make those experiences more readily available to others. Please write to us at 10 E. 53rd St., New York, NY 10022.

We sincerely hope to hear from you.

ALEXANDRA MAYES BIRNBAUM

How to Use This Guide

A great deal of care has gone into the special organization of this guidebook, and we believe it represents a real breakthrough in the presentation of travel material. Our aim is to create a new, more modern generation of travel books, and to make this guide the most useful and practical travel tool available today.

Our text is divided into four basic sections in order to present information in the best way on every possible aspect of a vacation to Vancouver. This organization itself should alert you to the vast and varied opportunities available, as well as indicate all the specific data necessary to plan a successful visit. You won't find much of the conventional "swaying palms and shimmering sands" text here; we've chosen instead to deliver more useful and practical information. Prospective itineraries tend to speak for themselves, and with so many diverse travel opportunities, we feel our main job is to highlight what's where and to provide basic information — how, when, where, how much, and what's best — to assist you in making the most intelligent choices possible.

Here is a brief summary of the four basic sections of this book, and what you can expect to find in each. We believe that you will find both your travel planning and en route enjoyment enhanced by having this book at your side.

GETTING READY TO GO

This mini-encyclopedia of practical travel facts is a sort of know-it-all companion with all the precise information necessary to create a successful trip to Vancouver. There are entries on more than 25 separate topics, including how to get where you're going, what preparations to make before leaving, what to expect, what your trip is likely to cost, and how to avoid prospective problems. The individual entries are specific, realistic, and, where appropriate, cost-oriented. Except where noted, all prices in this book are in US dollars.

We expect you to use this section most in the course of planning your trip, for its ideas and suggestions are intended to simplify this often confusing period. Entries are intentionally concise, in an effort to get to the meat of the matter with the least extraneous prose. These entries are augmented by extensive lists of specific sources from which to obtain even more specialized data, plus some suggestions for obtaining travel information on your own.

THE CITY

The individual report on Vancouver has been prepared with the assistance of researchers, contributors, professional journalists, and other experts who live in the city. Although useful at the planning stage, THE CITY is really designed to be taken along and used on the spot. The report offers a short-stay guide, including an essay introducing the city as a historic entity and as a contemporary place to visit. *At-a-Glance* material is actually a site-by-site survey of the most important, interesting, and sometimes most eclectic sights to see and things to do. *Sources and Resources* is a concise listing of pertinent tourist information meant to answer myriad potentially pressing questions as they arise — from simple things such as the address of the local tourism office, how to get around, which sightseeing tours to take, and when special events occur, to something more difficult, like where to find the best nightspot or hail a taxi, which are the chic places to shop and where to find the more irresistible bargains, and where the best museums and theaters are to be found. *Best in Town* lists our cost-and-quality choices of the best places to eat and sleep on a variety of budgets.

DIVERSIONS

This section is designed to help travelers find the best places in which to pursue a wide range of physical and cerebral activities, without having to wade through endless pages of unrelated text. This very selective guide lists the broadest possible range of activities, including all the best places to pursue them.

We start with a list of special places to stay and eat, and move to activities that require some perspiration — sports preferences and other rigorous pursuits — and go on to report on a number of more spiritual vacation opportunities. In every case, our suggestion of a particular location — and often our recommendation of a specific hotel — is intended to guide you to that special place where the quality of experience is likely to be highest. Whether you seek a historic hotel or museum or the best place to shop or ski, each category is the equivalent of a comprehensive checklist of the absolute best in Vancouver.

DIRECTIONS

Here are six walks that cover Vancouver, along its main thoroughfares and side streets, past its most spectacular landmarks and magnificent parks. This is the only section of the book that is organized geographically; itineraries can be "connected" for longer sojourns, or used individually for short, intensive explorations.

Although each of this book's sections has a distinct format and a special function, they have all been designed to be used together to provide a complete inventory of travel information. To use this book to full advantage, take a few minutes to read the table of contents and random entries in each section to get a firsthand feel for how it all fits together.

Pick and choose needed information. Assume, for example, that you always wanted to visit Vancouver and partake of the best salmon or the most delicious dim sum on this side of the Pacific, but never really knew how to organize it or where to go. Choose specific restaurants from the selections offered in *Eating Out* in THE CITY, add some of those noted in each walking tour in DIRECTIONS, and cross-reference with those in the roundup of the best in the city in the *Vancouver Victuals* section in DIVERSIONS.

In other words, the sections of this book are building blocks designed to help you put together the best possible trip. Use them selectively as a tool, a source of ideas, a reference work for accurate facts, and a guidebook to the best buys, the most exciting sights, the most pleasant accommodations, the tastiest food — *the best travel experience* that you can possibly have.

PACIFIC
OCEAN

Vancouver

PA(99)

Third Beach

Stanley
Park

Los
Lag

Second Beach

N

ENGLISH
BAY

English Beach

**MacMillan Planetarium
and Vancouver Museum**

| 0 | miles | 1.2 |

**Maritime
Museum**

| 0 | kilometers | 2 |

NORTHWEST MARINE DR.

Vanier
Park

Jericho
Beach
Park

POINT GREY RD.

CORNWALL AVE.

4TH AVE.

4TH AVE.

To Point Grey,
University of British Coloumbia,
Museum of Anthropology,
← Nitobe Memorial Gardens

BROADWAY

BROADWAY

10TH AVE.

BURRARD ST.

ALMA ST.

12TH AVE.

16TH AVE.

16TH AVE.

MACDONALD ST.

ARBUTUS ST.

KING EDWARD AVE.

University
Endowment
Lands Park

CROWN ST.

DUNBAR ST.

BLENHEIM ST.

To Richmond
And Stevestor

33RD AVE.

SOUTHWEST MARINE DR.

To North Vancouver
Capilano River,
Grouse Mountain Skyride.
To West Vancouver and
Lighthouse Park

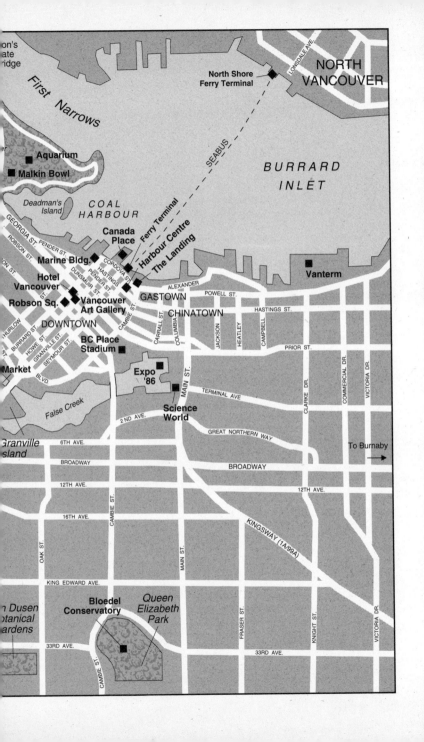

GETTING READY TO GO

When and How to Go

When to Go

 There really isn't a "best" time to visit Vancouver. Although the months of May through October traditionally have been the most popular vacation time, it is important to emphasize that more and more travelers who have the choice are enjoying the substantial advantages of off-season travel. Though some tourist attractions may close during the slower seasons, the majority remain open and tend to be less crowded. What's more, while winter sports such as skiing in the nearby Canadian Rockies are in full swing, travel to and from Vancouver during these seasons generally is less expensive.

For some, the most convincing argument in favor of off-season travel is the economic one. Getting there and staying there is more affordable during less popular travel periods as airfares, hotel rooms, and car rental rates go down and less expensive package tours become available; the independent traveler can go farther on less, too.

A definite bonus to visiting during the off-season is that even the most basic services are performed more efficiently. In theory, off-season service is identical to that offered during high season, but the fact is that the absence of demanding crowds inevitably begets much more thoughtful and personal attention.

Even during the off-season, high-season rates also may prevail because of an important local event. Particularly in Vancouver, special events and major trade shows or conferences held at the time of your visit also are sure to affect not only the availability of discounts on accommodations, but the basic availability of a place to stay.

In short, like many other popular places in Canada, the vacation appeal of Vancouver has become multi-seasonal. But the noted exceptions notwithstanding, most travel destinations are decidedly less heavily trafficked and less expensive during the winter.

WEATHER: Vancouver is a delight year-round. The range of temperature is not as great as in other regions, varying between the 30s F in the winter and the high 60s and 70s F in summer. In general, this region is best seen in late spring, summer, or early fall when the weather is warm. Comparatively, Vancouver almost always is warmer than New York City or Chicago in winter. Spring and autumn are pleasant, but again quite damp.

Travelers can get current readings and extended forecasts through the *Weather Channel Connection,* the worldwide weather report center of the *Weather Channel,* a cable television station. By dialing 900-WEATHER and punching in either the first four letters of the city name or the area code for over 600 cities, an up-to-date recording will provide such information as current temperature, barometric pressure, relative humidity, and wind speed, as well as a general 2-day forecast. Boating and highway reports are also provided for some locations. Weather information for over 225 international destinations can be obtained by punching in the first 4 letters of the city name. To hear the weather report for Vancouver, punch in VANC. (To find out which cities or locations in a given country are covered, enter the first four letters of the *country* name.) Callers also can access information on the weather patterns for any time of the year in the area requested, as well as international travel information such as visa requirements, US State Department travel advisories, tipping, and voltage requirements. This 24-hour service can be accessed from any touch-tone phone in the US, and costs 95¢ per minute. The charge will show up on your phone bill. For additional information, contact the *Weather Channel Connection,* 2600 Cumberland Pkwy., Atlanta, GA 30339 (phone: 404-434-6800).

SPECIAL EVENTS: On January 1st Canadians from this region ring in the New Year with a splash at the annual *Polar Bear Swim* in English Bay. For runners, there's the *Vancouver International Marathon* in May. And music lovers will enjoy the *Du Maurier International Jazz Festival* held in June which highlights top jazz greats. In September, moviegoers will enjoy the star-studded *Vancouver International Film Festival* where films from the world over vie for the coveted "best picture" award.

Traveling by Plane

 Flying usually is the quickest and most efficient way to get to Vancouver. When all costs are taken into account for traveling any substantial distance, plane travel usually is less expensive per mile than traveling by car. It also is the most economical way to go in terms of time. Although touring by car, bus, or train certainly is the most scenic way to travel, air travel is far faster and more direct — the less time spent in transit, the more time spent at your destination.

Despite recent attempts at price simplification by a number of major US carriers, the airlines offering flights to Canada continue to sell seats at a variety of prices under a vast spectrum of requirements and restrictions. Since you probably will spend more for your airfare than for any other single item in your travel budget, try to take advantage of the lowest available fare. You should know what kinds of flights are available, the rules and regulations pertaining to air travel, and all the special package options.

SCHEDULED FLIGHTS: Air service to Vancouver is provided by two Canadian airlines and a number of US carriers. *Air Canada* flies from Chicago, Portland, and Seattle. *Canadian Airlines International* flies from Honolulu, Los Angeles, San Francisco, and Seattle. *American* provides service only from Dallas and San Jose. *Continental* flies from Spokane and Denver. *Delta* has flights from Los Angeles, Phoenix, Portland, Salt Lake City, and San Francisco. *Horizon Air* provides service from Portland and Seattle. *Northwest* flies from Portland and Seattle. And *United* flies from Chicago, Los Angeles, Seattle, and San Francisco.

Tickets – When traveling on one of the many regularly scheduled flights, a full-fare ticket provides maximum travel flexibility (although at considerable expense), because there are no advance booking requirements. A prospective passenger can buy a ticket for a flight right up to the minute of takeoff — if a seat is available. If your ticket is for a round trip, you can make the return reservation whenever you wish — months before you leave, or the day before you return. Assuming the foreign immigration requirements are met, you can stay at your destination for as long as you like. (Tickets generally are good for a year and can be renewed if not used.) On some airlines, you also may be able to cancel your flight at any time without penalty; on others, cancellation — even of a full-fare ticket — may be subject to a variety of restrictions. It pays to check with the individual carrier *before* booking your flight. In addition, while it is true that this category of ticket can be purchased at the last minute, it is advisable to reserve well in advance during popular vacation periods and around holiday times.

Fares – Airfares continue to change so rapidly that even the experts find it difficult to keep up with them. This ever-changing situation is due to a number of factors, including airline deregulation (in both the US and Canada), volatile labor relations, increasing fuel costs, and vastly increased competition.

Perhaps the most common misconception about fares on scheduled airlines is that the cost of the ticket determines how much service will be provided on the flight. This is true only to a certain extent. A far more realistic rule of thumb is that the less you pay for your ticket, the more restrictions and qualifications are likely to come into play before you board the plane (as well as after you get off). These qualifying aspects relate to the months (and the days of the week) during which you must travel, how far in advance you must purchase your ticket, the minimum and maximum amount of time you may or must remain away, your willingness to decide on a return date at the time of booking — and your ability to stick to that decision. It is not uncommon for passengers sitting side by side on the same wide-body jet to have paid fares varying by hundreds of dollars, and all too often the traveler paying more would have been equally willing (and able) to accept the terms of the far less expensive ticket.

In general, the great variety of US domestic fares, Canadian domestic fares, and fares between the two countries can be reduced to four basic categories, including first class, coach (also called economy or tourist class), and excursion or discount fares. A fourth category, called business class, has been added by many airlines in recent years. In addition, Advance Purchase Excursion (APEX) fares offer savings under certain conditions.

A **first class** ticket is your admission to the special section of the aircraft, with larger seats, more legroom, sleeperette seating on some wide-body aircraft, better (or at least more elaborately served) food, free drinks and headsets for movies and music channels, and, above all, personal attention. First class fares are about twice those of full-fare economy, although both first class passengers and those paying full economy fares are entitled to reserve seats and are sold tickets on an open reservation system. Sometimes, a first class ticket offers the additional advantage of allowing travelers to schedule any number of stops en route to or from their most distant destination — provided that certain set, but generous, restrictions regarding maximum mileage limits and flight schedules are respected.

Not too long ago, there were only two classes of air travel, first class and all the rest, usually called economy or tourist. Then **business class** came into being — one of the most successful recent airline innovations. At first, business class passengers were merely curtained off from the other economy passengers. Now a separate cabin or cabins — usually toward the front of the plane — is the norm. While standards of comfort and service are not as high as in first class, they represent a considerable improvement over conditions in the rear of the plane, with roomier seats, more leg and shoulder space between passengers, and fewer seats abreast. Free liquor and headsets, a choice of meal entrées, and a separate counter for speedier check-in are other inducements. As in first class, a business class passenger may travel on any scheduled flight he or she wishes, buy a one-way or round-trip ticket, and have the ticket remain valid for a year. There are no minimum or maximum stay requirements, no advance booking requirements, and sometimes (depending on the carrier), no cancellation penalties. If the particular airline allows first class passengers unlimited free stopovers, this privilege generally also is extended to those flying business class. Though airlines often have their own names for their business class service, such as Executive Class on *Air Canada* or Medallion Class on *Delta, Canadian Airlines International* simply refers to it as business class.

The terms of the **coach** or **economy** fare may vary slightly from airline to airline, and in fact from time to time airlines may be selling more than one type of economy fare. Coach or economy passengers sit more snugly, as many as 10 in a single row on a wide-body jet, behind the first class and business class sections. Normally, alcoholic drinks are not free, nor are the headsets. If there are two economy fares on the books, one (often called "regular economy") still may include a number of free stopovers. The other, less expensive fare (often called "special economy") may limit stopovers to one or two, with a charge (typically $25) for each one.

Like first class passengers, however, passengers paying the full coach fare are subject to none of the restrictions that usually are attached to less expensive excursion and discount fares. There are no advance booking requirements, no minimum stay requirements, and often, no cancellation penalties — but beware, the rules regarding cancellation vary from carrier to carrier. Tickets are sold on an open reservation system: They can be bought for a flight right up to the minute of takeoff (if seats are available), and if the ticket is round trip, the return reservation can be made anytime you wish. Both first class and coach tickets generally are good for a year, after which they can be renewed if not used, and if you ultimately decide not to fly at all, your money may be refunded (again, policies vary). The cost of economy and business class tickets does not change much in the course of the year between the US and Canada, though on some routes they vary from a basic (low-season) price in effect most of the year to a peak (high-season) price — these seasonal demarcations vary according to the destination.

Excursion and other **discount** fares are the airlines' equivalent of a special sale and usually apply to round-trip bookings only. These fares generally differ according to the season and the number of travel days permitted. They are only a bit less flexible than full-fare economy tickets and are, therefore, often useful for both business and holiday travelers. Most round-trip excursion tickets include strict minimum and maximum stay requirements and reservations can be changed only within the specified time limits. So don't count on extending a ticket beyond the prescribed time of return or staying less time than required. Again, different airlines may have different regulations concerning stopover privileges and sometimes excursion fares are less expensive midweek. The availability of these reduced-rate seats is most limited at busy times such as holidays. Discount or excursion fare ticket holders sit with the coach passengers and, for all intents and purposes, are indistinguishable from them. They receive all the same basic services, even though they may have paid anywhere between 30% and 55% less for the trip. Obviously, it's wise to make plans early enough to qualify for this less expensive transportation if possible.

These discount or excursion fares may masquerade under a variety of names, and they may vary from city to city (from the East Coast to the West Coast, especially), but they invariably have strings attached. A common requirement is that the ticket be purchased a certain number of days — usually between 7 and 21 days — in advance of departure, though it may be booked weeks or months in advance (it has to be "ticketed," or paid for, shortly after booking, however). The return reservation usually has to be made at the time of the original ticketing and often cannot be changed later than a certain number of days (again, usually 7 to 21 days) before the return flight. If events force a change in the return reservation after the date allowed, the passenger may have to pay the difference between the round-trip excursion rate and the round-trip coach rate, although some carriers permit such scheduling changes for a nominal fee. In addition, some airlines also may allow passengers to use their discounted fares by standing by for an empty seat, even if they don't otherwise have standby fares. Another common condition is a minimum and maximum stay requirement: for example 1 to 6 days or 6 to 14 days (but including at least a Saturday night). Last, cancellation penalties of up to 50% of the full price of the ticket have been assessed — if a refund is offered at all — so careful planning is imperative. Check the specific penalty in effect when you purchase your discount/excursion ticket.

On some airlines, the ticket bearing the lowest price of all the current discount fares is the ticket where no change at all in departure and/or return flights is permitted, and where the ticket price is totally nonrefundable. If you do buy such a nonrefundable ticket, you should be aware of a policy followed by *some* airlines that may make it easier to change your plans if necessary. For a fee — set by each airline and payable at the airport when checking in — you *may* be able to change the time or date of a return flight on a nonrefundable ticket. However, if the nonrefundable ticket price for the replacement flight is higher than that of the original (as often is the case when trading in a weekday for a weekend flight), you will have to pay the difference. Any such change must be made a certain number of days in advance — in some cases as little as 2 days — of either the original or the replacement flight, whichever is earlier; restrictions are set by the individual carrier. (Travelers holding a nonrefundable or other restricted ticket who must change their plans due to a family emergency should know that some carriers may make special allowances in such situations; for further information, see *Staying Healthy,* in this section.)

■ **Note:** Due to recent changes in many US airlines' policies, nonrefundable tickets are now available that carry none of the above restrictions. Although passengers still may *not* be able to obtain a refund for the price paid, the time or date of a departing or return flight may be changed at any time (assuming seats are available) for a nominal service charge.

There also is a newer, often less expensive type of excursion fare, the **APEX**, or **Advance Purchase Excursion,** fare. As with traditional excursion fares, passengers paying an APEX fare sit with and receive the same basic services as any other coach or economy passengers, even though they may have paid up to 50% less for their seats. In return, they are subject to certain restrictions. In the case of flights to Canada the ticket usually is good for a minimum of approximately 4 days away (spanning at least 1 weekend), and a maximum, currently, of 1 month to 1 year (depending on the airline and the destination); as its name implies, it must be "ticketed," or paid for in its entirety, a certain period of time before departure — usually somewhere between 7 and 21 days.

The drawback to some APEX fares is that they penalize travelers who change their minds — and travel plans. Usually, the return reservation must be made at the time of the original ticketing, and if for some reason you change your schedule you will have to pay a penalty of $100 or 10% of the ticket value, whichever is greater, as long as you travel within the validity period of your ticket. More flexible APEX fares recently have been introduced that allow travelers to make changes in the date or time of their flights for a nominal charge (as low as $25).

With either type of APEX fare, if you change your return to a date less than the minimum stay or more than the maximum stay, the difference between the round-trip

APEX fare and the full round-trip coach rate will have to be paid. There also is a penalty of anywhere from $50 to $100 or more for canceling or changing a reservation *before* travel begins — check the specific penalty in effect when you purchase your ticket. No stopovers are allowed on an APEX ticket. Depending on the destination, APEX tickets to Canada may be sold at basic and peak rates (the peak season will vary) and may include surcharges for weekend flights.

Standby fares, at one time the rock-bottom price at which a traveler could fly to Canada, have become elusive. At the time of this writing, most major scheduled airlines did not regularly offer standby fares on direct flights to Canada. Because airline fares and their conditions constantly change, however, bargain hunters should not hesitate to ask if such a fare exists at the time they plan to travel.

While the definition of standby varies somewhat from airline to airline, it generally means that you make yourself available to buy a ticket for a flight (usually no sooner than the day of departure), then literally stand by on the chance that a seat will be empty. Once aboard, however, a standby passenger has the same meal service and frills (or lack of them) enjoyed by others in the economy class compartment.

Something else to check is the possibility of qualifying for a **GIT** (Group Inclusive Travel) fare, which requires that a specific dollar amount of ground arrangements be purchased, in advance, along with the ticket. The requirements vary as to number of travel days and stopovers permitted, and the minimum number of passengers required for a group. The actual fares also vary, but the cost will be spelled out in brochures distributed by the tour operators handling the ground arrangements. In the past, GIT fares were among the least expensive available from the established carriers, but the prevalence of discount fares has caused group fares to all but disappear from some air routes. Travelers reading brochures on group package tours to Canada will find that, in almost all cases, the applicable airfare given as a sample (to be added to the price of the land package to obtain the total tour price) is an APEX fare, the same discount fare available to the independent traveler.

The major airlines serving Canada from the US also may offer individual fare excursion rates similar to GIT fares, which are sold in conjunction with ground accommodation packages. Previously called ITX and sometimes referred to as individual tour-basing fares, these fares generally are offered as part of "air/hotel/car/ transfer packages," and can reduce the cost of an economy fare by more than a third. The packages are booked for a specific amount of time, with return dates specified; rescheduling and cancellation restrictions and penalties vary from carrier to carrier. At the time of this writing, these fares were offered to popular destinations throughout Canada by *Air Canada, American, Canadian Airlines International, Delta, Horizon Air,* and *Northwest.* Note that their offerings may or may not represent substantial savings over standard economy fares, so check at the time you plan to travel. (For further information on package options, see *Package Tours,* in this section.)

Travelers looking for the least expensive possible airfares should, finally, scan the pages of their hometown newspapers (especially the Sunday travel section) for announcements of special promotional fares. Most airlines offer their most attractive special fares to encourage travel during slow seasons and to inaugurate and publicize new routes. Even if none of these factors applies, prospective passengers can be fairly sure that the number of discount seats per flight at the lowest price is strictly limited, or that the fare offering includes a set expiration date — which means it's absolutely necessary to move fast to enjoy the lowest possible price.

Among other special airline promotional deals for which you should be on the lookout are discount or upgrade coupons sometimes offered by the major carriers and found in mail-order merchandise catalogues. For instance, airlines sometimes issue coupons that typically cost around $25 each and are good for a percentage discount or an upgrade on an international airline ticket — including flights to Canada. The only requirement beyond the fee generally is that a coupon purchaser must buy at least one item from the catalogue. There usually are some minimum airfare restrictions before the coupon is redeemable, but in general these are worthwhile offers. Restrictions often include certain blackout days (when the coupon cannot be used at all), usually imposed during peak travel periods. These coupons are particularly valuable to business travelers who tend to buy full-fare tickets, and while the coupons are issued in the buyer's name, they can be used by others who are traveling on the same itinerary.

It's always wise to ask about discount or promotional fares and about any conditions that might restrict booking, payment, cancellation, and changes in plans. Check the prices from neighboring cities. A special rate may be offered in a nearby city but not in yours, and it may be enough of a bargain to warrant your leaving from that city. Ask if there is a difference in price for midweek versus weekend travel, or if there is a further discount for traveling early in the morning or late at night. Also be sure to investigate package deals, which are offered by virtually every airline. These may include a car rental, accommodations, and dining and/or sightseeing features, in addition to the basic airfare, and the combined cost of packaged elements usually is considerably less than the cost of the exact same elements when purchased separately.

If in the course of your research you come across a deal that seems too good to be true, keep in mind that logic may not be a component of deeply discounted airfares — there's not always any sane relationship between miles to be flown and the price to get there. More often than not the level of competition on a given route dictates the degree of discount, so don't be dissuaded from accepting an offer that sounds irresistible, just because it also sounds illogical. Better to buy that inexpensive fare while it's being offered and worry about the sense — or absence thereof — while you're flying to your desired destination.

When you're satisfied that you've found the lowest possible price for which you can conveniently qualify (you may have to call the airline more than once, because different airline reservations clerks have been known to quote different prices), make your booking. Then, to protect yourself against fare increases, purchase and pay for your ticket as soon as possible after you've received a confirmed reservation. Airlines generally will honor their tickets, even if the operative price at the time of your flight is higher than the price you paid; if fares go up between the time you *reserve* a flight and the time you *pay* for it, you likely will be out of luck. Finally, with excursion or discount fares, it is important to remember that when a reservations clerk says that you must purchase a ticket by a specific date, this is an absolute deadline. Miss the deadline and the airline may automatically cancel your reservation without telling you.

■ **Note:** Another wrinkle in the airfare scene is that if the fares go *down* after you purchase your ticket, you *may* be entitled to a refund of the difference. However, this is only possible in certain situations — availability and advance purchase restrictions pertaining to the lower rate are set by the airline. If you suspect that you may be able to qualify for such a refund, check with your travel agent or the airline.

Frequent Flyers – The leading carriers serving Vancouver — *Air Canada, American, Canadian Airlines International, Delta, Northwest,* and *United* — offer a bonus system to frequent travelers. After the first 10,000 miles, for example, a passenger might be eligible for a first class seat for the coach fare; after another 10,000 miles, he or she might receive a discount on his or her next ticket purchase. The value of the bonuses continues to increase as more miles are logged.

Bonus miles also may be earned by patronizing affiliated car rental companies or hotel chains, or by using one of the credit cards that now offer this reward. In deciding whether to accept such a credit card from one of the issuing organizations that tempt you with frequent flyer mileage bonuses on a specific airline, first determine whether the interest rate charged on the unpaid balance is the same as (or less than) possible alternate credit cards, and whether the annual "membership" fee also is equal or lower. If these charges are slightly higher than those of competing cards, weigh the difference against the potential value in airfare savings. Also ask about any bonus miles awarded just for signing up — 1,000 is common, 5,000 generally the maximum.

For the most up-to-date information on frequent flyer bonus options, you may want to send for the monthly newsletter *Frequent.* Issued by Frequent Publications, it provides current information about frequent flyer plans in general, as well as specific data about promotions, awards, and combination deals to help you keep track of the profusion — and confusion — of current and upcoming availabilities. For a year's subscription, send $33 to Frequent Publications, 4715-C Town Center Dr., Colorado Springs, CO 80916 (phone: 800-333-5937).

There also is a monthly magazine called *Frequent Flyer,* but unlike the newsletter mentioned above, its focus is primarily on newsy articles of interest to business travelers and other frequent flyers. Published by Official Airline Guides (PO Box 58543, Boulder, CO 80322-8543; phone: 800-323-3537), *Frequent Flyer* is available for $24 for a 1-year subscription.

Low-Fare Airlines – Increasingly, the stimulus for special fares is the appearance of airlines associated with bargain rates. On these airlines, all seats on any given flight generally sell for the same price, which tends to be somewhat below the lowest discount fare offered by the larger, more established airlines. It is important to note that tickets offered by these smaller companies frequently are not subject to the same restrictions as some of the discounted fares offered by the more established carriers. They may not require advance purchase or minimum and maximum stays, may involve no cancellation penalties, and may be available one way or round trip. A disadvantage to some low-fare airlines, however, is that when something goes wrong, such as delayed baggage or a flight cancellation due to equipment breakdown, their smaller fleets and fewer flights mean that passengers may have to wait longer for a solution than they would on one of the equipment-rich major carriers.

Taxes and Other Fees – Travelers who have shopped for the best possible flight at the lowest possible price should be warned that a number of extras will be added to that price and collected by the airline or travel agent who issues the ticket. For instance, the $6 International Air Transportation Tax is a departure tax paid by all passengers flying from the US to a foreign destination.

Still another fee is charged by some airlines to cover more stringent security procedures, prompted by recent terrorist incidents. The 10% federal US Transportation Tax applies to travel within the US or US territories. It does not apply to passengers flying between US cities or territories en route to a foreign destination, unless the trip includes a stopover of more than 12 hours at a US point. Someone flying from New York to San Francisco and stopping in San Francisco for more than 12 hours before boarding a flight to Canada, for instance, would pay the 10% tax on the domestic portion of the trip. When flying from Canada back to the US, a Canadian Departure Tax also is charged; this amounts to 5% of the ticket cost, plus CN$4, the total of which may not exceed CN\$19. Note that these taxes *usually* (but not always) are included in advertised fares and in the prices quoted by airline reservations clerks.

Reservations – For those who don't have the time or patience to investigate personally all possible air departures and connections for a proposed trip, a travel agent can be of inestimable help. A good agent should have all the information on which flights go where and when, and which categories of tickets are available on each. Most have computerized reservation links with the major carriers, so that a seat can be reserved and confirmed in minutes. An increasing number of agents also possess fare-comparison computer programs, so they often are very reliable sources of detailed competitive price data. (For more information, see *How to Use a Travel Agent,* in this section.)

When making plane reservations through a travel agent, ask the agent to give the airline your home phone number, as well as your daytime business phone number. All too often the agent uses the agency number as the official contact for changes in flight plans. Especially during the winter, weather conditions hundreds or even thousands of miles away can wreak havoc with flight schedules. Aircraft are constantly in use, and a plane delayed in the Orient or on the West Coast can miss its scheduled flight from the East Coast the next morning. The airlines are fairly reliable about getting this sort of information to passengers if they can reach them; diligence does little good at 10 PM if the airline has only the agency's or an office number.

Reconfirmation is strongly recommended for all international flights (though it is not usually required on US domestic flights) and, in the case of flights to Canada, it is essential to confirm your round-trip reservations — especially the return leg — as well as any point-to-point flights within the country. Some (though increasingly fewer) reservations to and from international destinations are automatically canceled after a required reconfirmation period (typically 72 hours) has passed — even if you have a confirmed, fully paid ticket in hand. It always is wise to call ahead to make sure that the airline did not slip up in entering your original reservations, or in registering any changes you may have made since, and that it has your seat reservation and/or special meal request in the computer. If you look at the printed information on your ticket, you'll see the airline's reconfirmation policy stated explicitly. Don't be lulled into a false sense of security by the "OK" on your ticket next to the number and time of the flight. This only means that a reservation has been entered; a reconfirmation still may be necessary. If in doubt — call.

If you plan not to take a flight on which you hold a confirmed reservation, by all means inform the airline. Because the problem of "no-shows" is a constant expense for airlines, they are allowed to overbook flights, a practice that often contributes to the threat of denied boarding for a certain number of passengers (see "Getting Bumped," below).

Seating – For most types of tickets, airline seats usually are assigned on a first-come, first-served basis at check-in, although some airlines make it possible to reserve a seat at the time of ticket purchase. Always check in early for your flight, even with advance seat assignments. A good rule of thumb for international flights is to arrive at the airport *at least* 2 hours before the scheduled departure to give yourself plenty of time in case there are long lines.

Most airlines furnish seating charts, which make choosing a seat much easier, but there are a few basics to consider. You must decide whether you prefer a window, aisle, or middle seat. On flights where smoking is permitted, you also should indicate if you prefer the smoking or nonsmoking section.

The amount of legroom provided (as well as chest room, especially when the seat in front of you is in a reclining position) is determined by something called "pitch," a measure of the distance between the back of the seat in front of you and the front of the back of your seat. The amount of pitch is a matter of airline policy, not the type of plane you fly. First class and business class seats have the greatest pitch, a fact that figures prominently in airline advertising. In economy class or coach, the standard pitch ranges from 33 to as little as 31 inches — downright cramped.

The number of seats abreast, another factor determining comfort, depends on a combination of airline policy and airplane dimensions. First class and business class have the fewest seats per row. Economy generally has 9 seats per row on a DC-10 or an L-1011, making either one slightly more comfortable than a 747, on which there normally are 10 seats per row. Charter flights on DC-10s and L-1011s, however, often have 10 seats per row and can be noticeably more cramped than 747 charters, on which the seating normally remains at 10 per row.

Airline representatives claim that most aircraft are more stable toward the front and midsection, while seats farthest from the engines are quietest. Passengers who have long legs and are traveling on a wide-body aircraft might request a seat directly behind a door or emergency exit, since these seats often have greater than average pitch, or a seat in the first row of a given section, which offers extra legroom — although these seats are increasingly being reserved for passengers who are willing (and able) to perform certain tasks in the event of emergency evacuation. It often is impossible, however, to see the movie from these seats, which are directly behind the plane's exits. Be aware that seats in the first row of the economy section (called "bulkhead" seats) on a conventional aircraft (not a widebody) do *not* offer extra legroom, since the fixed partition will not permit passengers to slide their feet under it, and that watching a movie from these first-row seats can be difficult and uncomfortable. These bulkhead seats do, however, provide ample room to use a bassinet or safety seat and often are reserved for families traveling with children.

Despite all these rules of thumb, finding out which specific rows are near emergency exits or at the front of a wide-body cabin can be difficult because seating arrangements on two otherwise identical planes vary from airline to airline. There is, however, a quarterly publication called the *Airline Seating Guide* that publishes seating charts for most major US airlines and many foreign carriers as well. Your travel agent should have a copy, or you can buy the US edition for $39.95 per year and the international edition for $44.95. Order from Carlson Publishing Co., Box 888, Los Alamitos, CA 90720 (phone: 800-728-4877 or 213-493-4877).

Simply reserving an airline seat in advance, however, actually may guarantee very little. Most airlines require that passengers arrive at the departure gate at least 45 minutes (sometimes more) ahead of time to hold a seat reservation. *Air Canada,* for example, may cancel seat assignments and may not honor reservations of passengers who have not checked in some period of time — usually around 20 to 30 minutes, depending on the airport — before the scheduled departure time, and they *ask* travelers to check in at least 1 hour before all domestic flights and 2 hours before international flights. It pays to read the fine print on your ticket carefully and plan ahead.

A far better strategy is to visit an airline ticket office (or one of a select group of travel agents) to secure an actual boarding pass for your specific flight. Once this has been issued, airline computers show you as checked in, and you effectively own the seat you have selected (although some carriers may not honor boarding passes of passengers arriving at the gate less than 10 minutes before departure). This also is good — but not foolproof — insurance against getting bumped from an overbooked flight and is, therefore, an especially valuable tactic at peak travel times.

Smoking – One decision regarding choosing a seat has been taken out of the hands of many travelers who smoke. Effective February 25, 1990, the US government imposed a ban that prohibits smoking on all flights scheduled for 6 hours or less within the US and its territories. The new regulation applies to both domestic and international carriers serving these routes.

In the case of flights to Canada, by law these rules do not apply to nonstop flights from the US to destinations in Canada, or those with a *continuous* flight time of over 6 hours between stops in the US or its territories. As we went to press, however, all major carriers flying from the US to Canada included such flights in their "domestic" category in terms of nonsmoking rules, and no smoking was allowed on flights between the US and Canada with a continuous flight time of under 6 hours. (Note that there is no smoking on any *Air Canada* flight or any *Canadian Airlines International* flight.)

For a wallet-size guide that notes in detail the rights of nonsmokers according to these regulations, send a self-addressed, stamped envelope to ASH (*Action on Smoking and Health*), Airline Card, 2013 H St. NW, Washington, DC 20006 (phone: 202-659-4310).

Meals – If you have specific dietary requirements, be sure to let the airline know well before departure time. The available meals include vegetarian, seafood, kosher, Muslim, Hindu, high-protein, low-calorie, low-cholesterol, low-fat, low-sodium, diabetic, bland, and children's menus (not all of these may be available on every carrier). There is no extra charge for this option. It usually is necessary to request special meals when you make your reservations — check-in time is too late. It's also wise to reconfirm that your request for a special meal has made its way into the airline's computer — the time to do this is 24 hours before departure. (Note that special meals generally are not available on intra-Canadian flights on small local carriers. If this poses a problem, try to eat before you board, or bring a snack with you.)

Baggage – Travelers from the US face two different kinds of rules. When you fly in on a US airline or on a major international carrier, US baggage regulations will be in effect. Though airline baggage allowances vary slightly, in general all passengers are allowed to carry on board, without charge, one piece of luggage that will fit easily under a seat of the plane or in an overhead bin and whose combined dimensions (length, width, and depth) do not exceed 45 inches. A reasonable amount of reading material, camera equipment, and a handbag also are allowed. In addition, all passengers are allowed to check two bags in the cargo hold: one usually not to exceed 62 inches when length, width, and depth are combined, the other not to exceed 55 inches in combined dimensions. Generally no single bag may weigh more than 70 pounds.

In general, baggage allowances follow these guidelines in Canada, but care should be exercised on regional and local airlines. If you are flying from the US to Canada and connecting to a domestic flight, you generally will be allowed the same amount of baggage as on the international flight. If you break your trip and then take a domestic flight, the local carrier's weight restrictions apply. Particularly if traveling to remote outposts, be aware that the smaller aircraft used by carriers serving these routes often have limited luggage capacity and also may have to carry mail and freight. When booking flights off the routes of major trunk carriers, always verify baggage allowances.

Charges for additional, oversize, or overweight bags usually are made at a flat rate; the actual dollar amount varies from carrier to carrier. If you plan to travel with any special equipment or sporting gear, be sure to check with the airline beforehand. Most have specific procedures for handling such baggage, and you may have to pay for transport regardless of how much other baggage you have checked. Golf clubs and skis may be checked through as luggage (most airlines are accustomed to handling them), but tennis rackets should be carried onto the plane. Some airlines require that bicycles be partially dismantled and packaged.

To reduce the chances of your luggage going astray, remove all airline tags from previous trips, label each bag inside and out — with your business address rather than your home address on the outside, to prevent thieves from knowing whose house might be unguarded. Lock everything and double-check the tag that the airline attaches to make sure that it is coded YZR for Vancouver International Airport.

If your bags are not in the baggage claim area after your flight, or if they're damaged, report the problem to airline personnel immediately. Keep in mind that policies regarding the specific time limit within which you have to make your claim vary from carrier to carrier. Fill out a report form on your lost or damaged luggage and keep a copy of it and your original baggage claim check. If you must surrender the check to claim a damaged bag, get a receipt for it to prove that you did, indeed, check your baggage on the flight. If luggage is missing, be sure to give the airline your destination and/or a telephone number where you can be reached. Also take the name and number of the person in charge of recovering lost luggage.

Most airlines have emergency funds for passengers stranded away from home without their luggage, but if it turns out your bags are truly lost and not simply delayed, do not then and there sign any paper indicating you'll accept an offered settlement. Since the airline is responsible for the value of your bags within certain statutory limits ($1,250 per passenger for lost baggage on a US domestic flight; $9.07 per pound or $20 per kilo for checked baggage, and up to $400 per passenger for unchecked baggage on an international flight), you should take some time to assess the extent of your loss (see *Insurance,* in this section). It's a good idea to keep records indicating the value of the contents of your luggage. A wise alternative is to take a Polaroid picture of the most valuable of your packed items just after putting them in your suitcase.

Considering the increased incidence of damage to baggage, it's now more than ever a good idea to keep the sales slips that confirm how much you paid for your bags. These are invaluable in establishing the value of damaged luggage and eliminating any arguments. A better way to protect your precious gear from the luggage-eating conveyers is to try to carry it on board wherever possible.

Airline Clubs – Some US and foreign carriers often have clubs for travelers who pay for membership. These clubs are not solely for first class passengers, although a first class ticket *may* entitle a passenger to lounge privileges. Membership entitles the traveler to use the private lounges at airports along their route, to refreshments served in those lounges, and to check-cashing privileges at most of their counters. Extras include special telephone numbers for individual reservations, embossed luggage tags, and a membership card for identification. Airlines serving Canada that offer membership in such clubs include the following:

   American: The *Admiral's Club.* Single yearly membership $225 for the first year; $125 yearly thereafter; spouse an additional $70 per year.

   Continental: The *President's Club.* Single yearly membership $150 for the first year; $100 yearly thereafter; spouse an additional $50 per year.

   Delta: The *Crown Club.* Single yearly membership $150; spouse an additional $50 per year; 3-year and lifetime memberships also available.

   Northwest: The *World Club.* Single yearly membership $140 (plus a one time $50 initiation fee); spouse an additional $50 per year; 3-year and lifetime memberships also available.

   United: The *Red Carpet Club.* Single yearly membership $125 (plus a one time $100 initiation fee); spouse an additional $70; 3-year and lifetime memberships also available.

In addition, *very* frequent travelers who have flown over 60,000 miles on *Air Canada* and are members of the carrier's frequent flyer program — called *Aeroplan* (membership costs CN$20) — may use the carrier's *Maple Leaf Lounges* at major airports across Canada. Club members with an *Aeroplan Elite* card also may bring a guest.

Note that the companies above do not have club facilities in all airports. Other airlines also may offer a variety of special services in many airports.

Getting Bumped – A special air travel problem is the possibility that an airline will accept more reservations (and sell more tickets) than there are seats on a given flight. This is entirely legal and is done to make up for "no-shows," passengers who don't show up for a flight for which they have made reservations and bought tickets. If the airline has oversold the flight and everyone does show up, there simply aren't enough seats. When this happens, the airline is subject to stringent rules designed to protect travelers.

In such cases, the airline first seeks ticket holders willing to give up their seats voluntarily in return for a negotiable sum of money or some other inducement, such as an offer of upgraded seating on the next flight or a voucher for a free trip at some other time. If there are not enough volunteers, the airline may bump passengers against their wishes.

Anyone inconvenienced in this way, however, is entitled to an explanation of the criteria used to determine who does and does not get on the flight, as well as compensation if the resulting delay exceeds certain limits. If the airline can put the bumped passengers on an alternate flight that is *scheduled to arrive* at their original destination within 1 hour of their originally scheduled arrival time, no compensation is owed. If the delay is more than 1 hour but less than 2 hours on a domestic US flight, they must be paid denied-boarding compensation equivalent to the one-way fare to their destination (but not more than $200). If the delay is more than 2 hours beyond the original arrival time on a domestic flight or more than 4 hours on an international flight, the compensation must be doubled (not more than $400). The airline also may offer bumped travelers a voucher for a free flight instead of the denied-boarding compensation. The passenger may be given the choice of either the money or the voucher, the dollar value of which may be no less than the monetary compensation to which the passenger would be entitled. The voucher is not a substitute for the bumped passenger's original ticket; the airline continues to honor that as well.

Keep in mind that the above regulations and policies are only for flights leaving the US, and do *not* apply to charters or to inbound flights originating abroad, even on US carriers.

To protect yourself as best you can against getting bumped, arrive at the airport early, allowing plenty of time to check in and get to the gate. If the flight is oversold, ask immediately for the written statement explaining the airline's policy on denied-boarding compensation and its boarding priorities. If the airline refuses to give you this information, or if you feel it has not handled the situation properly, file a complaint with both the airline and the appropriate government agency.

Delays and Cancellations – The above compensation rules also do not apply if the flight is canceled or delayed, or if a smaller aircraft is substituted due to mechanical problems. Each airline has its own policy for assisting passengers whose flights are delayed or canceled or who must wait for another flight because their original one was overbooked. Most airline personnel will make new travel arrangements if necessary. If the delay is longer than 4 hours, the airline may pay for a phone call or telegram, a meal, and, in some cases, a hotel room and transportation to it.

■ **Caution:** If you are bumped or miss a flight, be sure to ask the airline to notify other airlines on which you have reservations or connecting flights. When your name is taken off the passenger list of your initial flight, the computer usually cancels all of your reservations automatically, unless *you* take steps to preserve them.

CHARTER FLIGHTS: By booking a block of seats on a specially arranged flight, charter tour operators offer travelers air transportation for a substantial reduction over the full coach or economy fare. These operators may offer air-only charters (selling transportation alone) or charter packages (the flight plus a combination of land arrangements such as accommodations, meals, tours, or car rentals). Charters are especially attractive to people living in smaller cities or out-of-the-way places, because they frequently take off from nearby airports, saving travelers the inconvenience and expense of getting to a major gateway.

From the consumer's standpoint, charters differ from scheduled airlines in two main respects: You generally need to book and pay in advance, and you can't change the itinerary or the departure and return dates once you've booked the flight. In practice, however, these restrictions don't always apply. Today, although most charter flights still require advance reservations, some permit last-minute bookings (when there are unsold seats available), and some even offer seats on a standby basis.

Some things to keep in mind about the charter game are:

1. It cannot be repeated often enough that if you are forced to cancel your trip, you can lose much (and possibly all) of your money unless you have cancellation insurance, which is a *must* (see *Insurance,* in this section). Frequently, if the cancellation occurs far enough in advance (often 6 weeks or more), you may forfeit only a $25 or $50 penalty. If you cancel only 2 or 3 weeks before the flight, there may be no refund at all unless you or the operator can provide a substitute passenger.

2. Charter flights may be canceled by the operator up to 10 days before departure for any reason, usually underbooking. Your money is returned in this event, but there may be too little time for you to make new arrangements.

3. Most charters have little of the flexibility of regularly scheduled flights regarding refunds and the changing of flight dates; if you book a return flight, you must be on it or lose your money.

4. Charter operators are permitted to assess a surcharge, if fuel or other costs warrant it, of up to 10% of the airfare up to 10 days before departure.

5. Because of the economics of charter flights, your plane almost always will be full, so you will be crowded, though not necessarily uncomfortable. (There is, however, a new movement among charter airlines to provide flight accommodations that are more comfort-oriented, so this situation may change in the near future.)

To avoid problems, *always* choose charter flights with care. When you consider a charter, ask your travel agent who runs it and carefully check the company. The Better Business Bureau in the company's home city can report on how many complaints, if any, have been lodged against it in the past. Protect yourself with trip cancellation and interruption insurance, which can help safeguard your investment if you, or a traveling companion, are unable to make the trip and must cancel too late to receive a full refund from the company providing your travel services. (This is advisable whether you're buying a charter flight alone or a tour package for which the airfare is provided by charter or scheduled flight.)

Booking – If you do fly on a charter, read the contract's fine print carefully and pay particular attention to the following:

Instructions concerning the payment of the deposit and its balance and to whom the check is to be made payable. Ordinarily, checks are made out to an escrow account, which means the charter company can't spend your money until your flight has safely returned. This provides some protection for you. To ensure the safe handling of your money, make out your check to the escrow account, the number of which must appear by law on the brochure, though all too often it is on the back in fine print. Write the details of the charter, including the destination and dates, on the face of the check; on the back, print "For Deposit Only." Your travel agent may prefer that you make out your check to the agency, saying that it will then pay the tour operator the fee minus commission. It is perfectly legal to write the check as we suggest, however, and if your agent objects too vociferously (he or she should trust the tour operator to send the proper commission), consider taking your business elsewhere. If you don't make your check out to the escrow account, you lose the protection of that escrow should the trip be canceled. Furthermore, recent bankruptcies in the travel industry have served to point out that even the protection of escrow may not be enough to safeguard a traveler's investment. More and more, insurance is becoming a necessity. The charter company should be bonded (usually by an insurance company), and if you want to file a claim against it, the claim should be sent to the bonding agent. The contract will set a time limit within which a claim must be filed.

Specific stipulations and penalties for cancellations. Most charters allow you to cancel up to 45 days in advance without major penalty, but some cancellation dates are 50 to 60 days before departure.

Stipulations regarding cancellation and major changes made by the charterer. US rules say that charter flights may not be canceled within 10 days of departure except when circumstances — such as natural disasters or political upheavals — make it physically impossible to fly. Charterers may make "major changes," however, such as in the date or place of departure or return, but you are entitled to cancel and receive a full refund if you don't wish to accept these changes. A price increase of more than 10% at any time up to 10 days before departure is considered a major change; no price increase at all is allowed during the last 10 days immediately before departure.

Canadian Airlines International offers charter flights through its subsidiary *Canadian Holidays* (191 The West Mall, Etobicoke, Ontario M9C 5K8, Canada; phone: 800-237-0314 from the US; call local offices in Canada), both within Canada and to foreign destinations. Bookings can be made through *Canadian Airlines International* or through a travel agent. *Travel Charter* (1120 E. Longlake Rd., Detroit, MI 48098; phone: 313-528-3570) also sometimes offers charters to Canada.

You also may want to subscribe to the travel newsletter *Jax Fax,* which regularly features a list of charter companies and packagers offering seats on charter flights and may be a source for other charter flights to and within Canada. For a year's subscription send a check or money order for $12 to *Jax Fax,* 397 Post Rd., Darien, CT 06820 (phone: 203-655-8746).

DISCOUNTS ON SCHEDULED FLIGHTS: Promotional fares often are called discount fares because they cost less than what used to be the standard airline fare — full-fare economy. Nevertheless, they cost the traveler the same whether they are bought through a travel agent or directly from the airline. Tickets that cost less if bought from some outlet other than the airline do exist, however. While it is likely that the vast majority of travelers flying to Canada in the near future will be doing so on a promotional fare or charter rather than on a "discount" air ticket of this sort, it still is a good idea for cost-conscious consumers to be aware of the latest developments in the budget airfare scene. Note that the following discussion makes clear-cut distinctions among the types of discounts available based on how they reach the consumer; in actual practice, the distinctions are not nearly so precise.

Net Fare Sources – The newest notion for reducing the costs of travel services comes from travel agents who offer individual travelers "net" fares. Defined simply, a net fare is the bare minimum amount at which an airline or tour operator will carry a prospective traveler. It doesn't include the amount that normally would be paid to the travel agent as a commission. Traditionally, such commissions amount to about 10% on domestic fares and from 10% to 20% on international fares — not counting significant additions to these commission levels that are paid retroactively when agents sell more than a specific volume of tickets or trips for a single supplier. At press time, at least one travel agency in the US was offering travelers the opportunity to purchase tickets and/or tours for a net price. Instead of earning its income from individual commissions, this agency assesses a fixed fee that may or may not provide a bargain for travelers; it requires a little arithmetic to determine whether to use the services of a net travel agent or those of one who accepts conventional commissions. One of the potential drawbacks of buying from agencies selling travel services at net fares is that some airlines refuse to do business with them, thus possibly limiting your flight options.

Travel Avenue is a fee-based agency that rebates its ordinary agency commission to the customer. For domestic flights, they will find the lowest retail fare, then rebate 7% to 10% (depending on the airline selected) of that price minus a $10 ticket-writing charge. The rebate percentage for international flights varies from 5% to 16% (again depending on the airline), and the ticket-writing fee is $25. The ticket-writing charge is imposed per ticket; if the ticket includes more than eight separate flights, an additional $10 or $25 fee is charged. Customers using free flight coupons pay the ticket-writing charge, plus an additional $5 coupon-processing fee.

Travel Avenue will rebate its commissions on all tickets, including heavily discounted fares and senior citizen passes. Available 7 days a week, reservations should be made far enough in advance to allow the tickets to be sent by first class mail, since extra charges accrue for special handling. It's possible to economize further by making your own airline reservation, then asking *Travel Avenue* only to write/issue your ticket. For travelers outside the Chicago area, business may be transacted by phone and purchases charged to a credit card. For information, contact *Travel Avenue* at 641 W. Lake St., Suite 201, Chicago, IL 60606-1012 (phone: 312-876-1116 in Illinois; 800-333-3335 elsewhere in the US).

Consolidators and Bucket Shops – Other vendors of travel services can afford to sell tickets to their customers at an even greater discount because the airline has sold the tickets to them at a substantial discount (usually accomplished by sharply increasing commissions to that vendor), a practice in which many airlines indulge, albeit discreetly, preferring that the general public not know they are undercutting their own "list" prices. Airlines anticipating a slow period on a particular route sometimes sell off a certain portion of their capacity at a very great discount to a wholesaler, or consolidator. The wholesaler sometimes is a charter operator who resells the seats to the public as though they were charter seats, which is why prospective travelers perusing the brochures of charter operators with large programs frequently see a number of flights designated as "scheduled service." As often as not, however, the consolidator, in turn, sells the seats to a travel agency specializing in discounting. Airlines also can sell seats directly to such an agency, which thus acts as its own consolidator. The airline offers the seats either at a net wholesale price, but without the volume-purchase requirement that would be difficult for a modest retail travel agency to fulfill, or at the standard price, but with a commission override large enough (as high as 50%) to allow both a profit and a price reduction to the public.

Travel agencies specializing in discounting sometimes are called "bucket shops," a term once fraught with connotations of unreliability in this country. But in today's highly competitive travel marketplace, more and more conventional travel agencies are selling consolidator-supplied tickets, and the old bucket shops' image is becoming respectable. Agencies that specialize in discounted tickets exist in most large cities, and usually can be found by studying the smaller ads in the travel sections of Sunday newspapers.

Before buying a discounted ticket, whether from a bucket shop or a conventional, full-service travel agency, keep the following considerations in mind: To be in a position to judge how much you'll be saving, first find out the "list" prices of tickets to your destination. Then do some comparison shopping among agencies. Also bear in mind that a ticket that may not differ much in price from one available directly from the airline may, however, allow the circumvention of such things as the advance-purchase requirement. If your plans are less than final, be sure to find out about any other restrictions, such as penalties for canceling a flight or changing a reservation. Most discount tickets are non-endorsable, meaning they can be used only on the airline that issued them, and they usually are marked "nonrefundable" to prevent their being cashed in for a list price refund.

A great many bucket shops are small businesses operating on a thin margin, so it's a good idea to check the local Better Business Bureau for any complaints registered against the one with which you're dealing — before parting with any money. If you still do not feel reassured, consider buying discounted tickets only through a conventional travel agency, which can be expected to have found its own reliable source of consolidator tickets — some of the largest consolidators, in fact, sell only to travel agencies.

A few bucket shops require payment in cash — we strongly advise *against* this — or by certified check or money order, but if credit cards are accepted, use that option. Note, however, if buying from a charter operator selling both scheduled and charter flights, that the scheduled seats are not protected by the regulations — including the use of escrow accounts — governing the charter seats. Well-established charter operators, nevertheless, may extend the same protection to their scheduled flights and, when this is the case, consumers should be sure that the payment option selected directs their money into the escrow account.

The following is a list of companies active in the North American market. Although, at press time, none offered discount fares to Canada, it might prove useful to call when planning your trip to see if Vancouver is among the destinations served at the time.

Bargain Air (655 Deep Valley Dr., Suite 355, Rolling Hills, CA 90274; phone: 800-347-2345 or 213-377-2919).

Council Charter (205 E. 42nd St., New York, NY 10017; phone: 800-223-7402 or 212-661-0311).

TFI Tours International (34 W. 32nd St., 12th Floor, New York, NY 10001; phone: 212-736-1140).

Travac Tours and Charters (989 Ave. of the Americas, New York, NY 10018; phone: 800-TRAV-800 or 212-563-3303).

25 West Tours (2490 Coral Way, Miami, FL 33145; phone: 305-856-0810 in Florida; 800-925-0250 elsewhere in the US).

Unitravel (1177 N. Warson Rd., St. Louis, MO 63132; phone: 314-569-2501 in Missouri; 800-325-2222 elsewhere in the US).

■ **Note:** Although rebating and discounting are becoming increasingly common, there is some legal ambiguity concerning them. Strictly speaking, it is legal to discount domestic tickets, but not international tickets. On the other hand, the law that prohibits discounting, the Federal Aviation Act of 1958, is consistently ignored these days, in part because consumers benefit from the practice and in part because many illegal arrangements are indistinguishable from legal ones. Since the line separating the two is so fine that even the authorities can't always tell the difference, it is unlikely that most consumers would be able to do so, and in fact it is not illegal to *buy* a discounted ticket. If the issue of legality bothers you, ask the agency whether any ticket you're about to buy would be permissible under the above-mentioned act.

Last-Minute Travel Clubs – Still another way to take advantage of bargain airfares is open to those who have a flexible schedule. A number of organizations, usually set up as last-minute travel clubs and functioning on a membership basis, routinely keep in touch with travel suppliers to help them dispose of unsold inventory at discounts of between 15% and 60%. A great deal of the inventory consists of complete package tours and cruises, but some clubs offer air-only charter seats and, occasionally, seats on scheduled flights.

Members pay an annual fee and receive a toll-free hotline telephone number to call for information on imminent trips. In some cases, they also receive periodic mailings with information on bargain travel opportunities for which there is more advance notice. Despite the suggestive names of the clubs providing these services, last-minute travel does not necessarily mean that you cannot make plans until literally the last minute. Trips can be announced as little as a few days or as much as 2 months before departure, but the average is from 1 to 4 weeks' notice.

Among the organizations regularly offering such discounted travel opportunities to Canada are the following:

Discount Travel International (152 W. 72nd St., Suite 223, New York, NY 10023; phone: 212-362-3636). Annual fee: $45 per household.

Encore/Short Notice (4501 Forbes Blvd., Lanham, MD 20706; phone: 301-459-8020; 800-638-0930 for customer service). Annual fee: $36 per family for its Short Notice program only; $48 per family to join the Encore program, which provides additional travel services.

Last Minute Travel (1249 Boylston St., Boston MA 02215; phone: 800-LAST-MIN or 617-267-9800). No fee.

Moment's Notice (425 Madison Ave., New York, NY 10017; phone: 212-486-0503). Annual fee: $45 per family.

Spur-of-the-Moment Tours and Cruises (10780 Jefferson Blvd., Culver City, CA 90230; phone: 310-839-2418 in Southern California; 800-343-1991 elsewhere in the US). No fee.

Traveler's Advantage (3033 S. Parker Rd., Suite 1000, Aurora, CO 80014; phone: 800-835-8747). Annual fee: $49 per family.

Vacations to Go (2411 Fountain View, Suite 201, Houston, TX 77057; phone: 800-338-4962). Annual fee: $19.95 per family.

Worldwide Discount Travel Club (1674 Meridian Ave., Miami Beach, FL 33139; phone: 305-534-2082). Annual fee: $40 per person; $50 per family.

■ **Note:** For additional information on last-minute travel discounts, a new "900" number telephone service called *Last Minute Travel Connection* (phone: 900-446-8292) provides recorded advertisements (including contact information) for discount offerings on airfares, package tours, cruises, and other travel opportunities. Since companies update their advertisements as often as every hour, listings are current. This 24-hour service is available to callers using touch-tone phones; the cost is $1 per minute (the charge will show up on your phone bill). For more information, contact *La Onda, Ltd.* (601 Skokie Blvd., Suite 224, Northbrook, IL 60062; phone: 708-498-9216).

Generic Air Travel – Organizations that apply the same flexible-schedule idea to air travel only and sell tickets at literally the last minute also exist. Their service sometimes is known as "generic" air travel, and it operates somewhat like an ordinary airline standby service except that the organizations running it offer seats on not one but several scheduled and charter airlines.

One pioneer of generic flights is *Airhitch* (2790 Broadway, Suite 100, New York, NY 10025; phone: 212-864-2000). Prospective travelers stipulate a range of at least five consecutive departure dates and their desired destination, along with alternate choices, and pay the fare in advance. They are then sent a voucher good for travel *on a space-available basis* on flights to their destination *region* (i.e., not necessarily the specific destination requested) during this time period. The week before this range of departure dates begins, travelers must contact *Airhitch* for specific information about flights that will probably be available and instructions on how to proceed for check-in. (Return flights are arranged in the same manner as the outbound flights — a specified period of travel is decided upon, and a few days before this date range begins, prospective passengers contact *Airhitch* for details about flights that may be available.) If the client does not accept any of the suggested flights or cancels his or her travel plans after selecting a flight, the amount paid can be applied toward a future fare or the flight arrangements can be transferred to another individual (although, in both cases, an additional fee may be charged). No refunds are offered unless the prospective passenger does not ultimately get on any flight in the specified date range; in such a case, the full fare is refunded. (Note that *Airhitch*'s slightly more expensive "Target" program, which provides confirmed reservations on specific dates to specific destinations, offers passengers greater — but not guaranteed — certainty regarding flight arrangements.) At the time of this writing, *Airhitch* did not offer flights between the US and Canada, but do check at the time you plan to travel.

Bartered Travel Sources – Suppose a hotel buys advertising space in a newspaper. As payment, the hotel gives the publishing company the use of a number of hotel rooms in lieu of cash. This is barter, a common means of exchange among hotels, airlines, car rental companies, cruise lines, tour operators, restaurants, and other travel service companies. When a bartering company finds itself with empty airline seats (or excess hotel rooms, or cruise ship cabin space, and so on) and offers them to the public, considerable savings can be enjoyed.

Bartered travel clubs often offer discounts of up to 50% to members, who pay an annual fee (approximately $50 at press time) that entitles them to select from the flights, cruises, hotel rooms, or other travel services that the club obtained by barter. Members usually present a voucher, club credit card, or scrip (a dollar-denomination voucher negotiable only for the bartered product) to the hotel, which in turn subtracts the dollar amount from the bartering company's account.

Selling bartered travel is a perfectly legitimate means of retailing. One advantage to club members is that they don't have to wait until the last minute to obtain flight or room reservations.

Among the companies specializing in bartered travel, two that offer members travel services to and in Canada are *IGT (In Good Taste) Services* (1111 Lincoln Rd., 4th Floor, Miami Beach, FL 33139; phone: 800-444-8872 or 305-534-7900), with an annual fee of $48 per family, and *Travel Guild* (18210 Redmond Way, Redmond, WA 98052; phone: 206-861-1900), which charges $48 per family per year.

OTHER DISCOUNT TRAVEL SOURCES: An excellent source of information on economical travel opportunities is the *Consumer Reports Travel Letter,* published monthly by Consumers Union. It keeps abreast of the scene on a wide variety of fronts, including package tours, rental cars, insurance, and more, but it is especially helpful for its comprehensive coverage of airfares, offering guidance on all the options from scheduled flights on major or low-fare airlines to charters and discount sources. For a year's subscription, send $37 ($57 for 2 years) to *Consumer Reports Travel Letter* (PO Box 53629, Boulder, CO 80322-3629; phone: 800-234-1970). For information on other travel newsletters, see *Books, Magazines, and Newsletters,* in this section.

On Arrival

FROM THE AIRPORT TO THE CITY: Vancouver International Airport, which handles both domestic and international flights, is located 11 miles (18 km) south of downtown.

    Taxi – In Vancouver, it takes about 20 minutes to get from Vancouver International Airport to the center of town; the fare is about CN$24.

Public Transportation – The most convenient way to get from Vancouver International Airport to downtown Vancouver is to take the shuttle bus *Airporter,* which operates a shuttle bus that goes to all the major hotels. It takes about 20 minutes, and costs CN$8.25.

CAR RENTAL: Unless planning to drive round-trip from home, most travelers who want to drive while on vacation simply rent a car.

    Renting a car in Canada is not inexpensive, but it is possible to economize by determining your own needs and then shopping around among the car rental companies until you find the best deal. Ask about special rates or promotional deals, such as weekend or weekly rates, bonus coupons for airline tickets, or 24-hour rates that include gas and unlimited mileage.

Renting from the US – Travel agents can arrange foreign rentals for clients, but it is just as easy to call and rent a car yourself. Listed below are some of the major international rental companies that have representation in Vancouver and have information and reservations numbers that can be dialed toll-free from the US:

    Avis (phone: 800-331-1084 throughout the US; 800-268-2310 in Canada). Has a representative at the airport and 2 others in downtown Vancouver.

    Budget (phone: 800-527-0700 in the US; 800-268-8900 in Canada). Has a representative at the airport and 8 other locations in Vancouver.

    Hertz (phone: 800-654-3001 in the US; 800-263-0600 in Canada). Has a representative at the airport and 2 others in the city.

    National Car Rental (phone: 800-CAR-RENT throughout the US and Canada). Has a representative at the airport and 3 other locations in Vancouver.

    Sears Rent-A-Car (phone: 800-527-0770 in the US; 800-268-8900 in Canada). Has a representative at the airport and 4 other locations in Vancouver.

    Thrifty Rent-A-Car (phone: 800-367-2277 in the US and Canada). Has a representative at the airport and one location downtown.

    Tilden Rent-A-Car System Largest Canadian firm, affiliated with *National* in the US; for *National,* or reservations through them with *Tilden* in Canada, call 800-CAR-RENT throughout the US and Canada.

It also is possible to rent a car before you go by contacting any number of smaller or less well-known US companies that do not operate worldwide. These organizations may specialize in North American auto travel, including leasing and car purchase in addition to car rental, or may actually be tour operators with a well-established Canadian car rental program.

Requirements – Whether you decide to rent a car in advance from a large international rental company with Canadian branches or wait to rent from a local company, you should know that renting a car is rarely as simple as signing on the dotted line and roaring off into the night. To drive in Vancouver, you need certain documents (see below), and will have to convince the renting agency that (1) you are personally creditworthy, and (2) you will bring the car back at the stated time. This will be easy if you have a major credit card; most rental companies accept credit cards in lieu of a cash deposit, as well as for payment of your final bill. If you prefer to pay in cash, leave your credit card imprint as a "deposit," then pay your bill in cash when you return the car.

If you are planning to rent a car once you're in Canada, *Avis, Budget, Hertz,* and other US rental companies usually *will* rent to travelers paying in cash and leaving either a credit card imprint or a substantial amount of cash as a deposit. This is not necessarily standard policy, however, as some of the other international chains and a number of local and regional Canadian companies will *not* rent to an individual who doesn't have a valid credit card. In this case, you will have to call around to find a company that accepts cash.

Also keep in mind that although the minimum age to drive a car in Vancouver is 16 years, the minimum age to rent a car is set by the rental company. (Restrictions vary from company to company, as well as at different locations.) Many firms have a minimum age requirement of 21 years, some raise that to between 23 and 25 years, and for some models of cars it rises to 30 years. The upper age limit at many companies is between 69 and 75; others have no upper limit or may make drivers above a certain age subject to special conditions.

Don't forget that all car rentals in the province of British Columbia are subject to a 6% province tax, as well as the Canadian Goods and Services Tax (GST) of 7%. This tax rarely is included in the rental price that's advertised or quoted, but it always must be paid —. whether you pay in advance in the US or pay it when you drop off the car.

Driving Documents – A valid driver's license from his or her own state of residence is required for a US citizen to drive in Canada. Proof of liability also is required and is a standard part of any car rental contract. Car rental companies also make provisions for breakdowns, emergency service, and assistance; ask for a number to call when you pick up the vehicle.

Rules of the Road – Driving in Canada is on the right side of the road, as in the US. Passing is on the left; the left turn signal must be flashing before and while passing, and the right indicator must be used when pulling back to the right.

According to law, those coming from the right at intersections have the right of way, as in the US, and pedestrians, provided they are in marked crosswalks, have priority over all vehicles.

In the city, speed limits usually are 50 kmh (about 30 mph). Outside the city, the speed limit is 100 kmh (about 60 mph) on freeways and 80 kmh (about 50 mph) on highways.

Gasoline – The major oil companies have stations in Canada: *Chevron, Exxon, Gulf, Shell, Sunoco,* and *Texaco.* Even more common are Canadian companies, like *Petro-Canada.* Gas is sold by the liter, which is slightly more than 1 quart; approximately 3.8 liters equal 1 US gallon. As in the US, regular, leaded, and diesel gas generally are available in several grades, and self-service (where you do the pumping) often is less expensive than full service. Similarly, gas paid for in cash often costs less than when you pay for it with a credit card.

Package Tours

If the mere thought of buying a package for your visit to Vancouver conjures up visions of a trip marching in lockstep with a horde of frazzled fellow travelers, remember that packages have come a long way. For one thing, not all packages necessarily are escorted tours, and the one you buy does not have to include any organized touring at all — nor will it necessarily include traveling companions. If it does, however, you'll find that people of all sorts — many just like yourself — are taking advantage of packages today because they are economical and convenient, and save you an immense amount of planning time. Given the high cost of travel these days, packages have emerged as a particularly wise buy.

In essence, a package is just an amalgam of travel services that can be purchased in a single transaction. A Vancouver package (tour or otherwise) may include any or all of the following: round-trip transportation, local transportation (and/or car rentals), accommodations, some or all meals, sightseeing, entertainment, transfers to and from the hotel, taxes, tips, escort service, and a variety of incidental features that might be offered as options at additional cost. In other words, a package can be any combination of travel elements, from a fully escorted tour offered at an all-inclusive price to a simple fly/drive booking that allows you to move about totally on your own. Its principal advantage is that it saves money: The cost of the combined arrangements invariably is well below the price of all of the same elements if bought separately, and, particularly if transportation is provided by discount flight, the whole package could cost less than just a round-trip economy airline ticket on a regularly scheduled flight. A package provides more than economy and convenience: It releases the traveler from having to make individual arrangements for each separate element of a trip.

Tour programs generally can be divided into two categories — "escorted" (or locally hosted) and "independent." An escorted tour means that a guide will accompany the group from the beginning of the tour through to the return flight; a locally hosted tour means that the group will be met upon arrival at each location by a different local host. On independent tours, there generally is a choice of hotels, meal plans, and sightseeing trips, as well as a variety of special excursions. The independent plan is for travelers who do not want a totally set itinerary, but who do prefer confirmed hotel reservations. Whether you choose an escorted or an independent tour, always bring along complete contact information for your tour operator in case a problem arises, although US tour operators often have local affiliates who can give additional assistance or make other arrangements on the spot.

To determine whether a package — or more specifically, *which* package — fits your travel plans, start by evaluating your interests and needs, deciding how much and what you want to spend, see, and do. Gather brochures on Vancouver tours. Be sure that you take the time to read each brochure *carefully* to determine precisely what is included. Keep in mind that they are written to entice you into signing up for a package tour. Often the language is deceptive and devious. For example, a brochure may quote the lowest prices for a package tour based on facilities that are unavailable during the off-season, undesirable at any season, or just plain nonexistent. Information such as "breakfast included" (as it often is in packages to Canada) or "plus tax" (which can add up) should be taken into account. Note, too, that the prices quoted in brochures almost always are based on double occupancy: The rate listed is for each of two people sharing a double room, and if you travel alone the supplement for single accommodations can raise the price considerably (see *Hints for Single Travelers,* in this section).

In this age of erratic airfares, the brochure most often will *not* include the price of an airline ticket in the price of the package, though sample fares from various gateway cities usually will be listed separately, as extras to be added to the price of the ground arrangements. Before figuring your actual costs, check the latest fares with the airlines, because the samples invariably are out of date by the time you read them. If the brochure gives more than one category of sample fares per gateway city — such as an individual tour-basing fare, a group fare, an excursion, APEX, or other discount ticket — your travel agent or airline tour desk will be able to tell you which one applies to the package you choose, depending on when you travel, how far in advance you book, and other factors. (An individual tour-basing fare is a fare computed as part of a package that includes land arrangements, thereby entitling a carrier to reduce the air portion almost to the absolute minimum. Though it always represents a saving over full-fare coach or economy, lately the individual tour-basing fare has not been as inexpensive as the excursion and other discount fares that also are available to individuals. The group fare usually is the least expensive fare, and it is the tour operator, not you, who makes up the group.) When the brochure does include round-trip transportation in the package price, don't forget to add the cost of round-trip transportation from your home city to the departure city to come up with the total cost of the package.

Finally, read the general information regarding terms and conditions and the responsibility clause (usually in fine print at the end of the descriptive literature) to determine the precise elements for which the tour operator is — and is not — liable. Here the tour operator frequently expresses the right to change services or schedules as long as equivalent arrangements are offered. This clause also absolves the operator of responsibility for circumstances beyond human control, such as floods, avalanches, earthquakes, or injury to you or your property. While reading, ask the following questions:

1. Does the tour include airfare or other transportation, sightseeing, meals, transfers, taxes, baggage handling, tips, or any other services? Do you want all these services?
2. If the brochure indicates that "some meals" are included, does this mean a welcoming and farewell dinner, two breakfasts, or every evening meal?
3. What classes of hotels are offered? If you will be traveling alone, what is the single supplement?
4. Does the tour itinerary or price vary according to the season?
5. Are the prices guaranteed; that is, if costs increase between the time you book and the time you depart, can surcharges unilaterally be added?
6. Do you get a full refund if you cancel? If not, be sure to obtain cancellation insurance.
7. Can the operator cancel if too few people join? At what point?

One of the consumer's biggest problems is finding enough information to judge the reliability of a tour packager, since individual travelers seldom have direct contact with the firm putting the package together. Usually, a retail travel agent is interposed between customer and tour operator, and much depends on his or her candor and cooperation. So ask a number of questions about the tour you are considering. For example:

- Has the travel agent ever used a package provided by this tour operator?
- How long has the tour operator been in business? Check the Better Business Bureau in the area where the tour operator is based to see if any complaints have been filed against it.
- Is the tour operator a member of the *United States Tour Operators Association* (*USTOA;* 211 E. 51st St., Suite 12B, New York, NY 10022; phone: 212-944-5727)? *USTOA* will provide a list of its members on request; it also offers a useful brochure called *How to Select a Package Tour.*

- How many and which companies are involved in the package?
- If air travel is by charter flight, is there an escrow account in which deposits will be held; if so, what is the name of the bank?

This last question is very important. US law requires that tour operators deposit every charter passenger's deposit and subsequent payment in a proper escrow account (see "Charter Flights," above).

■ **A word of advice:** Purchasers of vacation packages who feel they're not getting their money's worth are more likely to get a refund if they complain in writing to the operator — and bail out of the whole package immediately. Alert the tour operator to the fact that you are dissatisfied, that you will be leaving for home as soon as transportation can be arranged, and that you expect a refund. They may have forms to fill out detailing your complaint; otherwise, state your case in a letter. Even if difficulty in arranging immediate transportation home detains you, your dated, written complaint should help in procuring a refund from the operator.

SAMPLE PACKAGES IN VANCOUVER: As discussed above, a typical package tour to Vancouver might include round-trip transportation, accommodations, a sightseeing tour, and several meals. Although some packages just cover arrangements at a specific hotel, others offer more extensive arrangements and may be built around activities such as fishing, hunting, or skiing, or special interests such as history, archaeology, or nature exploration.

Following is a list of some of the major tour operators that offer packages to Vancouver. Most tour operators offer several departure dates, depending on the length of the tour and areas visited. As indicated, some operators are wholesalers only, and will deal only with a travel agent.

American Express Travel Related Services (offices throughout the US; phone: 800-241-1700 for information and local branch offices). Offers city packages to Montreal and Quebec City, as well as an 11-day Eastern Highlights tour that includes stops in US and Canadian cities. The tour operator is a wholesaler, so use a travel agent.

Brenden Tours (15137 Califa St., Van Nuys, CA 91411-3021; phone: 818-785-9696 or 800-421-8446). Offers an 11-day city package to Vancouver.

Cartan Tours (1304 Parkview Ave., Suite 210, Manhattan Beach, CA 90266; phone: 800-422-7826). Offers a variety of Canada packages that include the 11-day "Best of the Rockies" with stops in Calgary, Jasper, Lake Louise, Banff, Victoria, and Vancouver.

Collette Tours (162 Middle St., Pawtucket, RI 02860; phone: 800-752-2655 in Rhode Island, 800-832-4656 elsewhere in the US). Offers 7- to 11-day city packages that include stops in Vancouver, Victoria, Kamloops, Lake Louise, Jasper, Banff, and Calgary.

Maupintour (PO Box 807, Lawrence, KS 66044; phone: 800-255-4266). Offers 1- to 2-week escorted tours throughout Canada, including several packages that include Vancouver and the Canadian Rockies. The operator is a wholesaler, so use a travel agent.

Tauck Tours (PO Box 5027, Westport, CT 06881-5027; phone: 800-451-4708 in Connecticut, 800-468-2825 elsewhere in the US). Offers several tours of Canada, including an 11-day "Grand Canadian Rockies" with stops in Vancouver and Seattle.

■ **Note:** Frequently, the best city packages are offered by the hotels, which are trying to attract guests during the weekends, when business travel drops off, and during other off-periods. These packages are sometimes advertised in local newspapers and in the Sunday travel sections of major metropolitan papers, such as *The New York Times,* which has a national edition available in most parts of the US. It's worthwhile asking about packages, especially family and special-occasion offerings, when you call to make a hotel reservation. Calling several hotels can garner you a variety of options from which to choose.

How to Use a Travel Agent

Preparing

How to Use a Travel Agent

 A reliable travel agent remains the best source of service and information for planning a trip, whether you have a specific itinerary and require an agent only to make reservations or you need extensive help in sorting through the maze of airfares, tour offerings, hotel packages, and the scores of other arrangements that may be involved in a trip to Canada.

Know what you want from a travel agent so that you can evaluate what you are getting. It is perfectly reasonable to expect your travel agent to be a thoroughly knowledgeable travel specialist, with information about your destination and, even more crucial, a command of current airfares, ground arrangements, and other wrinkles in the travel scene.

Most travel agents work through computer reservations systems (CRS). These are used to assess the availability and cost of flights, hotels, and car rentals; reservations can be booked through them as well. Despite reports of "computer bias," in which a computer may favor one airline over another, the CRS should provide agents with the entire spectrum of flights available to a given destination, and the complete range of fares, in considerably less time than it takes to telephone the airlines individually — and at no extra cost to the client.

Make the most intelligent use of a travel agent's time and expertise; understand the economics of the industry. As a client, traditionally you pay nothing for the agent's services; with few exceptions, it's all free, from hotel bookings to advice on package tours. Any money the travel agent makes on the time spent arranging your itinerary — booking hotels, resorts, or flights, or suggesting activities — comes from commissions paid by the suppliers of these services — the airlines, hotels, and so on. These commissions generally run from 10% to 15% of the total cost of the service, although suppliers often reward agencies that sell their services in volume with an increased commission called an override.

A conventional travel agent sometimes may charge a fee for special services. These chargeable items may include long-distance telephone costs incurred in making a booking, for reserving a room in a place that does not pay a commission (such as a small, out-of-the-way hotel), or for special attention such as planning a highly personalized itinerary. A fee also may be assessed in instances of deeply discounted airfares.

Choose a travel agent with the same care with which you would choose a doctor or lawyer. You will be spending a good deal of money on the basis of the agent's judgment, so you have a right to expect that judgment to be mature, informed, and interested. At the moment, unfortunately, there aren't many standards within the travel agent industry to help you gauge competence, and the quality of individual agents varies enormously.

At present, only nine states have registration, licensing, or other forms of travel agent–related legislation on their books. Rhode Island licenses travel agents; Florida, Hawaii, Iowa, and Ohio register them; and California, Illinois, Oregon, and Washington have laws governing the sale of transportation or related services. While state licensing of agents cannot absolutely guarantee competence, it can at least ensure that an agent has met some minimum requirements.

Perhaps the best way to find a travel agent is by word of mouth. If the agent (or agency) has done a good job for your friends over a period of time, it probably indicates a certain level of commitment and competence. Always ask for the name of the company *and* the name of the specific agent with whom your friends dealt, for it is that individual who will serve you, and quality can vary widely within a single agency.

Entry Requirements and Documents

 ENTRY REQUIREMENTS: The only requirement for citizens and legal residents of the US crossing the US-Canada border in either direction is that they present one form of identification. For native US citizens, this can be a valid passport or a driver's license, original or certified birth certificate, baptismal certificate, voter registration card or draft card, or other identification that officially verifies their US citizenship. Proof of current residency also may be required. Naturalized US citizens should carry their naturalization certificate or some other evidence of citizenship. Permanent residents of the US who are not American citizens should have Alien Registration Receipt cards (US Form I-151 or Form I-551). Visitors under 18 years of age not accompanied by an adult should carry a letter from a parent or guardian giving them permission to travel to Canada.

Any visitor to Canada who is not a US citizen or a permanent resident of the US must have a valid passport from some other nation. In addition, a visa may be required of visitors other than British citizens. Foreign visitors to the US who cross into Canada and then return to the US should check with the US Immigration and Naturalization Service to make sure that they have all the papers they need for reentry into the US.

DUTY AND CUSTOMS: As a general rule, the requirements for bringing the majority of items *into Canada* is that they must be in quantities small enough not to imply commercial import. Among the items that each person may take into Canada duty free are 50 cigars, 200 cigarettes, and 2.2 pounds (1 kilo) of manufactured tobacco, as well as 40 ounces (1.1 liters) of liquor or wine or 24 12-ounce cans or bottles of beer or ale. Personal effects and sports equipment appropriate for a pleasure trip also are allowed.

If you are bringing along a computer, camera, or other electronic equipment for your own use that you will be taking back to the US, you should register the item with the US Customs Service to avoid paying duty both entering and returning from Canada (see *Customs and Returning to the US,* in this section). For information on this procedure, as well as for a variety of pamphlets on US customs regulations, contact the local office of the US Customs Service or the central office, PO Box 7474, Washington, DC 20044 (phone: 202-566-8195).

■**One rule to follow:** When passing through customs, it is illegal not to declare dutiable items; penalties range from stiff fines and seizure of goods to prison terms. So don't try to sneak anything through — it just isn't worth it.

Insurance

 It is unfortunate that most decisions to buy travel insurance are impulsive and usually are made without any real consideration of the traveler's existing policies. Therefore, the first person with whom you should discuss travel insurance is your own insurance broker, not a travel agent or the clerk behind the airport insurance counter. You may discover that the insurance you already carry — homeowner's policies and/or accident, health, and life insurance — protects you adequately while you travel and that your real needs are in the more mundane areas of excess value insurance for baggage or trip cancellation insurance.

TYPES OF INSURANCE: To make insurance decisions intelligently, however, you first should understand the basic categories of travel insurance and what they cover. Then you can decide what you should have in the broader context of your personal insurance needs, and you can choose the most economical way of getting the desired protection: through riders on existing policies; with onetime, short-term policies; through a special program put together for the frequent traveler; through coverage that's part of a travel club's benefits; or with a combination policy sold by insurance companies through brokers, automobile clubs, tour operators, and travel agents.

There are seven basic categories of travel insurance:

1. Baggage and personal effects insurance
2. Personal accident and sickness insurance
3. Trip cancellation and interruption insurance
4. Default and/or bankruptcy insurance
5. Flight insurance (to cover injury or death)
6. Automobile insurance (for driving your own or a rented car)
7. Combination policies

Baggage and Personal Effects Insurance – Ask your insurance agent if baggage and personal effects are included in your current homeowner's policy, or if you will need a special floater to cover you for the duration of a trip. The object is to protect your bags and their contents in case of damage or theft anytime during your travels, not just while you're in-flight, where only limited protection is provided by the airline. Baggage liability varies from carrier to carrier, but generally speaking, on domestic flights, luggage usually is insured to $1,250 — that's per passenger, not per bag. For most international flights, including domestic portions of international flights, the airline's liability limit is approximately $9.07 per pound or $20 per kilo (which comes to about $360 per 40-pound suitcase) for checked baggage and up to $400 per passenger for unchecked baggage. Canadian airlines insure baggage for up to a maximum of $750 on domestic flights and $640 on flights originating in the US that cross the Canadian border only. These limits should be specified on your airline ticket, but to be awarded the specified amount, you'll have to provide an itemized list of lost property, and if you're including new and/or expensive items, be prepared for a request that you back up your claim with sales receipts or other proofs of purchase.

If you are carrying goods worth more than the maximum protection offered by the airline, consider excess value insurance. Additional coverage is available from airlines at an average, currently, of $1 to $2 per $100 worth of coverage, up to a maximum of $5,000. This insurance can be purchased at the airline counter when you check in, though you should arrive early enough to fill out the necessary forms and avoid holding up other passengers.

Major credit card companies provide coverage for lost or delayed baggage — and this coverage often also is over and above what the airline will pay. The basic coverage usually is automatic for all cardholders who use the credit card to purchase tickets, but to qualify for additional coverage, cardholders generally must enroll.

Additional baggage and personal effects insurance also is included in certain of the combination travel insurance policies discussed below.

■**A note of warning:** Be sure to read the fine print of any excess value insurance policy; there often are specific exclusions, such as cash, tickets, furs, gold and silver objects, art, and antiques. Insurance companies ordinarily will pay only the depreciated value of the goods rather than their replacement value. The best way to protect your property is to take photos of your valuables, and keep a record of the serial numbers of such items as cameras, typewriters, laptop computers, radios, and so on. If an airline loses your luggage, you will be asked to fill out a Property Irregularity Report before you leave the airport. Also, report the loss to the police (since the insurance company will check with the police when processing your claim).

Personal Accident and Sickness Insurance – This covers you in case of illness during your trip or death in an accident. Most policies insure you for hospital and doctors' expenses, lost income, and so on. In most cases, it is a standard part of existing health insurance policies, though you should check with your insurance broker to be sure of the conditions for which your policy will pay. If your coverage is insufficient, take out a separate vacation accident policy or an entire vacation insurance policy that includes health and life coverage.

Two examples of such comprehensive health and life insurance coverage are the travel insurance packages offered by *Wallach & Co.:*

  HealthCare Abroad: This program is available to individuals up to age 75. For $3 per day (minimum 10 days, maximum 90 days), policy holders receive $100,000 medical insurance and a $25,000 death benefit.

  HealthCare Global: This insurance package, which can be purchased for periods of 10 to 180 days, is offered for two age groups: Men and women up to age 75 receive $25,000 medical insurance and a $50,000 death benefit; those from age 75 to 84 are eligible for $12,500 medical insurance and a $25,000 death benefit. For either policy, the cost for a 10-day period is $25, with decreasing rates up to 75 days, after which the rate is $1.50 per day.

Both of these basic programs also may be bought in combination with trip cancellation and baggage insurance at extra cost. For further information, write to *Wallach & Co.,* 107 W. Federal St., Box 480, Middleburg, VA 22117-0480 (phone: 703-687-3166 in Virginia; 800-237-6615 elsewhere in the US).

Trip Cancellation and Interruption Insurance – Most package tour passengers pay for their travel well before departure. The disappointment of having to miss a vacation because of illness or any other reason pales before the awful prospect that not all (and sometimes none) of the money paid in advance might be returned. So cancellation insurance for any package tour is a must.

Although cancellation penalties vary (they are listed in the fine print in every tour brochure, and before you purchase a package tour you should know exactly what they are), rarely will a passenger get more than 50% of this money back if forced to cancel within a few weeks of scheduled departure. Therefore, if you book a package tour, you should have trip cancellation insurance to guarantee full reimbursement or refund should you, a traveling companion, or a member of your immediate family get sick, forcing you to cancel your trip or *return home early.*

The key here is *not* to buy just enough insurance to guarantee full reimbursement for the cost of the package in case of cancellation. The proper amount of coverage should be sufficient to reimburse you for the cost of having to catch up with a tour after its departure or having to travel home at the full economy airfare if you have to forgo the return flight tied to the package. There usually is quite a discrepancy between an excursion or other special fare and the amount charged to travel the same distance on a regularly scheduled flight at full economy fare.

Trip cancellation insurance is available from travel agents and tour operators in two forms: as part of a short-term, all-purpose travel insurance package (sold by the travel agent); or as specific cancellation insurance designed by the tour operator for a specific charter tour. Generally, tour operators' policies are less expensive, but also less inclusive. Cancellation insurance also is available directly from insurance companies or their agents as part of a short-term, all-inclusive travel insurance policy.

Before you decide on a policy, read each one carefully. (Either type can be purchased from a travel agent when you book the charter or package tour.) Be sure to check the fine print for stipulations concerning "family members" and "pre-existing medical conditions," as well as allowances for living expenses if you must delay your return due to injury or illness.

Default and/or Bankruptcy Insurance – Although trip cancellation insurance usually protects you if *you* are unable to complete — or begin — your trip, a fairly recent innovation is coverage in the event of default and/or bankruptcy on the part of the tour operator, airline, or other travel supplier. In some travel insurance packages, this contingency is included in the trip cancellation portion of the coverage; in others, it is a separate feature. Either way, it is becoming increasingly important. Whereas sophisticated travelers have long known to beware of the possibility of default or bankruptcy when buying a tour package, in recent years more than a few respected airlines unexpectedly have revealed their shaky financial condition, sometimes leaving hordes of stranded ticket holders in their wake. While default/bankruptcy insurance will not ordinarily result in reimbursement in time to pay for new arrangements, it can ensure that you will get your money back, and even independent travelers buying no more than an airplane ticket may want to consider it.

Flight Insurance – Airlines have carefully established limits of liability for injury to or the death of passengers on international flights. For all international flights to, from, or with a stopover in the US, all carriers are liable for up to $75,000 per passenger. For all other international flights, the liability is based on where you purchase the ticket: If booked in advance in the US, the maximum liability is $75,000; if arrangements are made abroad, the liability is $10,000. But remember, these liabilities are not the same thing as insurance policies; every penny that an airline eventually pays in the case of death or injury may be subject to a legal battle.

But before you buy last-minute flight insurance from an airport vending machine, consider the purchase in light of your total existing insurance coverage. A careful review of your current policies may reveal that you already are amply covered for accidental death. Be aware that airport insurance, the kind typically bought at a counter or from a vending machine, is among the most expensive forms of life insurance coverage, and that even within a single airport, rates for approximately the same coverage vary widely.

If you buy your plane ticket with a major credit card, you generally receive automatic insurance coverage at no extra cost. Additional coverage usually can be obtained at extremely reasonable prices, but a cardholder must sign up for it in advance.

Automobile Insurance – All drivers in Canada are required by law to have automobile insurance for their car. The minimum coverage is determined by provincial law, but this minimum usually is too low for adequate protection. Your insurance agent can advise you on the proper amount of insurance necessary. There are several kinds of coverage you should have in Canada:

1. *Liability Insurance:* This provides protection if you are sued for injuring someone or his or her property. US motorists driving in Canada should obtain a Canadian Non-Resident Inter-Province Motor Vehicle Liability Insurance Card, which provides evidence of financial responsibility by a valid automobile liability insurance policy. This card is available only through insurance agents in the US. (There usually is no charge for this card.) All provinces in Canada require visiting

motorists to produce evidence of financial responsibility should they be involved in an accident. Minimum liability requirements can be as much as CN$200,000 in some Canadian provinces. Information and advice regarding auto insurance may be obtained from the *Insurance Bureau of Canada,* 181 University Ave., Toronto, Ontario M5H 3M7, Canada (phone: 416-362-2031).

2. *Accident Insurance:* This protects against payments for death or bodily injury and includes loss of pay, medical expenses, and so on. These policies also include coverage against uninsured motorists.

3. *Comprehensive and Collision Insurance:* This protects against loss of or damage to your car. There usually is a deductible amount indicated for this coverage; it either is paid by the policy holder toward the cost of repairs or deducted from the loss settlement.

When you rent a car, the rental company is required to provide you with collision protection. In your car rental contract, you'll see that for about $10 to $13 a day you may buy optional collision damage waiver (CDW) protection. Some companies such as *Hertz* and *Avis* call the option a loss damage waiver (LDW).

If you do not accept the CDW coverage, you may be liable for as much as the full retail value of the rental car if it is damaged or stolen; by paying for the CDW you are relieved of all responsibility for any damage to the car. Before agreeing to this coverage, however, check with your own broker about your own existing personal automobile insurance policy. It very well may cover your entire liability exposure without any additional cost, or you automatically may be covered by the credit card company to which you are charging the cost of your rental. To find out the amount of rental car insurance provided by major credit cards, contact the issuing institutions.

You also should know that an increasing number of the major international car rental companies automatically are including the cost of the CDW in their basic rates. Car rental prices have increased to include this coverage, although rental company ad campaigns may promote this as a new, improved rental package "benefit." The disadvantage of this inclusion is that you may not have the option to turn down the CDW — even if you already are adequately covered by your own insurance policy or through a credit card company.

Combination Policies – Short-term insurance policies, which may include a combination of any or all of the types of insurance discussed above, are available through retail insurance agencies, automobile clubs, and many travel agents. These combination policies are designed to cover you for the duration of a single trip.

Companies offering policies of this type include the following:

Access America International (PO Box 90310, Richmond, VA 23230; phone: 800-424-3391 or 804-215-3300).

Carefree Travel Insurance (Arm Coverage, 120 Mineola Blvd., Mineola, NY 11501; phone: 800-645-2424 or 516-294-0220).

NEAR Services (450 Prairie Ave., Suite 101, Calumet City, IL 60409; phone: 708-868-6700 in the Chicago area; 800-654-6700 elsewhere in the US and Canada).

Tele-Trip (3201 Farnam St., Omaha, NE 68131; phone: 402-345-2400 in Nebraska; 800-228-9792 elsewhere in the US).

Travel Assistance International (1133 15th St. NW, Suite 400, Washington, DC 20005; phone: 202-331-1609 in Washington, DC; 800-821-2828 elsewhere in the US).

Travel Guard International (1145 Clark St., Stevens Point, WI 54481; phone: 715-345-0505 in Wisconsin; 800-826-1300 elsewhere in the US).

Travel Insurance PAK c/o The Travelers Companies (Travelers Insurance Company, Travel Insurance Division 10NB, One Tower Sq., Hartford, CT 06183-5040; phone: 203-277-2319 in Connecticut; 800-243-3174 elsewhere in the US).

Hints for Handicapped Travelers

 From 40 to 50 million people in the US alone have some sort of disability, and over half this number are physically handicapped. Like everyone else today, they — and the uncounted disabled millions around the world — are on the move. More than ever before, they are demanding facilities they can use comfortably, and they are being heard.

With the 1990 passage of the Americans with Disabilities Act, the physically handicapped increasingly will be finding better access to places and services throughout the US. The provisions of the act relating to public accommodations and transportation, which took effect in January 1992, mandate that means of access be provided except where the cost would be prohibitive, and creative alternatives are being encouraged. As the impact of the law spreads across the country, previous barriers to travel in the US should be somewhat ameliorated.

PLANNING: Make your travel arrangements well in advance and specify to all services involved the exact nature of your condition or restricted mobility. The best way to find out if your intended destination can accommodate a handicapped traveler is to write or call the local tourist authority or hotel and ask specific questions.

It is also advisable to call the hotel you are considering and ask specific questions. If you require a corridor of a certain width to maneuver a wheelchair or if you need handles on the bathroom walls for support, ask the hotel manager (many large hotels have rooms designed for the handicapped). A travel agent or the local chapter or national office of the organization that deals with your particular disability — for example, the *American Foundation for the Blind* or the *American Heart Association* — will supply the most up-to-date information on the subject.

The following organizations offer general information on access:

ACCENT on Living (PO Box 700, Bloomington, IL 61702; phone: 309-378-2961). This information service for persons with disabilities provides a free list of travel agencies specializing in arranging trips for the disabled; for a copy send a self-addressed, stamped envelope. It also offers a wide range of publications, including a quarterly magazine ($10 per year; $17.50 for 2 years; $25 for 3 years) for persons with disabilities.

Canadian Paraplegic Association (520 Sutherland Dr., Toronto, Ontario M4G 3V9, Canada; phone: 416-422-5644) is a good source of information on travel for the mobility-disabled. The association has a comprehensive library, offers accessibility information, and provides referral services.

Information Center for Individuals with Disabilities (27-43 Wormwood St., Ft. Point Pl., 1st Floor, Boston, MA 02210; phone: 800-462-5015 in Massachusetts; 617-727-5540/1 elsewhere in the US; both numbers provide voice and TDD — telecommunications device for the deaf). The center offers information and referral services on disability-related issues, publishes fact sheets on travel agents, tour operators, and other travel resources, and can help you research your trip.

Mobility International USA (*MIUSA;* PO Box 3551, Eugene, OR 97403; phone: 503-343-1284; both voice and TDD). This US branch of *Mobility International* (the main office is at 228 Borough High St., London SE1 1JX, England; phone:

011-44-71-403-5688), a nonprofit British organization with affiliates worldwide, offers members advice and assistance — including information on accommodations and other travel services, and publications applicable to the traveler's disability. *Mobility International* also offers a quarterly newsletter and a comprehensive sourcebook, *A World of Options for the 90s: A Guide to International Education Exchange, Community Service and Travel for Persons with Disabilities* ($14 for members; $16 for non-members). Membership includes the newsletter and is $20 a year; subscription to the newsletter alone is $10 annually.

National Rehabilitation Information Center (NRIC; 8455 Colesville Rd., Suite 935, Silver Spring, MD 20910; phone: 301-588-9284). A general information, resource, research, and referral service.

Paralyzed Veterans of America (PVA; PVA/ATTS Program, 801 18th St. NW, Washington, DC 20006; phone: 202-416-7708 in Washington, DC, 800-424-8200 elsewhere in the US). The members of this national service organization all are veterans who have suffered spinal-cord injuries, but it offers advocacy services and information to all persons with a disability. *PVA* also sponsors *Access to the Skies (ATTS),* a program that coordinates the efforts of the national and international air travel industry in providing airport and airplane access for the disabled. Members receive several helpful publications, as well as regular notification of conferences on subjects of interest to the disabled traveler.

Royal Association for Disability and Rehabilitation (RADAR; 25 Mortimer St., London W1N 8AB, England; phone: 44-71-637-5400). Offers a number of publications for the handicapped, including *Holidays and Travel Abroad 1993/94 — A Guide for Disabled People,* a comprehensive guidebook focusing on international travel. This publication can be ordered by sending payment in British pounds to *RADAR.* As we went to press, it cost just over £3; call for current pricing before ordering.

Society for the Advancement of Travel for the Handicapped (SATH; 347 Fifth Ave., Suite 610, New York, NY 10016; phone: 212-447-7284). To keep abreast of developments in travel for the handicapped as they occur, you may want to join *SATH,* a nonprofit organization whose members include consumers as well as travel service professionals who have experience (or an interest) in travel for the handicapped. For an annual fee of $45 ($25 for students and travelers who are 65 and older) members receive a quarterly newsletter and have access to extensive information and referral services. *SATH* also offers two useful publications: *Travel Tips for the Handicapped* (a series of informative fact sheets) and *The United States Welcomes Handicapped Visitors* (a 48-page guide covering domestic transportation and accommodations, as well as useful hints for travelers with disabilities abroad); to order, send a self-addressed, #10 envelope and $1 per title for postage.

Travel Information Service (Moss Rehabilitation Hospital, 1200 W. Tabor Rd., Philadelphia, PA 19141-3099; phone: 215-456-9600 for voice; 215-456-9602 for TDD). This service assists physically handicapped people in planning trips and supplies detailed information on accessibility for a nominal fee.

Blind travelers should contact the *American Foundation for the Blind* (15 W. 16th St., New York, NY 10011; phone: 212-620-2147 or 800-829-0500) and *The Seeing Eye* (PO Box 375, Morristown, NJ 07963-0375; phone: 201-539-4425); both provide useful information on resources for the visually impaired. *Note:* Seeing Eye dogs accompanied by their owners may enter Canada without certification or other restrictions.

The American Society for the Prevention of Cruelty to Animals (ASPCA; Education Dept., 424 E. 92 St., New York, NY 10128; phone: 212-876-7700) offers a useful booklet, *Traveling With Your Pet,* which lists inoculation and other requirements by country and territory. It is available for $5 (including postage and handling).

In addition, there are a number of publications — from travel guides to magazines — of interest to handicapped travelers. Among these are the following:

Access to the World, by Louise Weiss, offers sound tips for the disabled traveler. Published by Facts on File (460 Park Ave. S., New York, NY 10016; phone: 212-683-2244 in New York State; 800-322-8755 elsewhere in the US; 800-443-8323 in Canada), it costs $16.95. Check with your local bookstore; it also can be ordered by phone with a credit card.

The Diabetic Traveler (PO Box 8223 RW, Stamford, CT 06905; phone: 203-327-5832) is a useful quarterly newsletter for travelers with diabetes. Each issue highlights a single destination or type of travel and includes information on general resources and hints for diabetics. A 1-year subscription costs $18.95. When subscribing, ask for the free fact sheet including an index of special articles; back issues are available for $4 each.

Guide to Traveling with Arthritis, a free brochure available by writing to the Upjohn Company (PO Box 307-B, Coventry, CT 06238), provides lots of good, commonsense tips on planning your trip and how to be as comfortable as possible when traveling by car, bus, train, cruise ship, or plane.

Handicapped Travel Newsletter is regarded as one of the best sources of information for the disabled traveler. It is edited by wheelchair-bound Vietnam veteran Michael Quigley, who has traveled to 93 countries around the world. Issued every 2 months (plus special issues), a subscription is $10 per year. Write to *Handicapped Travel Newsletter,* PO Box 269, Athens, TX 75751 (phone: 903-677-1260).

Handi-Travel: A Resource Book for Disabled and Elderly Travellers, by Cinnie Noble, is a comprehensive travel guide full of practical tips for those with disabilities affecting mobility, hearing, or sight. To order this book, send $12.95, plus shipping and handling, to the *Canadian Rehabilitation Council for the Disabled,* 45 Sheppard Ave. E., Suite 801, Toronto, Ontario M2N 5W9, Canada (phone: 416-250-7490; both voice and TDD).

The Itinerary (PO Box 2012, Bayonne, NJ 07002-2012; phone: 201-858-3400). This quarterly travel magazine for people with disabilities includes information on accessibility, listings of tours, news of adaptive devices, travel aids, and special services, as well as numerous general travel hints. A subscription costs $10 a year.

The Physically Disabled Traveler's Guide, by Rod W. Durgin and Norene Lindsay, rates accessibility of a number of travel services and includes a list of organizations specializing in travel for the disabled. It is available for $9.95, plus $2 shipping and handling, from Resource Directories, 3361 Executive Pkwy., Suite 302, Toledo, OH 43606 (phone: 419-536-5353 in the Toledo area; 800-274-8515 elsewhere in the US).

Ticket to Safe Travel offers useful information for travelers with diabetes. A reprint of this article is available free from local chapters of the *American Diabetes Association.* For the nearest branch, contact the central office at 1660 Duke St., Alexandria, VA 22314 (phone: 703-549-1500 in Virginia; 800-232-3472 elsewhere in the US).

Travel for the Patient with Chronic Obstructive Pulmonary Disease, a publication of the George Washington University Medical Center, provides some sound practical suggestions for those with emphysema, chronic bronchitis, asthma, or other lung ailments. To order, send $2 to Dr. Harold Silver, 1601 18th St. NW, Washington, DC 20009 (phone: 202-667-0134).

Traveling Like Everybody Else: A Practical Guide for Disabled Travelers, by Jacqueline Freedman and Susan Gersten, offers the disabled tips on traveling by car, cruise ship, and plane, as well as lists of accessible accommodations, tour operators specializing in tours for disabled travelers, and other resources. It is available for $11.95, plus postage and handling, from Modan Publishing, PO Box 1202, Bellmore, NY 11710 (phone: 516-679-1380).

Travel Tips for Hearing-Impaired People, a free pamphlet for deaf and hearing-impaired travelers, is available from the *American Academy of Otolaryngology* (One Prince St., Alexandria, VA 22314; phone: 703-836-4444). For a copy, send a self-addressed, stamped, business-size envelope to the academy.

Travel Tips for People with Arthritis, a 31-page booklet published by the *Arthritis Foundation,* provides helpful information regarding travel by car, bus, train, cruise ship or plane, planning your trip, medical considerations, and ways to conserve your energy while traveling, and includes listings of helpful resources, such as associations and travel agencies that operate tours for disabled travelers. For a copy, contact your local *Arthritis Foundation* chapter, or send $1 to the national office, 1314 Spring St. NW, Atlanta, GA 30309 (phone: 404-872-7100 or 800-283-7800).

A few more basic resources to look for are *Travel for the Disabled,* by Helen Hecker ($19.95) and, by the same author, *Directory of Travel Agencies for the Disabled* ($19.95). *Wheelchair Vagabond,* by John G. Nelson, is another useful guide for travelers confined to a wheelchair (hardcover, $14.95; paperback, $9.95). All three titles are published by Twin Peaks Press, PO Box 129, Vancouver, WA 98666 (phone: 800-637-CALM or 206-694-2462). For $2, the publisher also will send you a catalogue of 26 books on travel for the disabled.

PLANE: The US Department of Transportation (DOT) has ruled that US airlines must accept all passengers with disabilities. As a matter of course, US airlines were pretty good about accommodating handicapped passengers even before the ruling, although each airline has somewhat different procedures. Canadian airlines also are good about accommodating the disabled traveler, but, again, policies may vary somewhat from carrier to carrier. Ask for specifics when you book your flight.

Disabled passengers always should make reservations well in advance, and should provide the airline with all relevant details of their conditions. These details include information on mobility and equipment that you will need the airline to supply — such as a wheelchair for boarding or portable oxygen for in-flight use. Be sure that the person to whom you speak fully understands the degree of your disability — the more details provided, the more effective help the airline can give you.

On the day before the flight, call back to make sure that all arrangements have been prepared, and arrive early on the day of the flight so that you can board before the rest of the passengers. It's a good idea to bring a medical certificate with you, stating your specific disability or the need to carry particular medicine.

Because most airports have jetways (corridors connecting the terminal with the door of the plane), a disabled passenger usually can be taken as far as the plane, and sometimes right onto it, in a wheelchair. If not, a narrow boarding chair may be used to take you to your seat. Your own wheelchair, which will be folded and put in the baggage compartment, should be tagged as escort luggage to assure that it's available at planeside upon landing rather than in the baggage claim area. Travel is not quite as simple if your wheelchair is battery-operated: Unless it has non-spillable batteries, it might not be accepted on board, and you will have to check with the airline ahead of time to find out how the batteries and the chair should be packaged for the flight. Usually people in wheelchairs are asked to wait until other passengers have disembarked. If you are making a tight connection, be sure to tell the attendant.

Passengers who use oxygen may not use their personal supply in the cabin, though it may be carried on the plane as cargo when properly packed and labeled (the tank must be emptied). If you will need oxygen during the flight, the airline will supply it to you (there is a charge) provided you have given advance notice — 24 hours to a few days, depending on the carrier.

Useful information on every stage of air travel, from planning to arrival, is provided in the booklet *Incapacitated Passengers Air Travel Guide.* To receive a free copy, write to the *International Air Transport Association* (Publications Sales Department, 2000 Peel St., Montreal, Quebec H3A 2R4, Canada; phone: 514-844-6311). Another helpful publication is *Air Transportation of Handicapped Persons,* which explains the general guidelines that govern air carrier policies. For a copy of this free booklet, write to the US Department of Transportation (Distribution Unit, Publications Section, M-443-2, Washington, DC 20590) and ask for "Free Advisory Circular #AC-120-32." *Access Travel: A Guide to the Accessibility of Airport Terminals,* a free publication of the *Airport Operators Council International,* provides information on more than 500 airports worldwide — including major airports in Canada — and offers ratings of 70 features, such as wheelchair accessibility to bathrooms, corridor width, and parking spaces. For a copy, contact the Consumer Information Center, Dept. 563W, Pueblo, CO 81009 (phone: 719-948-3334).

Among the major carriers serving Canada, the following airlines have TDD toll-free lines for the hearing-impaired:

Air Canada: 800-361-8071 only in Canada.
American: 800-582-1573 in Ohio; 800-543-1586 elsewhere in the US.
Canadian Airlines International: 800-465-3611 only in Canada.
Delta: 800-831-4488 throughout the US.
Northwest: 800-328-2298 throughout the US.
USAir: 800-245-2966 throughout the US.

GROUND TRANSPORTATION: Perhaps the simplest solution to getting around is to travel with an able-bodied companion who can drive. If you are accustomed to driving your own hand-controlled car and want to rent one, you may be in luck. Some rental car companies will fit cars with hand controls. *Avis* (phone: 800-331-1084) can convert a car to hand controls with as little as 24 hours' notice, though it's a good idea to make arrangements more than one day in advance. *Hertz* (phone: 800-654-3001) requires 4 days to install the controls. Neither company charges extra for hand controls, but will fit them only on mid- or full-size cars — which tend to be among the most expensive models to rent. Both companies can provide hand-controlled cars in Vancouver. But remember, hand controls often are installed only at some locations of a given company, and there usually are a limited number of these devices available, so make arrangements as early as possible.

The *American Automobile Association (AAA)* publishes a useful book, *The Handicapped Driver's Mobility Guide.* Contact the central office of your local *AAA* club for availability and pricing, which may vary at different branch offices.

TOURS: Programs designed for the physically impaired are run by specialists who have researched hotels, restaurants, and sites to be sure they present no insurmountable obstacles. The following travel agencies and tour operators specialize in making group and individual arrangements for travelers with physical or other disabilities:

Access: The Foundation for Accessibility by the Disabled (PO Box 356, Malverne, NY 11565; phone: 516-887-5798). A travelers' referral service that acts as an intermediary with tour operators and agents worldwide, and provides information on accessibility at various locations. A membership program, *Access* charges a one-time $35 registration fee.

Accessible Journeys (35 W. Sellers Ave., Ridley Park, PA 19078; phone: 215-747-0171). Arranges for medical professionals to be traveling companions — registered or licensed practical nurses, therapists, or doctors (all are experienced travelers). Several prospective companions' profiles and photos are sent to the client for perusal and, if one is acceptable, the "match" is made. The client usually pays all travel expenses for the companion, plus a set fee to compensate for wages the companion would be making at his or her usual job.

Accessible Tours/Directions Unlimited (720 N. Bedford Rd., Bedford Hills, NY 10507; phone: 914-241-1700 in New York State; 800-533-5343 elsewhere in the continental US). Arranges group or individual tours for disabled persons traveling in the company of able-bodied friends or family members. Accepts the unaccompanied traveler if completely self-sufficient.

Evergreen Travel Service (4114 198th St. SW, Suite 13, Lynnwood, WA 98036-6742; phone: 206-776-1184 or 800-435-2288 throughout the US and Canada). It offers worldwide tours for people who are disabled (Wings on Wheels Tours), sight-impaired/blind (White Cane Tours), hearing-impaired/deaf (Flying Fingers Tours), or mentally disabled (Happiness Tours). It also offers programs for people who are not disabled but who want a slower pace (Lazybones Tours), and arranges special programs for people who need dialysis.

Flying Wheels Travel (143 W. Bridge St., Box 382, Owatonna, MN 55060; phone: 507-451-5005 or 800-535-6790 throughout the US and Canada). Handles both tours and individual arrangements.

Sprout (893 Amsterdam Ave., New York, NY 10025; phone: 212-222-9575). Arranges travel programs for mildly and moderately disabled teens and adults.

USTS Travel Horizons (11 E. 44th St., New York, NY 10017; phone: 212-687-5121 in New York State or 800-487-8787 elsewhere in the US). Travel agent and registered nurse Mary Ann Hamm designs trips for individual travelers requiring all types of kidney dialysis and handles arrangements for the dialysis.

Whole Person Tours (PO Box 1084, Bayonne, NJ 07002-1084; phone: 201-858-3400). Owner Bob Zywicki travels the world with his wheelchair and offers a lineup of escorted tours (many conducted by him) for the disabled. Call for a current itinerary at the time you plan to travel. *Whole Person Tours* also publishes *The Itinerary,* a quarterly newsletter for disabled travelers (see the publication source list above).

Travelers who would benefit from being accompanied by a nurse or physical therapist also can hire a companion through *Traveling Nurses' Network,* a service provided by Twin Peaks Press (PO Box 129, Vancouver, WA 98666; phone: 800-637-CALM or 206-694-2462). For a $10 fee, clients receive the names of three nurses, whom they can then contact directly; for a $125 fee, the agency will make all the hiring arrangements for the client. Travel arrangements also may be made in some cases — the fee for this further service is determined on an individual basis.

A similar service is offered by *MedEscort International* (ABE International Airport, PO Box 8766, Allentown, PA 18105; phone: 800-255-7182 in the continental US; elsewhere, call 215-791-3111). Clients can arrange to be accompanied by a nurse, paramedic, respiratory therapist, or physician through *MedEscort.* The fees are based on the disabled traveler's needs. This service also can assist in making travel arrangements.

Hints for Single Travelers

Just about the last trip in human history on which the participants were neatly paired was the voyage of Noah's Ark. Ever since, passenger lists and tour groups have reflected the same kind of asymmetry that occurs in real life, as countless individuals set forth to see the world unaccompanied (or unencumbered, depending on your outlook) by spouse, lover, companion, or relative. Unfortunately, traveling alone can turn a traveler into a second class citizen.

The truth is that the travel industry is not very fair to people who vacation by themselves. People traveling alone almost invariably end up paying more than individuals traveling in pairs. Most travel bargains, including package tours, accommodations, resort packages, and cruises, are based on *double occupancy* rates. This means that the per-person price is offered on the basis of two people traveling together and sharing a double room (which means they each will spend a good deal more on meals and extras). The single traveler will have to pay a surcharge, called a single supplement, for exactly the same package. In extreme cases, this can add as much as 35% — and sometimes more — to the basic per-person rate.

Don't despair, however. In Vancouver, there are scores of smaller hotels and other hostelries where, in addition to a cozier atmosphere, prices still are quite reasonable for the single traveler.

The obvious, most effective alternative is to find a traveling companion. Even special "singles' tours" that promise no supplements usually are based on people sharing double rooms. Perhaps the most recent innovation along these lines is the creation of organizations that "introduce" the single traveler to other single travelers. Some charge fees, while others are free, but the basic service offered is the same: to match an unattached person with a compatible travel mate. Among such organizations are the following:

Odyssey Network (118 Cedar St., Wellesley, MA 02181; phone: 617-237-2400). Originally founded to match single women travelers, this company now includes men in its enrollment. *Odyssey* offers a quarterly newsletter for members who are seeking a travel companion, and occasionally organizes small group tours. Membership (which includes newsletter subscription) is $50.

Partners-in-Travel (PO Box 491145, Los Angeles, CA 90049; phone: 213-476-4869). Members receive a list of singles seeking traveling companions; prospective companions make contact through the agency. The membership fee is $40 per year and includes a chatty newsletter (6 issues per year).

Travel Companion Exchange (PO Box 833, Amityville, NY 11701; phone: 516-454-0880). This group publishes a newsletter for singles and a directory of individuals looking for travel companions. On joining, members fill out a lengthy questionnaire and write a small listing (much like an ad in a personal column). Based on these listings, members can request copies of profiles and contact prospective traveling companions. It is wise to join well in advance of your planned vacation so that there's enough time to determine compatibility and plan a joint trip. Membership fees, including the newsletter, are $30 for 6 months or $60 a year for a single-sex listing.

Travel in Two's (239 N. Broadway, Suite 3, N. Tarrytown, NY 10591; phone: 914-631-8409). For city programs, this company matches up solo travelers and then customizes programs for them. The firm also puts out a quarterly *Singles Vacation Newsletter,* which costs $5 per issue or $15 per year.

In addition, a number of tour packagers cater to single travelers. These companies offer packages designed for individuals interested in vacationing with a group of single travelers or in being matched with a traveling companion. Among the better established of these agencies are the following:

Cosmos This tour operator offers a number of package tours with a guaranteed-share plan whereby singles who wish to share rooms (and avoid paying the single supplement) are matched by the tour escort with individuals of the same sex and charged the basic double-occupancy tour price. Contact the firm at one of its three North American branches: 95-25 Queens Blvd., Rego Park, NY 11374 (phone: 800-221-0090 or 718-268-7000); 5301 S. Federal Circle, Littleton, CO 80123 (phone 800-221-0090); 1061 Eglinton Ave. W., Toronto, Ontario M6C 2C9, Canada (phone: 416-787-1281). *Cosmos* offers package tours to Vancouver including the "Canadian Rockies" tour.

Grand Circle Travel (347 Congress St., Boston, MA 02210; phone: 617-350-7500 or 800-221-2610). Arranges extended vacations, escorted tours and cruises for the over-50 traveler. Membership, which is automatic when you book a trip through *Grand Circle,* includes travel discounts and other extras, such as a Pen Pals service for singles seeking travel companions.

Marion Smith Singles (611 Prescott Pl., N. Woodmere, NY 11581; phone: 516-791-4852, 516-791-4865, or 212-944-2112). Specializes in tours for singles ages 20 to 50, who can choose to share accommodations to avoid paying single-supplement charges.

Saga International Holidays (222 Berkeley St., Boston MA 02116; phone: 617-451-6808 or 800-343-0273). A subsidiary of a British company specializing in older travelers, many of them single, *Saga* offers a broad selection of packages for people age 60 and over or those 50 to 59 traveling with someone 60 or older. Although anyone can book a *Saga* trip, a club membership (no fee) includes a subscription to their newsletter, as well as other publications and travel services — such as a matching service for single travelers. Several tour packages include a 16-day "Western Canada" which begins and ends in Vancouver; and the 14-day "Vancouver Island and the Cascades" that highlights San Francisco, Sacramento, Portland, and Vancouver.

Singles in Motion (545 W. 236th St., Suite 1D, Riverdale, NY 10463; phone: 718-884-4464). Offers a number of packages for single travelers, including tours, cruises, and excursions focusing on outdoor activities such as hiking and biking.

A good book for single travelers is *Traveling On Your Own,* by Eleanor Berman, which offers tips on traveling solo and includes information on trips for singles. Available in bookstores, it also can be ordered by sending $12.95, plus postage and handling, to Random House, Order Dept., 400 Hahn Rd., Westminster, MD 21157 (phone: 800-733-3000).

Single travelers also may want to subscribe to *Going Solo,* a newsletter that offers helpful information on going on your own. Issued eight times a year, a subscription costs $29. Contact Doerfer Communications, PO Box 1035, Cambridge, MA 02239 (phone: 617-876-2764).

Hints for Older Travelers

Special discounts and more free time are just two factors that have given Americans over age 65 a chance to see the world at affordable prices. Senior citizens make up an ever-growing segment of the travel population, and the trend among them is to travel more frequently and for longer periods of time.

PLANNING: When planning a vacation, prepare your itinerary with one eye on your own physical condition and the other on your interests. One important factor to keep in mind is not to overdo anything and to be aware of the effects that the weather may have on your capabilities.

Older travelers may find the following publications of interest:

Going Abroad: 101 Tips for the Mature Traveler offers tips on preparing for your trip, commonsense precautions en route, and some basic travel terminology. This concise free booklet is available from *Grand Circle Travel,* 347 Congress St., Boston, MA 02210 (phone: 800-221-2610 or 617-350-7500).

The International Health Guide for Senior Citizen Travelers, by Dr. W. Robert Lange, covers such topics as trip preparations, food and water precautions, adjusting to weather and climate conditions, finding a doctor, motion sickness, jet lag, and so on. Also includes a list of resource organizations that provide medical assistance for travelers. It is available for $4.95 plus $1 in postage, from Pilot Books, 103 Cooper St., Babylon, NY 11702 (phone: 516-422-2225).

Mature Traveler is a monthly newsletter that provides information on travel discounts, places of interest, useful tips, and other topics of interest for travelers 49 and up. To subscribe, send $24.95 to GEM Publishing Group, PO Box 50820, Reno, NV 89513 (phone: 702-786-7419).

Senior Citizen's Guide To Budget Travel In The US And Canada, by Paige Palmer, provides specific information on economical travel options for senior citizens. To order, send $4.95, plus postage and handling, to Pilot Books (address above).

Take a Camel to Lunch and Other Adventures for Mature Travelers, by Nancy O'Connell, offers offbeat and unusual adventures for travelers over 50. Available at bookstores or directly from Bristol Publishing Enterprises for $8.95 (plus shipping and handling), PO Box 1737, San Leandro, CA 94577 (phone: 800-346-4889 or 510-895-4461).

Travel Tips for Older Americans is a useful booklet that provides good, basic advice. This US State Department publication (stock number: 044-000-02270-2) can be ordered by sending a check or money order for $1 to the Superintendent of Documents (US Government Printing Office, Washington, DC 20420) or by calling 202-783-3238 and charging the order to a credit card.

Unbelievably Good Deals & Great Adventures That You Absolutely Can't Get Unless You're Over 50, by Joan Rattner Heilman, offers travel tips for older travelers, including discounts on accommodations and transportation, as well as a list of organizations for seniors. It is available for $7.95 (plus shipping and handling) from Contemporary Books, 180 N. Michigan Ave., Chicago, IL 60601 (phone: 312-782-9181).

HEALTH: Health facilities generally are maintained by individual Canadian provinces, but Blue Cross usually is honored throughout Canada. Pre-trip medical and dental checkups are strongly recommended. In addition, be sure to take along any prescription medication you need, enough to last *without a new prescription* for the duration of your trip; pack all medications with a note from your doctor for the benefit of airport authorities. If you have specific medical problems, bring prescriptions and a "medical file" composed of the following:

1. A summary of your medical history and current diagnosis.
2. A list of drugs to which you are allergic.
3. Your most recent electrocardiogram, if you have heart problems.
4. Your doctor's name, address, and telephone number.

DISCOUNTS AND PACKAGES: Since guidelines change from place to place, it is a good idea to inquire in advance about discounts on accommodations, transportation, tickets to theater and concert performances and movies, entrance fees to museums, national monuments, and other attractions. Senior citizens with identification are eligible for a large variety of discounts across Canada. Some discounts are only available to Canadians, but many others are available to anyone over 65. For instance, depending on the local management, discounts of 10% to 25% often are available at a variety of hotel chains, including *Holiday Inn, Howard Johnson, Rodeway Inn,* and *Sheraton.* In addition, both *Air Canada* and *Canadian Airlines International* offer discounts on fares to senior citizens 62 and over (and often one traveling companion per senior). Given the continuing changes in the airline industry, however, these discounted fares may not be available when you purchase your tickets. For more information on current prices and applicable restrictions, contact the individual carriers.

Some discounts, however, are extended only to bona fide members of certain senior citizens organizations. Because the same organizations frequently offer package tours to both domestic and international destinations, the benefits of membership are twofold: Those who join can take advantage of discounts as individual travelers and also reap the savings that group travel affords. In addition, because the age requirements for some of these organizations are quite low (or nonexistent), the benefits can begin to accrue early.

In order to take advantage of these discounts, you should carry proof of your age or eligibility (for Canadians, a special card issued by the province — for older visitors from the US and other countries, a driver's license, passport, birth certificate, membership card in a recognized senior citizens organization, or a Medicare card should be sufficient). Among the organizations dedicated to helping older travelers see the world are the following:

American Association of Retired Persons (AARP; 601 E St. NW, Washington, DC 20049; phone: 202-434-2277). The largest and best-known of these organizations. Membership is open to anyone 50 or over, whether retired or not; dues are $8 a year, $20 for 3 years, or $45 for 10 years, and include spouse. The *AARP* Travel Experience Worldwide program, available through *American Express Travel Related Services,* offers members travel programs designed exclusively for older travelers. Members can book these services by calling *American Express* at 800-927-0111 for land and air travel.

Mature Outlook (Customer Service Center, 6001 N. Clark St., Chicago, IL 60660; phone: 800-336-6330). Through its *Travel Alert,* tours, cruises, and other vacation packages are available to members at special savings. Hotel and car rental discounts and travel accident insurance also are available. Membership is open to anyone 50 years of age or older, costs $9.95 a year, and includes a bimonthly newsletter and magazine, as well as information on package tours.

National Council of Senior Citizens (1331 F St. NW, Washington, DC 20004; phone: 202-347-8800). Here, too, the emphasis is on keeping costs low. This nonprofit organization offers members a different roster of package tours each year, as well as individual arrangements. Although most members are over 50, membership is open to anyone (regardless of age) for an annual fee of $12 per person or couple, or $30 for 3 years. Lifetime membership costs $150. For information, contact its affiliated travel agency *Vantage Travel Service* (phone: 800-322-6677).

Certain travel agencies and tour operators offer special trips geared to older travelers. Among them are the following:

Evergreen Travel Service (4114 198th St. SW, Suite 13, Lynnwood, WA 98036-6742; phone: 206-776-1184 or 800-435-2288 throughout the US and Canada.) This specialist in trips for persons with disabilities recently introduced Lazybones Tours, a program offering leisurely trips for older travelers. Most programs are first class or deluxe, and include an escort.

Gadabout Tours (700 E. Tahquitz, Palm Springs, CA 92262; phone: 619-325-5556 or 800-521-7309 in California; 800-952-5068 elsewhere in the US). Offers escorted tours and cruises throughout Canada including an 18-day "Canadian Rockies Roundup" with a stopover in Vancouver.

Grand Circle Travel (347 Congress St., Boston, MA 02210; phone: 800-221-2610 or 617-350-7500). Caters exclusively to the over-50 traveler and packages a large variety of escorted tours, including the 15-day "Northwest National Parks", cruises, and extended vacations. Membership, which is automatic when you book a trip through *Grand Circle,* includes discount certificates on future trips and other travel services, such as a matching service for single travelers and a helpful free booklet, *Going Abroad: 101 Tips for Mature Travelers* (see the source list above).

OmniTours (104 Wilmot Rd., Deerfield, IL 60015; phone: 800-962-0060 or 708-374-0088). Offers combination air and rail group tours designed for travelers 50 years and older. Their itineraries include a 14-day "Pacific Northwest" tour with stops in Seattle, Vancouver, and Lake Louise.

Saga International Holidays (120 Boylston St., Boston MA 02116; phone: 617-451-6808 or 800-343-0273). A subsidiary of a British company catering to older travelers, *Saga* offers a broad selection of packages for people age 60 and over or those 50 to 59 traveling with someone 60 or older. Although anyone can book a *Saga* trip, a $15 club membership includes a subscription to their newsletter, as well as other publications and travel services.

Many travel agencies, particularly the larger ones, are delighted to make presentations to help a group of senior citizens select destinations. A local chamber of commerce should be able to provide the names of such agencies. Once a time and place are determined, an organization member or travel agent can obtain group quotations for transportation, accommodations, meal plans, and sightseeing. Larger groups usually get the best breaks.

Another choice open to older travelers is a trip that includes an educational element. *Elderhostel,* a nonprofit organization, offers educational programs at schools worldwide. Most Canadian programs run for 1 week, and include double occupancy accommodations in hotels or student residence halls and all meals. Elderhostelers must be at least 60 years old (younger if a spouse or companion qualifies), in good health, and not in need of special diets. For a free catalogue describing the program and current offerings, contact *Elderhostel* (75 Federal St., Boston, MA 02110; phone: 617-426-7788) or *Elderhostel Canada* (308 Wellington St., Kingston, Ontario K7K 7A7, Canada; phone: 613-530-2222). Those interested in the program also can borrow slides at no charge or purchase an informational videotape for $5.

Hints for Traveling with Children

 What better way to encounter the world's variety than in the company of the young, wide-eyed members of your family? Their presence does not have to be a burden or an excessive expense. The current generation of discounts for children and family package deals can make a trip together quite reasonable.

A family trip to Vancouver will be an investment in your children's future, making geography and history come alive to them, and leaving a sure memory that will be among the fondest you will share with them someday. Their insights will be refreshing to you; their impulses may take you to unexpected places with unexpected dividends.

PLANNING: Here are several hints for making a trip with children easy and fun:

1. Children, like everyone else, will derive more pleasure from a trip if they know something about their destination before they arrive. Begin their education about a month before you leave. Using maps, travel magazines, and books, give children a clear idea of where you are going and how far away it is.
2. Children should help to plan the itinerary, and where you go and what you do should reflect some of their ideas. If they already know something about the sites they'll visit, they will have the excitement of recognition when they arrive.
3. Familiarize your children with Canadian dollars. Give them an allowance for the trip and be sure they understand just how far it will or won't go.
4. Give children specific responsibilities: The job of carrying their own flight bags and looking after their personal things, along with some other light chores, will give them a stake in the journey.
5. Give each child a travel diary or scrapbook to take along.

Children's books about Canada provide an excellent introduction to the country and culture and can be found at many general bookstores and in libraries.

And for parents, *Travel With Your Children* (*TWYCH;* 45 W. 18th St., 7th Floor, New York, NY 10011; phone: 212-206-0688) publishes a newsletter, *Family Travel Times,* that focuses on families with young travelers and offers helpful hints. An annual subscription (10 issues) is $35 and includes a copy of the "Airline Guide" issue (updated every other year), which focuses on the subject of flying with children. This special issue also is available separately for $10.

Another newsletter devoted to family travel is *Getaways.* This quarterly publication provides reviews of family-oriented literature, activities, and useful travel tips. To subscribe, send $25 to *Getaways,* Att. Ms. Brooke Kane, PO Box 8282, McLean, VA 22107 (phone: 703-534-8747).

Also of interest to parents traveling with their children is *How to Take Great Trips With Your Kids,* by psychologist Sanford Portnoy and his wife, Joan Flynn Portnoy. The book includes helpful tips from fellow family travelers, tips on economical accommodations, and touring by car, recreational vehicle, and train, as well as over 50 games to play with your children en route. It is available for $8.95, plus shipping and handling, from Harvard Common Press, 535 Albany St., Boston, MA 02118 (phone: 617-423-5803).

Another book on family travel, *Travel with Children* by Maureen Wheeler, offers a wide range of practical tips on traveling with children, and includes accounts of the author's family travel experiences. It is available for $10.95, plus shipping and handling, from Lonely Planet Publications, 155 Filbert St., Oakland, CA 94607 (phone: 510-893-8555).

Adventure Travel North America, by Pat Dickerman (Adventure Guides, 36 E. 57th St., New York, NY 10022; phone: 800-252-7899 or 212-355-6334; $18, plus shipping and handling), is a good source of companies featuring family travel adventures. Also see *Great Vacations with Your Kids,* by Dorothy Jordan (Dutton; $12.95), *What to Do with the Kids This Year: One Hundred Family Vacation Places with Time Off for You!,* by Jane Wilford and Janet Tice (Globe Pequot Press; $8.95), and *Super Family Vacations,* by Martha Shirk (HarperCollins; $14).

Finally, parents arranging a trip with their children may want to contact *Let's Take the Kids* (1268 Devon Ave., Los Angeles, CA 90024; phone: 800-726-4349 or 213-274-7088), an information service specializing in family travel. Although they do not arrange or book trips, this organization provides parents with information and advice on questions they may have about accommodations, itineraries, transportation, and other aspects of a planned vacation. They also offer a parent travel network, whereby parents who have been to a particular destination can evaluate it for others.

PLANE: Begin early to investigate all available discounts and charter flights, as well as any package deals and special rates offered by the major airlines. Booking is sometimes required up to 2 months in advance. You may well find that charter companies offer no reductions for children, or not enough to offset the risk of last-minute delays or other inconveniences to which charters are subject. The major scheduled airlines, on the other hand, almost invariably provide hefty discounts for children.

When you make your reservations, tell the airline that you are traveling with a child. Children ages 2 through 11 generally travel at about a 20% to 30% discount off regular full-fare adult ticket prices on international flights. This children's fare, however, usually is much higher than the excursion fare, which is applicable to any traveler regardless of age. An infant under 2 years of age usually can travel free if it sits on an adult's lap. A second infant without a second adult would pay the fare applicable to children ages 2 through 11.

Although some airlines will, on request, supply bassinets for infants, most carriers encourage parents to bring their own safety seat on board, which then is strapped into the airline seat with a regular seat belt. This is much safer — and certainly more comfortable — than holding the child in your lap. If you do not purchase a seat for your baby, you have the option of bringing the infant restraint along on the off-chance that there might be an empty seat next to yours — in which case some airlines will let you use that seat at no charge for your baby and infant seat. However, if there is no empty seat available, the infant seat no doubt will have to be checked as baggage (and you may have to pay an additional charge), since it generally does not fit under the seat or in the overhead racks. The safest bet is to pay for a seat.

Be forewarned: Some safety seats designed primarily for use in cars do not fit into plane seats properly. Although nearly all seats manufactured since 1985 carry labels indicating whether they meet federal standards for use aboard planes, actual seat sizes may vary from carrier to carrier. At the time of this writing, the FAA was in the process of reviewing and revising the federal regulations regarding infant travel and safety devices — it was still to be determined if children should be *required* to sit in safety seats and whether the airlines will have to provide them.

If using one of these infant restraints, you should try to get bulkhead seats, which will provide extra room to care for your child during the flight. You also should request a bulkhead seat when using a bassinet — again, this is not as safe as strapping the child in. On some planes bassinets hook into a bulkhead wall; on others they are placed on the floor in front of you. (Note that bulkhead seats often are reserved for families traveling with children.) As a general rule, babies should be held during takeoff and landing.

Request seats on the aisle if you have a toddler or if you think you will need to use the bathroom frequently. Carry onto the plane all you will need to care for and occupy your children during the flight — formula, diapers, a sweater, books, favorite stuffed animals, and so on. Dress your baby simply, with a minimum of buttons and snaps, because the only place you may have to change a diaper is at your seat or in a small lavatory.

On some airlines, you also can ask for a hot dog, hamburger, or even a fruit plate instead of the airline's regular lunch or dinner if you give at least 24 hours' notice. Some, but not all, airlines have baby food aboard and the flight attendant can warm a bottle for you. While you should bring along toys from home, also ask about children's diversions. Some carriers have terrific free packages of games, coloring books, and puzzles.

When the plane takes off and lands, make sure your baby is nursing or has a bottle, pacifier, or thumb in its mouth. This sucking will make the child swallow and help to clear stopped ears. A piece of hard candy will do the same for an older child.

Parents traveling by plane with toddlers, children, or young teenagers may want to consult *When Kids Fly,* a free booklet published by Massport (Public Affairs Department, 10 Park Plaza, Boston, MA 02116-3971; phone: 617-973-5600), which includes helpful information on airfares for children, infant seats, what to do in the event of overbooked or cancelled flights, and so on.

■ **Note:** Newborn babies, whose lungs may not be able to adjust to the altitude, should not be taken aboard an airplane. And some airlines may refuse to allow a pregnant woman in her 8th or 9th month to fly. Check with the airline ahead of time, and carry a letter from your doctor stating that you are fit to travel — and indicating the estimated date of birth.

Things to Remember
1. If you are visiting many sites, pace the days with children in mind. Break the trip into half-day segments, with running around or "doing" time built in.
2. Don't forget that a child's attention span is far shorter than an adult's. Children don't have to see every sight or all of any sight to learn something from their trip; watching, playing with, and talking to other children can be equally enlightening.
3. Let your children lead the way sometimes; their perspective is different from yours, and they may lead you to things you would never have noticed on your own.
4. Remember the places that children love to visit: aquariums, zoos, amusement parks, nature trails, and so on. Among the activities that may pique their interest are bicycling, boat trips, visiting planetariums and children's museums, and viewing natural habitat exhibits. Children's favorites in Vancouver include the *Vancouver Aquatic Centre,* the children's zoo and miniature train at *Stanley Park,* and the *Maplewood Children's Farm.*

On the Road

Credit and Currency

 It may seem hard to believe, but one of the greatest (and least understood) costs of travel is money itself. Your one single objective in relation to the care and retention of your travel funds is to make them stretch as far as possible. When you do spend money, it should be on things that expand and enhance your travel experience, with no buying power lost due to carelessness or lack of knowledge. This requires more than merely ferreting out the best airfare or the most charming budget hotel. It means being canny about the management of money itself. Herewith, a primer on making money go as far as possible when traveling.

CURRENCY: Travelers from the US should have little difficulty with matters of exchange in Canada. Both countries have money systems based on 100 cents to the dollar, although the US dollar and the Canadian dollar are not equal in value. The value of Canadian currency in relation to the US dollar fluctuates daily, affected by a wide variety of phenomena.

Although US dollars usually are accepted in Canada, you certainly will lose a percentage of your dollar's buying power if you do not take the time to convert it into the local legal tender. By paying for goods and services in local currency, you save money by not negotiating invariably unfavorable exchange rates for every small purchase, and avoid difficulty where US currency is not readily — or happily — accepted. *Throughout this book, unless specifically stated otherwise, prices are given in US dollars.*

There is no limit to the amount of US currency that can be brought into Canada. To avoid problems anywhere along the line, it's advisable to fill out any customs forms provided when leaving the US on which you can declare all money you are taking with you — cash, traveler's checks, and so on. US law requires that anyone taking more than $10,000 into or out of the US must report this fact on customs form No. 4790, which is available at all international airports or from any office of US Customs. If taking over $10,000 out of the US, you must report this *before* leaving the US; if returning with such an amount, you should include this information on your customs declaration. Although travelers usually are not questioned by customs officials about currency when entering or leaving, the sensible course is to observe all regulations just to be on the safe side.

In Vancouver, as in the rest of Canada, you will find the official rate of exchange posted in banks, airports, money exchange houses, hotels, and some shops. As a general rule, expect to get more local currency for your US dollar at banks than at any other commercial establishment. Exchange rates do change from day to day, and most banks offer the same (or very similar) exchange rates. (In a pinch, the convenience of cashing money in your hotel — sometimes on a 24-hour basis — *may* make up for the difference in the exchange rate.) Don't try to bargain in banks or hotels — no one will alter the rates for you.

Money exchange houses are financial institutions that charge a fee for the service of exchanging dollars for local currency. When considering alternatives, be aware that although the rate varies among these establishments, the rates of exchange offered are bound to be less favorable than the terms offered at nearby banks — again, don't be surprised if you get fewer Canadian dollars for your US dollar than the rate published in the papers.

That said, however, the following rules of thumb are worth remembering:

Rule number one: Never (repeat: *never*) exchange more than $10 for foreign currency at hotels, restaurants, or retail shops. If you do, you are sure to lose a significant amount of your US dollar's buying power. If you do come across a storefront exchange counter offering what appears to be an incredible bargain, there's too much counterfeit specie in circulation to take the chance.

Rule number two: Estimate your needs carefully; if you overbuy, you lose twice — buying and selling back. Every time you exchange money, someone is making a profit, and rest assured it isn't you. Use up foreign notes before leaving, saving just enough for last-minute incidentals, and tips.

Rule number three: Learn the local currency quickly and keep abreast of daily fluctuations in the exchange rate. These are listed in the *International Herald Tribune* daily for the preceding day, as well as in every major newspaper in Canada. Rates change to some degree every day. For rough calculations, it is quick and safe to use round figures, but for purchases and actual currency exchanges, carry a small pocket calculator to help you compute the exact rate. Inexpensive calculators specifically designed to convert currency amounts for travelers are widely available.

When changing money, don't be afraid to ask how much commission you're being charged, and the exact amount of the prevailing exchange rate. In fact, in any exchange of money for goods or services, you should work out the rate before making any payment.

TRAVELER'S CHECKS: It's wise to carry traveler's checks instead of (or in addition to) cash, since it's possible to replace them if they are stolen or lost. Issued in various denominations and available in both US and Canadian dollars with adequate proof of identification (credit cards, driver's license, passport), traveler's checks are as good as cash in most hotels, restaurants, stores, and banks.

You will be able to cash traveler's checks fairly easily throughout Canada. However, even in metropolitan areas, don't assume that restaurants, small shops, and other establishments are going to be able to change checks of large denominations.

Although traveler's checks are available in some foreign currencies, such as Canadian dollars, the exchange rates offered by the issuing companies in the US generally are far less favorable than those available from banks both in the US and abroad. Therefore, it usually is better to carry the bulk of your travel funds abroad in US dollar–denomination traveler's checks.

Every type of traveler's check is legal tender in banks around the world, and each company guarantees full replacement if checks are lost or stolen. After that the similarity ends. Some charge a fee for purchase, others are free; you can buy traveler's checks at almost any bank, and some are available by mail. Most important, each traveler's check issuer differs slightly in its refund policy — the amount refunded immediately, the accessibility of refund locations, the availability of a 24-hour refund service, and the time it will take for you to receive replacement checks. For instance, *American Express* guarantees replacement of lost or stolen traveler's checks in under 3 hours at any *American Express* office — other companies may not be as prompt. (Travelers should keep in mind that *American Express*'s 3-hour policy is based on a traveler's being able to provide the serial numbers of the lost checks. Without these numbers, refunds can take much longer.)

We cannot overemphasize the importance of knowing how to replace lost or stolen checks. All of the traveler's check companies have agents around the world, both in their own name and at associated agencies (usually, but not necessarily, banks), where refunds can be obtained during business hours. Most of them also have 24-hour toll-free telephone lines, and some even will provide emergency funds to tide you over on a Sunday.

Be sure to make a photocopy of the refund instructions that will be given to you by the issuing institution at the time of purchase. To avoid complications should you need to redeem lost checks (and to speed up the replacement process), keep the purchase receipt and an accurate list, by serial number, of the checks that have been spent or cashed. You may want to incorporate this information in an "emergency packet," also including the numbers of the credit cards you are carrying, and any other bits of information you shouldn't be without. Always keep these records separate from the checks and the original records themselves (you may want to give them to a traveling companion to hold).

Several of the major traveler's check companies charge 1% for the acquisition of their checks; others don't. To receive fee-free traveler's checks you may have to meet certain qualifications — for instance, *Thomas Cook* checks issued in US currency are free if you make your travel arrangements through its travel agency; *American Express* traveler's checks are available without charge to members of the *American Automobile Association (AAA)*. Holders of some credit cards (such as the *American Express Platinum* card) also may be entitled to fee traveler's checks. The issuing institution (e.g., the particular bank at which you purchase them) may itself charge a fee. If you purchase traveler's checks at a bank in which you or your company maintains significant accounts (especially commercial accounts of some size), the bank may absorb the 1% fee as a courtesy.

American Express, Bank of America, Citicorp, MasterCard, Thomas Cook, and *Visa* all offer traveler's checks. Here is a list of the major companies issuing traveler's checks and the numbers to call in the event that loss or theft makes replacement necessary:

American Express: To report lost or stolen checks in the US and Canada, call 800-221-7282.

Bank of America: To report lost or stolen checks in the US, call 800-227-3460. In Canada, call 415-624-5400, collect, 24 hours.

Citicorp: To report lost or stolen checks in the US, call 800-645-6556. In Canada, call 813-623-1709, collect.

MasterCard: Note that *Thomas Cook Travel* (below) is now handling all *MasterCard* traveler's checks, inquiries, and refunds.

Thomas Cook MasterCard: To report lost or stolen checks in the US, call 800-223-7373; in Canada call 609-987-7300, collect.

Visa: To report lost or stolen checks throughout the US and Canada, call 800-227-6811.

CREDIT CARDS: Some establishments you may encounter during the course of your travels may not honor any credit cards and some may not honor all cards, so there is a practical reason to carry more than one. Most US credit cards, including the principal bank cards, are honored in Canada. The following is a list of credit cards that enjoy wide domestic and international acceptance:

American Express: Cardholders can cash personal checks for traveler's checks and cash at *American Express* or its representatives' offices in the US and Canada up to the following limits (within any 21-day period): $1,000 for *Green* and *Optima* cardholders; $5,000 for *Gold* cardholders; and $10,000 for *Platinum* cardholders. Check cashing also is available to cardholders who are guests at participating hotels in the US and Canada (up to $250) and, for holders of airline tickets, at participating airlines (up to $50). Free travel accident, baggage, and car rental insurance is provided if the ticket or rental is charged to the card; additional insurance also is available for additional cost. For further information or to report a lost or stolen *American Express* card, call 800-528-4800 throughout the continental US and Canada.

Carte Blanche: Free travel accident, baggage, and car rental insurance if ticket or rental is charged to card; additional insurance also is available at additional cost. For medical, legal, and travel assistance worldwide, call 800-356-3448 throughout the US and Canada. For further information or to report a lost or stolen *Carte Blanche* card, call 800-525-9135 throughout the US and Canada.

Diners Club: Emergency personal check cashing for cardholders staying at participating hotels and motels in the US (up to $250 per stay). Free travel accident, baggage, and car rental insurance if ticket or rental is charged to card; additional insurance also is available for an additional fee. For medical, legal, and travel assistance worldwide, call 800-356-3448 throughout the US and Canada. For further information or to report a lost or stolen *Diners Club* card, call 800-525-9135 throughout the US and Canada.

Discover Card: Offered by a subsidiary of *Sears, Roebuck & Co.,* it provides cardholders with cash advances at numerous automatic teller machines and *Sears* stores throughout the US. For further information and to report a lost or stolen *Discover* card, call 800-DISCOVER throughout the US; in Canada, call 302-323-7834, collect.

MasterCard: Cash advances are available at participating banks worldwide. Check with your issuing bank for information. *MasterCard* also offers a 24-hour emergency lost card service; call 800-826-2181 throughout the US and Canada; in Canada you can also call 314-275-6690, collect.

Visa: Cash advances are available at participating banks worldwide. Check with your issuing bank for information. *Visa* also offers a 24-hour emergency lost card service; call 800-336-8472 throughout the US. Once in Canada, call 415-570-3200, collect.

SENDING MONEY ABROAD: If you have used up your traveler's checks, cashed as many emergency personal checks as your credit card allows, drawn on your cash advance line to the fullest extent, and still need money, have it sent to you via one of the following services:

American Express (phone: 800-926-9400 for an operator). Offers a service called "MoneyGram," completing money transfers generally within 15 minutes. The sender can go to any *American Express Travel Office* or MoneyGram agent location in the US and transfer money by presenting cash or credit card — *Discover, MasterCard, Visa* or *American Express Optima* card (no other *American Express* or other credit cards are accepted). *American Express Optima* cardholders also can arrange for this transfer over the phone. To collect at the other end, the receiver must show identification (passport, driver's license, or other picture ID) or answer a test question at an *American Express Travel Office* (there are over 3,000) or at a branch of an affiliated bank in Canada. For further information on this service, call 800-543-4080.

Western Union Telegraph Company (phone: 800-325-4176 throughout the US). A friend or relative can go, cash in hand, to any *Western Union* office in the US, where, for a charge of $50 or less (it varies with the amount of the transaction), the funds will be transferred to one of *Western Union*'s branch offices. When the money arrives you will not be notified — you must go to the *Western Union* branch office to inquire. Transfers generally take only about 15 minutes. The funds will be turned over in Canadian currency, based on the rate of exchange in effect on the day of receipt. For a higher fee, the US party to this transaction may call *Western Union* with a *MasterCard* or *Visa* number to send up to $2,000.

If you are literally down to your last cent, and you have no other way to obtain cash, the nearest US consulate (see *Legal Aid and Consular Services,* in this section) will let you call home to set these matters in motion.

CASH MACHINES: Automatic teller machines (ATMs) are increasingly common worldwide. If your bank participates in one of the international ATM networks (most do), the bank will issue you a "cash card" along with a personal identification code or number (also called a PIC or PIN). You can use this card at any ATM in the same electronic network to check your account balances, transfer monies between checking and savings accounts, and — most important for a traveler — withdraw cash instantly. Network ATMs generally are located in banks, commercial and transportation centers, and near major tourist attractions.

Some financial institutions offer exclusive automatic teller machines for their own customers only at bank branches. At the time of this writing, ATMs which *are* connected generally belong to one of the following two international networks:

> *CIRRUS:* Has over 75,000 ATMs worldwide, including 61 in Vancouver. *Master-Card* and *Visa* cardholders also may use their cards to draw cash against their credit lines. For more information on the *CIRRUS* network and the location of the nearest ATM call 800-4-CIRRUS; for all other information contact your financial institution.

> *PLUS:* Has over 60,000 automatic teller machines worldwide, including 175 in Vancouver. *MasterCard* and *Visa* cardholders also may use their cards to draw cash against their credit lines. For a free directory listing the locations of these machines and further information on the *PLUS* network, call 800-THE-PLUS.

Information about these networks is available at member bank branches, where you can obtain free booklets listing the locations worldwide. Note that a recent change in banking regulations permits financial institutions to subscribe to *both* the *CIRRUS* and *PLUS* systems, allowing users of either network to withdraw funds from ATMs at participating banks.

Time Zones, Business Hours, and Public Holidays

TIME ZONES: Canada is divided into six time zones, but because the two most northeasterly zones — Newfoundland standard time and Atlantic standard time — are only a half hour apart, there is no more than a 5½-hour difference between its east and west coasts. Traveling west from Atlantic standard time, the zones get earlier by hour intervals.

Greenwich Mean Time — the time in Greenwich, England, at longitude 0°0′ — is the base from which all other time zones are measured. Areas in zones west of Greenwich have earlier times and are called Greenwich Minus; those to the east have later times and are called Greenwich Plus. For example, New York City — which falls into the Greenwich Minus 5 time zone — is 5 hours earlier than Greenwich, England.

Vancouver is in the Pacific Standard time zone, which means that the time is 8 hours earlier than it is in Greenwich, England.

Daylight savings time in Canada, as in the US, begins on the first Sunday in April and continues until the last Sunday in October.

Canadian timetables use a 24-hour clock to denote arrival and departure times, which means that hours are expressed sequentially from 1 AM. By this method, 9 AM is recorded as 0900, noon as 1200, 1 PM as 1300, 6 PM as 1800, midnight as 2400, and so on. For example, the departure of a train at 7 AM will be announced as "0700"; one leaving at 7 PM will be announced as "1900."

BUSINESS HOURS: In Vancouver, business hours are fairly standard and similar to those in the US: 9 AM to 5 PM, Mondays through Fridays. While an hour lunch break is customary, employees often take it in shifts so that service is not interrupted, especially at banks and other public service operations.

Banks traditionally are open from 10 AM to 3 PM, Mondays through Thursdays, and until 6 PM on Fridays, but, as in the US, the trend is toward longer hours. Banks generally are closed on Saturdays and Sundays, although in major cities such as Vancouver some banks offer services on Saturday mornings and afternoons.

Retail stores usually are open from 9 or 9:30 AM to 5 or 6PM. They often are open until 9 PM on Thursday or Friday nights. Most major stores are open on Saturdays.

PUBLIC HOLIDAYS: In Vancouver the public holidays (and their dates this year) are as follows:

New Year's Day (January 1)
Good Friday (April 9)
Easter Monday (April 12)
Victoria Day (May 24)
Canada Day (July 1)
British Columbia Day (August 2)
Labour Day (September 6)
Thanksgiving (October 11)
Remembrance Day (November 11)
Christmas Day (December 25)
Boxing Day (December 26)

Mail, Telephone, and Electricity

 MAIL: The main post office in Vancouver (349 W. Georgia St.; phone: 604-685-2692) is open from 8:30 AM to 5 PM, Mondays through Fridays. Other branch offices have postal services Saturdays and Sundays. Stamps also are available at most hotel desks. Vending machines for stamps are outside post offices and in shopping centers.

Letters between Canada and the US have been known to arrive in as short a time as 5 days, but it is a good idea to allow at least 10 days for delivery in either direction. If your correspondence is important, you may want to send it via a special courier service: *Federal Express* (820 Burrard St.; phone: 800-463-3339 or 604-273-1544); or *DHL* (4871 Miller Rd., Bldg. E; phone: 604-278-7131). The cost is considerably higher than sending something via the postal service — but the assurance of its timely arrival may be worth it.

There are several places that will receive and hold mail for travelers in Vancouver. Mail sent to you at a hotel and clearly marked "Guest Mail, Hold for Arrival" is one safe approach. Canadian post offices, including the main city offices, also will extend this service to you if the mail is sent to you in care of General Delivery. To inquire about this service, call the post office (phone: 604-685-2692). Also, don't forget to bring identification (driver's license, credit cards, birth certificate, or passport) with you when you go to collect it. Mail must be collected in person.

If you are an *American Express* customer (a cardholder, a carrier of *American Express* traveler's checks, or traveling on an *American Express Travel Related Services* tour) you can have mail sent to its office in Vancouver. Letters are held free of charge — registered mail and packages are not accepted. You must be able to show an *American Express* card, traveler's checks, or a voucher proving you are on one of the company's tours to qualify. Those who aren't clients cannot use the service. Mail should be addressed to you, care of *American Express,* and should be marked "Client Mail Service."

While the US Embassy and consulates in Canada will not under ordinary circumstances accept mail for tourists, they *may* hold mail for US citizens in an emergency situation or if the papers sent are particularly important. It is best to inform them either by separate letter or cable, or by phone (particularly if you are in the country already), that you will be using their address for this purpose.

 TELEPHONE: The procedure for calling any number in Canada is the same as when calling within the US: dial the area code + the local number. The reverse procedure — dialing a number in the US from Canada — is the same.

The area code for Vancouver is 604.

Public telephones are available just about everywhere in Vancouver — including transportation terminals, hotel lobbies, restaurants, drugstores, libraries, post offices, and other municipal buildings. They also may be found at rest stops along major highways, at major tourist centers, and in resort areas. Roadside booths can be found just about anywhere. The price of a local call in Vancouver is CN 25¢. *Note:* US coins can be used in pay phones.

Although you can use a telephone-company credit card number on any phone, pay phones that take major credit cards (*American Express, MasterCard, Visa,* and so on) are increasingly common, particularly in transportation and tourism centers. Also now available is the "affinity card," a combined telephone calling card/bank credit card that can be used for domestic and international calls. Cards of this type include the following:

> *AT&T/Universal* (phone: 800-662-7759).
> *Executive Telecard International* (phone: 800-950-3800).
> *Sprint Visa* (phone: 800-877-4646).

Similarly, *MCI VisaPhone* (phone: 800-866-0099) can add phone card privileges to the services available through your existing *Visa* card. This service allows you to use your *Visa* account number, plus an additional code, to charge calls on any touch-tone phone in the US and Canada.

The nationwide number for information is the same as in the US, 555-1212. If you need a number in another area code, dial the area code + 555-1212. (If you don't know the area code, simply dial 0 for an operator who can tell you.) In Vancouver, you also have the option of dialing 411 for local information.

Long-distance rates are charged according to when the call is placed: weekday daytime; weekday evenings; and nights, weekends, and holidays. Least expensive are the calls you dial yourself from a private phone at night, and on weekends and major holidays. It generally is more expensive to call from a pay phone than it is to call from a private phone, and you must pay for a minimum 3-minute call. If the operator assists you, calls are more expensive. This includes credit card, bill-to-a-third-number, collect, and time-and-charge calls, as well as person-to-person calls, which are the most expensive. Rates are fully explained in the front of the white pages of every telephone directory.

Hotel Surcharges – Avoiding operator-assisted calls can cut costs considerably and bring rates into a somewhat more reasonable range — except for calls made through hotel switchboards. One of the most unpleasant surprises travelers encounter in many foreign countries is the amount they find tacked on to their hotel bill for telephone calls, because foreign hotels routinely add on astronomical surcharges. Before calling from your hotel room, inquire about any surcharges the hotel may impose. These can be excessive, but are avoidable by calling collect, using a telephone credit card (see above), or calling from a public pay phone. (Note that when calling from your hotel room, even if the call is made collect or charged to a credit card number, some establishments still may add on a nominal line usage charge — so ask before you call.)

Emergency Number – As in the US, dial 911 in Vancouver in the event of an emergency. Operators at this number will get you the help you need from the police, fire department, or ambulance service.

■**Note:** An excellent resource for planning your trip is *AT&T's Toll-Free 800 Directory,* which lists thousands of companies with 800 numbers, both alphabetically (white pages) and by category (yellow pages), including a wide range of travel services — from travel agents to transportation and accommodations. Issued in a consumer edition for $9.95 and a business edition for $14.95, both are available from *AT&T Phone Centers* or by calling 800-426-8686. Another useful directory for use before you leave and on the road is the *Toll-Free Travel & Vacation Information Directory* ($4.95 postpaid from Pilot Books, 103 Cooper St., Babylon, NY 11702; phone: 516-422-2225).

ELECTRICITY: Canada has the same electrical current system as that in the US: 110 volts, 60 cycles, alternating current (AC). US appliances running on standard current can be used throughout Canada without adapters or convertors.

Staying Healthy

The surest way to return home in good health is to be prepared for medical problems that might occur while on vacation. Below we've outlined some things about which you need to think before you go.

BEFORE YOU GO: Older travelers or anyone suffering from a chronic medical condition such as diabetes, high blood pressure, cardiopulmonary disease, asthma, or ear, eye, or sinus trouble, should consult a physician before leaving home. Those with conditions requiring special consideration when traveling should think about seeing, in addition to their regular physician, a specialist in travel medicine. For a referral in a particular community, contact the nearest medical school or ask a local doctor to recommend such a specialist. Dr. Leonard Marcus, a member of the *American Committee on Clinical Tropical Medicine and Travelers' Health,* provides a directory of more than 100 travel doctors around the world. For a copy, send a 9- by 12-inch self-addressed, stamped envelope to Dr. Marcus at 148 Highland Ave., Newton, MA 02165 (phone: 617-527-4003).

Also be sure to check with your insurance company ahead of time about the applicability of your hospitalization and major medical policies away from home; many policies do not apply. Older travelers should know that Medicare does not make payments outside the US and its territories. If your medical policy does not protect you while you're traveling, there are comprehensive combination policies specifically designed to fill the gap. (For a discussion of medical insurance and a list of inclusive combination policies, see *Insurance,* in this section.)

First Aid – Put together a compact, personal medical kit including Band-Aids, first-aid cream, antiseptic, nose drops, insect repellent, aspirin, an extra pair of prescription glasses or contact lenses (and a copy of your prescription for glasses or contact lenses), sunglasses, over-the-counter remedies for diarrhea, indigestion, and motion sickness, a thermometer, and a supply of those prescription medicines you take regularly.

In a corner of your kit, keep a list of all the drugs you have brought and their purpose, as well as duplicate copies of your doctor's prescriptions (or a note from your doctor). As brand names may vary in different countries, it's a good idea to ask your doctor for the generic name of any drugs you use so that you can ask for their equivalent should you need a refill. It also is a good idea to ask your doctor to prepare a medical identification card that includes such information as your blood type, your social security number, any allergies or chronic health problems you have, and your medical insurance information. Considering the essential contents of your medical kit, keep it with you, rather than in your checked luggage.

MINIMIZING THE RISKS: Travelers to Canada do not face the same health risks as might be encountered in visiting some other destinations in this hemisphere (such as Mexico and South America). Certainly travel always entails *some* possibility of injury or illness, but neither is inevitable and, with some basic precautions, your trip should proceed untroubled by ill health.

Sunburn – Even in Canada the burning power of the sun can quickly cause severe sunburn or sunstroke. To protect yourself against these ills, wear sunglasses, take along a broad-brimmed hat and cover-up, and, most important, use a sunscreen lotion.

Food and Water – Tap water in Canada generally is quite pure, so feel free to drink it. However, in rural areas, the local water supply may not be thoroughly purified, and local residents either have developed immunities to the natural bacteria or boil the water for drinking. You also should avoid swimming in or drinking water from freshwater streams, rivers, or pools, as they may be contaminated with leptospira, which cause a bacterial disease called leptospirosis (the symptoms resemble influenza). Milk is pasteurized throughout Canada, and dairy products are safe to eat, as are fruit, vegetables, meat, poultry, and fish.

MEDICAL AID ABROAD: Nothing ruins a vacation or business trip more effectively than sudden injury or illness. Fortunately, should you need medical attention, competent health professionals perfectly equipped to handle any medical problem can be found throughout the country. All hospitals are prepared for emergency cases, and many hospitals also have walk-in clinics to serve people who do not really need emergency service, but who have no place to go for immediate medical attention. Medical institutes in Canada, especially in the larger cities, generally provide the same basic specialties and services that are available in the US.

Emergency Treatment – You will find, in the event of an emergency, that most tourist facilities — transportation companies and hotels — are equipped to handle the situation quickly and efficiently. If a bona fide emergency occurs, the fastest way to get attention may be to take a taxi to the emergency room of the nearest hospital. In

Vancouver, *St. Paul's Hospital* (1081 Burrard St.; phone: 604-682-2344) is equipped with advanced equipment and technology to deal with acute medical situations. An alternative is to dial the free "emergency" number — 911 in Canada — used to summon the police, fire department, or an ambulance.

Non-Emergency Care – If a doctor is needed for something less than an emergency, there are several ways to find one. If you are staying in a hotel or at a resort, ask for help in reaching a doctor or other emergency services, or for the house physician, who may visit you in your room or ask you to visit an office.

It also usually is possible to obtain a referral through a US consulate (see addresses and phone numbers below) or directly through a hospital, especially if it is an emergency.

Pharmacies and Prescription Drugs – If you have a minor medical problem, a pharmacist might offer some help. In Vancouver, one 24-hour drugstore is the *Shoppers Drug* (1125 Davie St.; phone: 604-631-2831).

Bring along a copy of any prescription you may have from your doctor in case you should need a refill. In the case of minor complaints, Canadian pharmacists *may* fill a foreign prescription; however, do not count on this. In most cases, you will need a local doctor to rewrite the prescription. Even in an emergency, a traveler will more than likely be given only enough of a drug to last until a local prescription can be obtained.

ADDITIONAL RESOURCES: Emergency assistance also is available from the various medical programs designed for travelers who have chronic ailments or whose illness requires them to return home:

> *International Association for Medical Assistance to Travelers* (*IAMAT;* 417 Center St., Lewiston, NY 14092; phone: 716-754-4883). Entitles members to the services of participating doctors around the world, as well as clinics and hospitals in various locations. Participating physicians agree to adhere to a basic charge of around $50 to see a patient referred by *IAMAT.* To join, simply write to *IAMAT;* in about 3 weeks you will receive a membership card, the booklet of members, and an inoculation chart. A nonprofit organization, *IAMAT* appreciates donations; with a donation of $25 or more, you will receive a set of worldwide climate charts detailing weather and sanitary conditions. (Delivery can take up to 5 weeks, so plan ahead.)

> *International Health Care Service* (New York Hospital–Cornell Medical Center, 525 E. 68th St., Box 210, New York, NY 10021; phone: 212-746-1601). This service provides a variety of travel-related health services, including a complete range of immunizations at moderate per-shot rates. A pre-travel counseling and immunization package costs $255 for the first family member and $195 for each additional member; a post-travel consultation is $175 to $275, plus lab work. Consultations are by appointment only, from 4 to 8 PM Mondays through Thursdays, although 24-hour coverage is available for urgent travel-related problems. In addition, sending $4.50 (with a self-addressed envelope) to the address above will procure the service's publication, *International Health Care Travelers Guide,* a compendium of facts and advice on health care and diseases around the world.

> *International SOS Assistance* (PO Box 11568, Philadelphia, PA 19116; phone: 800-523-8930 or 215-244-1500). Subscribers are provided with telephone access — 24 hours a day, 365 days a year — to a worldwide, monitored, multilingual network of medical centers. A phone call brings assistance ranging from a telephone consultation to transportation home by ambulance or aircraft, or, in some cases, transportation of a family member to wherever you are hospitalized. Individual rates are $35 for 2 weeks of coverage ($3.50 for each additional

day), $70 for 1 month, or $240 for 1 year; couple and family rates also are available.

Medic Alert Foundation (2323 N. Colorado, Turlock, CA 95380; phone: 800-ID-ALERT or 209-668-3333). If you have a health condition that may not be readily perceptible to the casual observer — one that might result in a tragic error in an emergency situation — this organization offers identification emblems specifying such conditions. The foundation also maintains a computerized central file from which your complete medical history is available 24 hours a day by phone (the telephone number is clearly inscribed on the emblem). The onetime membership fee (between $35 and $50) is based on the type of metal from which the emblem is made — the choices range from stainless steel to 10K gold-filled.

TravMed (PO Box 10623, Baltimore, MD 21204; phone: 800-732-5309 or 410-296-5225). For $3 per day, subscribers receive comprehensive medical assistance while abroad. Major medical expenses are covered up to $100,000, and special transportation home or of a family member to wherever you are hospitalized is provided at no additional cost.

Helpful Publications – Practically every phase of health care — before, during, and after a trip — is covered in *The New Traveler's Health Guide,* by Drs. Patrick J. Doyle and James E. Banta. It is available for $4.95, plus postage and handling, from Acropolis Books Ltd., 13950 Park Center Rd., Herndon, VA 22071 (phone: 800-451-7771 or 703-709-0006).

The *Traveling Healthy Newsletter,* which is published six times a year, also is brimming with health-related travel tips. For a year's subscription, which costs $24, contact Dr. Karl Neumann (108-48 70th Rd., Forest Hills, NY 11375; phone: 718-268-7290). A sample issue is available for $4. Dr. Neumann also is the editor of the useful free booklet *Traveling Healthy,* which is available by writing to the *Travel Healthy Program* (Clark O'Neill Inc., 1 Broad Ave., Fairview, NJ 07022; phone: 201-947-3400).

For more information regarding preventive health care for travelers, contact the *International Association for Medical Assistance to Travelers* (*IAMAT;* 417 Center St., Lewiston, NY 14092; phone: 716-754-4883). The Centers for Disease Control also publishes an interesting booklet, *Health Information for International Travel.* To order send a check or money order for $5 to the Superintendent of Documents (US Government Printing Office, Washington, DC 20402), or charge it to your credit card by calling 202-783-3238. For information on vaccination requirements, disease outbreaks, and other health information pertaining to traveling abroad, you also can call the Centers for Disease Control's 24-hour International Health Requirements and Recommendations Information Hotline: 404-332-4559.

■ **Note:** Those who are unable to take a reserved flight due to personal illness or who must fly home unexpectedly due to a family emergency should be aware that airlines may offer a discounted airfare (or arrange a partial refund) if the traveler can demonstrate that his or her situation is indeed a legitimate emergency. Your inability to fly, or the illness or death of an immediate family member, usually must be substantiated by a doctor's note or the name, relationship, and funeral home from which the deceased will be buried. In such cases, airlines often will waive certain advance purchase restrictions or you may receive a refund check or voucher for future travel at a later date. Be aware, however, that this bereavement fare may not necessarily be the least expensive fare available and, if possible, it is best to have a travel agent check all possible flights through a computer reservations system (CRS).

Legal Aid and Consular Services

There are crucial places to keep in mind when outside the US, namely, the US Embassy (100 Wellington St., Ottawa, Ontario K1P 5T1, Canada; phone: 613-238-4470) and the US consulate (1075 W. Pender St., Vancouver, BC V6E 4E9, Canada; phone: 604-685-4311).

If you are injured or become seriously ill, or if you encounter legal difficulties, the consulate is the first place to turn, although its powers and capabilities are limited. It will direct you to medical assistance and notify your relatives if you are ill; it can advise you of your rights and provide a list of English-speaking lawyers if you are arrested, but it cannot interfere with the local legal process.

For questions about US citizens arrested abroad, how to get money to them, and other useful information, call the *Citizen's Emergency Center* of the Office of Special Consular Services in Washington, DC, at 202-647-5225. (For further information about this invaluable hotline, see below.)

A consulate exists to aid citizens in serious matters, such as illness, destitution, and the above legal difficulties. It is not there to aid in trivial situations, such as canceled reservations or lost baggage, no matter how important these matters may seem to the victimized tourist. If you should get sick, the US consul can provide names of doctors and dentists, as well as the names of local hospitals and clinics; the consul also will contact family members in the US and help arrange special ambulance service for a flight home. In a situation involving "legitimate and proven poverty" of a US citizen stranded abroad without funds, the consul will contact sources of money (such as family or friends in the US), apply for aid to agencies in foreign countries, and in a last resort — which is *rarely* — arrange for repatriation at government expense, although this is a loan that must be repaid. And in case of natural disasters or civil unrest, consulates around the world handle the evacuation of US citizens if it becomes necessary.

As mentioned above, the US State Department operates a *Citizens' Emergency Center,* which offers a number of services to US citizens traveling abroad and their families at home. In addition to giving callers up-to-date information on trouble spots, the center will contact authorities abroad in an attempt to locate a traveler or deliver an urgent message. In case of illness, death, arrest, destitution, or repatriation of a US citizen on foreign soil, it will relay information to relatives at home if the consulate is unable to do so. Travel advisory information is available 24 hours a day to people with touch-tone phones (phone: 202-647-5225). Callers with rotary phones can get information at this number from 8:15 AM to 10 PM (eastern standard time) on weekdays; 9 AM to 3 PM on Saturdays. In the event of an emergency, this number also may be called during these hours. For emergency calls only, at all other times, call 202-634-3600 and ask for the duty officer.

Drinking and Drugs

DRINKING: The legal drinking age is 19 in Vancouver. Beer and wine are sold at retail grocery stores; hard liquor is available at government liquor stores.

Licensed restaurants, hotels, lounges, and bars are found throughout Vancouver, though some may sell only wine or beer. The hours during which bars and restaurants may serve liquor vary, though traditionally bar closing time is between midnight and 3 AM. Liquor stores are required to close on Sundays and holidays, but some alcoholic beverages may be purchased on Sundays, usually only with meals, at authorized dining rooms, restaurants, and private clubs.

Visitors to Canada may bring in 40 ounces (about 1 gallon) of liquor or wine, or 288 ounces of beer or ale (twenty-four 12-ounce cans, eighteen 16-ounce cans) as personal baggage, duty-free. Anything in excess of this amount is subject to duties and taxes and requires a provincial permit. If excess liquor is declared, it will be held by Canada Customs at the point of entry for 30 days. A receipt will be issued, and the owner can claim it upon return. People leaving Canada from a point other than their point of entry can make arrangements to have their property returned at the point of departure.

DRUGS: Illegal narcotics are as prevalent in Canada as in the US, but the moderate legal penalties and vague social acceptance that marijuana has gained in the US has no equivalent in Canada. Due to the international war on drugs, enforcement of drug laws is becoming increasingly strict throughout the world. Local Canadian narcotics officers and customs officials are renowned for their absence of understanding and lack of a sense of humor — especially where foreigners are involved.

Opiates and barbiturates, and other increasingly popular drugs — "white powder" substances like heroin and cocaine, and "crack" (the cocaine derivative) — continue to be of major concern to narcotics officials. It is important to bear in mind that the type or quantity of drugs involved is of minor importance. According to a spokesperson for the Royal Canadian Mounted Police, stiff penalties have been imposed on drug offenders convicted of possessing mere *traces* of illegal drugs. Persons arrested are subject to the laws of the country they are visiting, and there isn't much the US consulate can do for drug offenders beyond providing a list of lawyers. The best advice we can offer is this: Don't carry, use, buy, or sell illegal drugs.

Those who carry medicines that contain a controlled drug should be sure to have a current doctor's prescription with them. Ironically, travelers can get into almost as much trouble coming through US Customs with over-the-counter drugs picked up abroad that contain substances that are controlled in the US. Cold medicines, pain relievers, and the like often have codeine or codeine derivatives that are illegal, except by prescription, in the US. Throw them out before leaving for home.

■ **Be forewarned:** US narcotics agents warn travelers of the increasingly common ploy of drug dealers asking travelers to transport a "gift" or other package back to the US. Don't be fooled into thinking that the protection of US law applies abroad — accused of illegal drug trafficking, you will be considered guilty until you prove your innocence. In other words, do not, under any circumstances, agree to take anything across the border for a stranger.

Tipping

While tipping is at the discretion of the person receiving the service, CN 50¢ is the rock-bottom tip for anything, and CN$1 is the current customary minimum for small services. *(Please note that the gratuities suggested below are given in Canadian dollars.)*

In restaurants, tip between 10% and 20% of the bill's total before tax is added. For average service in an average restaurant, a 15% tip to the waiter is reasonable, although one should never hesitate to penalize poor service or reward excellent and efficient attention by leaving less or more.

Although it's not necessary to tip the maître d' of most restaurants — unless he or she has been especially helpful in arranging a special party or providing a table (slipping the maître d' something in a crowded restaurant *may,* however, get you seated sooner or procure a preferred table) — when tipping is appropriate, the least amount should be CN$5. In the finest restaurants, where a multiplicity of servers are present, plan to tip 5% to the captain. The sommelier (wine waiter) is entitled to a gratuity of approximately 10% of the price of the bottle of wine.

In allocating gratuities at a restaurant, pay particular attention to what has become the standard credit card charge form, which now includes separate places for gratuities for waiters and/or captains. If these separate boxes are not on the charge slip, simply ask the waiter or captain how these separate tips should be indicated. In some establishments, tips indicated on credit card receipts may not be given to the help, so you may want to leave tips in cash.

In a large hotel, where it's difficult to determine just who out of a horde of attendants actually performed particular services, it is perfectly proper for guests to ask to have an extra 10% to 15% added to their bill. For those who prefer to distribute tips themselves, a chambermaid generally is tipped at the rate of around CN$1 a day. Tip the concierge and hall porter for specific services only, with the amount of such gratuities dependent on the level of service provided. For any special service you receive in a hotel, a tip is expected — CN$1 being the minimum for a small service.

Bellhops, doormen, and porters at hotels and transportation centers generally are tipped at the rate of CN$1 per piece of luggage, along with a small additional amount if a doorman helps with a cab or car. Taxi drivers should get about 15% of the total fare. And if you arrive without Canadian currency, tip in US dollars.

Miscellaneous tips: Sightseeing tour guides should be tipped. If you are traveling in a group, decide together what you want to give the guide and present it from the group at the end of the tour ($1 per person is a reasonable tip). If you have been individually escorted, the amount paid should depend on the degree of your satisfaction, but it should not be less than 10% of the tour price. Museum and monument guides usually are tipped, and it is a nice touch to tip a caretaker who unlocks a small church or turns on the light in a chapel. In barbershops and beauty parlors tips also are expected, but the percentages vary according to the type of establishment — 10% in the most expensive salons; 15% to 20% in less expensive establishments. (As a general rule, the person who washes your hair should get a small additional tip.) Washroom attendants should get a small tip — they usually set out a little plate with a coin already on it indicating the suggested denomination.

Tipping always is a matter of personal preference. In the situations covered above, as well as in any others that arise where you feel a tip is expected or due, feel free to express your pleasure or displeasure. Again, never hesitate to reward excellent and efficient attention and to penalize poor service. Give an extra gratuity and a word of thanks when someone has gone out of his or her way for you. Either way, the more personal the act of tipping, the more appropriate it seems. And if you didn't like the service — or the attitude — don't tip.

Duty-Free Shopping and Goods and Services Tax

DUTY-FREE SHOPS: If common sense says that it always is less expensive to buy goods in an airport duty-free shop than to buy them at home or in the streets of a foreign city, travelers should be aware of some basic facts. Duty-free, first of all, does not mean that the goods travelers buy will be free of duty when they return to the US. Rather, it means that the shop has paid no import tax in acquiring goods of foreign make, because the goods are not to be used in the country where the shop is located. This is why duty-free goods are available only in the restricted, passengers-only area of international airports or are delivered to departing passengers on the plane. In a duty-free store, travelers save money only on goods of foreign make because they are the only items on which an import tax would be charged in any other store. There usually is no saving on locally made items, but in provinces such as British Columbia that impose provincial sales and goods and services taxes (see below) that is refundable to foreigners, the prices in airport duty-free shops also subtract this tax, sparing travelers the often cumbersome procedures they otherwise have to follow to obtain a GST refund.

Beyond this, there is little reason to delay buying locally made merchandise and/or souvenirs until reaching the airport. In fact, because airport duty-free shops usually pay high rents, the locally made goods they sell may well be more expensive than they would be in downtown stores. The real bargains are foreign goods, but — let the buyer beware — not all foreign goods are automatically less expensive in an airport duty-free shop. You can get a good deal on even small amounts of perfume, costing less than the usually required minimum purchase, tax-free. Other fairly standard bargains include spirits, smoking materials, cameras, clothing, watches, chocolates, and other food and luxury items — but first be sure to know what these items cost elsewhere. Terrific savings do exist (they are the reason for such shops, after all), but so do overpriced items that an unwary shopper might find equally tempting. In addition, if you wait to do your shopping at airport duty-free shops, you will be taking the chance that the desired item is out of stock or unavailable.

Duty-free shops are located at Vancouver International Airport.

GOODS AND SERVICES TAX: Commonly abbreviated as GST, this 7% tax is levied by Canada on a wide range of purchases and payments for services, including package tours, car rentals, accommodations, and meals.

The tax is intended for residents (and already is included in the price tag), but visitors also are required to pay it unless they have purchases shipped by the store directly to an address abroad. If visitors pay the tax and take purchases with them, however, they generally are entitled to a refund.

The amount of the tax rebate claimed must be for a minimum of CN$7 — which means your expenditures in Canada for accommodations and other applicable purchases (there's no GST refund for food) must be at least CN$100 (CN$107, including the tax). Visitors are entitled to make up to four rebate claims per year, or purchases can be accumulated on any number of visits and one claim made for the calendar year. Visitors can mail the rebate forms after returning home (again, forms are available where goods are purchased), or at instant-rebate centers at points of departure from Canada such as duty-free shops and border crossings. (Any rebate claim for tax on a day's expenditure of CN$500 or more must be processed by mail.) Note that rebates through the mail are issued in US dollars; instant rebates are in Canadian dollars. If you have any questions about the tax while you're in Canada, call the information hotline that has been set up by Revenue Canada: 800-267-6620. For the hearing impaired, call 800-465-5770 (in Canada only).

In addition, most provinces impose a Provincial Sales Tax (PST) on most items, including food and lodging. These taxes vary from province to province; in British Columbia it is 6%; however, there is no tax refund afforded visitors. One way to avoid paying the PST is to have goods shipped by the merchant directly to your home address.

■ **Buyer Beware:** You may come across shops *not* at airports that call themselves duty-free shops. These require shoppers to show a foreign passport but are subject to the same rules as other stores, including paying import duty on foreign items. What "tax-free" means in the case of these establishments is something of an advertising strategy. They are announcing loud and clear that they do, indeed, offer the GST refund service — sometimes on the spot (minus a fee for higher overhead). Prices may be no better at these stores, and could be even higher due to this service.

Customs and Returning to the US

 When you return to the United States, you must declare to the US Customs official at the point of entry everything you have bought or acquired while in Canada. To speed up the process, keep all your receipts handy and try to pack your purchases together in an accessible part of your suitcase.

DUTY-FREE ARTICLES: In general, the duty-free allowance for US visitors returning from abroad is $400. This duty-free limit covers purchases that accompany you and are for personal use. This limit includes items used or worn while in Canada, souvenirs for friends, and gifts received during the trip. A flat 10% duty based on the "fair retail value in country of acquisition" is assessed on the next $1,000 worth of merchandise brought in for personal use or gifts. Amounts above these two levels are dutiable at a variety of rates. The average rate for typical tourist purchases is about 12%, but you can find out rates on specific items by consulting *Tariff Schedules of the United States* in a library or at any US Customs Service office.

Families traveling together may make a joint declaration to customs, which permits one member to exceed his or her duty-free exemption to the extent that another falls short. Families also may pool purchases dutiable under the flat rate. A family of three, for example, would be eligible for up to a total of $3,000 at the 10% flat duty rate (after each member had used up his or her $400 duty-free exemption) rather than three separate $1,000 allowances. This grouping of purchases is extremely useful when considering the duty on a duty-tariff item, such as jewelry or a fur coat. (Keep in mind, however, that the $25 exemption may not be grouped with family members.)

Personal exemptions can be used once every 30 days; in order to be eligible, an individual must have been out of the country for more than 48 continuous hours. If any portion of the exemption has been used once within any 30-day period or if your trip is less than 48 hours long, the duty-free allowance is cut to $25.

There are certain articles, however, that are duty-free only up to certain limits. The $25 limit includes the following: 10 cigars (not Cuban), 50 cigarettes, and 4 ounces of perfume. Individuals eligible for the full $400 duty-free limit are allowed 1 carton of cigarettes (200), 100 cigars, and 1 liter of alcoholic beverages if the traveler is over 21. Under federal law, alcohol above this allowance is liable for both duty and an Internal Revenue tax. Note, however, that states are allowed to impose additional restrictions and penalties of their own, including (in Arizona and Utah, for example) confiscation of any quantities of liquor over the statutory limit. Antiques, if they are 100 or more years old and you have proof from the seller of that fact, are duty-free, as are paintings and drawings if done entirely by hand.

To avoid paying duty twice, register the serial number of computers, watches, and electronic equipment with the nearest US Customs bureau before departure; receipts of insurance policies also should be carried for other foreign-made items.

Gold, gold medals, bullion, and up to $10,000 in currency or negotiable instruments may be brought into the US without being declared. Sums over $10,000 must be declared in writing.

The allotment for individual "unsolicited" gifts mailed from abroad (no more than one per day per recipient) is $50 retail value per gift. These gifts do not have to be declared and are not included in your duty-free exemption (see below). Although you should include a receipt for the purchases with each package, the examiner is empowered to impose a duty based on his or her assessment of the value of the goods. The duty owed is collected by the US Postal Service when the package is delivered. More information on mailing packages home from abroad is contained in the US Customs Service pamphlet *Buyer Beware, International Mail Imports* (see below for where to write for this and other useful brochures).

CLEARING CUSTOMS: This is a simple procedure. If your purchases total no more than the $400 duty-free limit, you need only make an oral declaration to the customs inspector. If entering with more than $400 worth of goods, you must submit a written declaration.

It is illegal not to declare dutiable items; not to do so, in fact, constitutes smuggling, and the penalty can be anything from stiff fines and seizure of the goods to prison sentences. There is a basic rule to buying goods abroad, and it should never be broken: *If you can't afford the duty on something, don't buy it.* Your list or verbal declaration should include all items purchased in Canada, as well as gifts received there, purchases made at the behest of others, the value of repairs, and anything brought in for resale in the US.

Do not include in the list items that do not accompany you, i.e., purchases that you have mailed or had shipped home. These are dutiable in any case, even if for your own use and even if the items that accompany your return from the same trip do not exhaust your duty-free exemption. It is a good idea, if you have accumulated too much while abroad, to mail home any personal effects (made and bought in the US) that you no longer need rather than your foreign purchases. These personal effects pass through US Customs as "American goods returned" and are not subject to duty.

FORBIDDEN IMPORTS: US residents are prohibited from bringing certain goods into the US from Canada, including any Cuban-made goods and items from North Korea, Vietnam, or Cambodia.

Narcotics, plants (unless specifically exempt and free of soil), and many types of food are not allowed into the US. Drugs are totally illegal, with the exception of medication prescribed by a physician. It's a good idea not to travel with too large a quantity of any given prescription drug (however, in the event that a pharmacy is not open when you need it, bring along several extra doses) and to have the prescription on hand in case any question arises either abroad or when re-entering the US.

Tourists have long been forbidden to bring into the US foreign-made, US-trade-marked articles purchased abroad (if the trademark is recorded with US Customs) without written permission. It's now permissible to enter with one such item in your possession as long as it's for personal use.

Tourists who want to bring Canadian plants into the US should know that house-plants usually are permitted; however, those transporting outdoor plants and fruit trees must have a plant certificate from an office of Agriculture Canada. For more information, contact Plant Protection Division, Export Division, Food Production and Inspection Branch, Agriculture Canada, Ottawa, Ontario K1A 0C6, Canada (phone: 613-995-7900).

The US Customs Service implements the rigorous Department of Agriculture regulations concerning the importation of vegetable matter, seeds, bulbs, and the like. Living vegetable matter may not be imported without a permit, and everything must be inspected, permit or not. Approved items (which do not require a permit) include dried bamboo and woven items made of straw; beads made of most seeds (but not jequirity beans — the poisonous scarlet and black seed of the rosary pea) and some viable seeds; cones of pine and other trees; roasted coffee beans; most flower bulbs; flowers (without roots); dried or canned fruits, jellies, or jams; polished rice, dried beans and teas; herb plants (not witchweed); nuts (but not acorns, chestnuts, or any nuts with outer husks); dried lichens, mushrooms (including truffles), shamrocks, and seaweed; and most dried spices.

Other processed foods and baked goods usually are okay. Regulations on meat products generally depend on the country of origin and manner of processing. As a rule, commercially canned meat, hermetically sealed and cooked in the can so that it can be stored without refrigeration, is permitted, but not all canned meat fulfills this requirement.

The US Customs Service also enforces federal laws that prohibit the entry of articles made from the furs or hides of animals on the endangered species list. Beware of shoes, bags, and belts made of crocodile and certain kinds of lizard, and anything made of tortoiseshell; this also applies to preserved crocodiles, lizards, and turtles sometimes sold in gift shops. Most coral — particularly black coral — also is restricted (although small quanitities of coral incorporated into jewelry or other craft items usually are permitted). And if you're shopping for big-ticket items, beware of fur coats made from the skins of spotted cats. They are sold abroad, but they will be confiscated upon your return to the US, and there will be no refund. For information about other animals on the endangered species list, contact the Department of the Interior, US Fish and Wildlife Service (Publications Unit, 4401 N. Fairfax Dr., Room 130, Arlington, VA 22203; phone: 703-358-1711), and ask for the free publication *Facts About Federal Wildlife Laws.*

Also note that some foreign governments prohibit the export of items made from certain species of wildlife, and the US honors any such restrictions. Before you go shopping in any foreign country, check with the US Department of Agriculture (G110 Federal Bldg., Hyattsville, MD 20782; phone: 301-436-8010) and find out what items are prohibited from the country you will be visiting.

The US Customs Service publishes a series of free pamphlets with customs information. It includes *Know Before You Go,* a basic discussion of customs requirements pertaining to all travelers; *Buyer Beware, International Mail Imports; Travelers' Tips on Bringing Food, Plant, and Animal Products into the United States; Importing a Car; GSP and the Traveler; Pocket Hints; Currency Reporting; Pets, Wildlife, US Customs; Customs Hints for Visitors (Nonresidents);* and *Trademark Information for Travelers.* For the entire series or individual pamphlets, write to the US Customs Service (PO Box 7474, Washington, DC 20044) or contact any of the seven regional offices — in Boston, Chicago, Houston, Long Beach (California), Miami, New Orleans, and New York.

Note that the US Customs Service has a tape-recorded message whereby callers using touch-tone phones can obtain free pamphlets on various travel-related topics; the number is 202-566-8195. These pamphlets provide great briefing material, but if you still have questions when you're in Canada, contact the nearest US consulate or the US Embassy.

Religion on the Road

The surest source of information on religious services in an unfamiliar country is the desk clerk of the hotel or guesthouse in which you are staying; the local tourist information office, a US consul, or a church of another religious affiliation also may be able to provide this information. For a full range of options, joint religious councils often print circulars with the addresses and times of services of houses of worship in the area. These often are printed as part of general tourist guides provided by the local tourist and convention center, or as part of a "what's going on" guide to the city. Many newspapers also print a listing of religious services in their area in weekend editions. You also can check the yellow pages of the phone book under "Churches" and call for more information.

You may want to use your vacation to broaden your religious experience by joining an unfamiliar faith in its service. This can be a moving experience, especially if the service is held in a church, synagogue, or temple that is historically significant or architecturally notable. You almost always will find yourself made welcome and comfortable.

■ **Note:** For those interested in a spiritual stay while in Canada, *Catholic America: Self-Renewal Centers and Retreats,* by Patricia Christian-Meyer, lists approximately 20 self-renewal centers throughout Canada. To order, send $13.95 to John Muir Publications, PO Box 613, Sante Fe, NM 87504 (phone: 800-888-7504 or 505-982-4078).

Sources and Resources

Tourist Information Offices

 The Canadian tourist offices and consulates in the US generally are the best sources of local travel information, and most of their many, varied publications are free for the asking. For the best results, request general information on specific provinces or cities, as well as publications relating to your particular areas of interest: accommodations, special events, sports, guided tours, and facilities for specific sports. There is no need to send a self-addressed, stamped envelope with your request, unless specified. For information on Vancouver contact the Vancouver Travel InfoCentre (Pavillion Plaza, Four Bentall Centre, 1055 Dunsmuir St., Vancouver, BC V7X 1L3 Canada; phone: 800-888-8535 or 604-683-2000).

Canadian Embassy and Consulates in the US

The Canadian government maintains an embassy and several consulates in the US. These are empowered to sign official documents and to notarize copies of US documents, which may be necessary for those papers to be considered legal abroad. Below is a list of the Canadian Embassy and consulates in the US.

Atlanta: Canadian Consulate (1 CNN Center, Suite 400, South Tower, Atlanta, GA 30303; phone: 404-577-6810).

Dallas: Canadian Consulate (750 N. St. Paul St., Suite 1700, Dallas, TX 75201; phone: 214-922-9806).

Los Angeles: Canadian Consulate (300 S. Grand Ave., Los Angeles, CA 90071; phone: 213-687-7432).

New York City: Canadian Consulate (1251 Ave. of the Americas, New York, NY 10020; phone: 212-768-2442).

San Francisco: Canadian Consulate (50 Fremont St., Suite 2100, San Francisco, CA 94105; phone: 415-495-6021).

Washington, DC: Canadian Embassy (501 Pennsylvania Ave. NW, Washington, DC 20001; phone: 202-682-1740).

Theater and Special Event Tickets

As you read this book, you will learn about events that may spark your interest — everything from music festivals and special theater seasons to sporting championships — along with telephone numbers and addresses to which to write for descriptive brochures, reservations, or tickets. The Canadian government tourist offices can supply information on these and other special events and festivals that take place in Vancouver, though they cannot in all cases provide the actual program or detailed information on ticket prices.

Since many of these occasions often are fully booked well in advance, think about having your reservation in hand before you go. In some cases, tickets may be reserved over the phone and charged to a credit card, or you can send an international money order or foreign draft. If you do write, remember that any request from the US should be accompanied by an International Reply Coupon to ensure a response (send two of them for an airmail response). These international coupons, money orders, and drafts are available at US post offices.

Books, Magazines, and Newsletters

BOOKS: Throughout GETTING READY TO GO, numerous books and brochures have been recommended as good sources of further information on a variety of topics. In many cases, these are publications of the various tourism authorities and are available in any of their offices both here and abroad.

Suggested Reading – The list below comprises books we have come across and think worthwhile; it is by no means complete, but meant merely to start you on your way. Unless indicated, all the books listed here are in print, but you also may want to do some additional research at your local library. These titles include some informative guides to special interests, solid historical accounts, and books that call attention to things you might not notice otherwise.

General Travel

The Adventure Guide to Canada, by Pam Hobbs (Hunter Publishing; $15.95).

Birnbaum's Canada 1993, edited by Alexandra Mayes Birnbaum (HarperCollins; $17).

British Columbia Adventures: The Driver's Guide, (Western Traveller; $12.95).

Budget Traveler's Guide to Great Off-Beat Vacations in the US and Canada, by Paige Palmer (Pilot Books; $4.95).

Canada: A Travel Survival Kit, by Mark Lightbody and Tom Smallman (Lonely Planet; $19.95).

Canadian Bed and Breakfast Guide, by Gerda Pantel (Chicago Review Press; $12.95).

The Canadian Canoeing Companion: An Illustrated Guide to Paddling Canada's Wilderness, by Alex Narvey (Thunder Enlightening Press; $16.95).

The Canadian Rockies Access Guide, by John Dodd and Gail Helgason (Hunter Publishing; $15.95).

Country Inns, Lodges, and Historic Hotels, Canada, by Anthony Hitchcock (Burt Franklin Press; $10.95).

Guide to Western Canada, by Frederick Pratson (Globe Pequot Press; $14.95).

O Canada: Travels in an Unknown Country, by Jan Morris (HarperCollins Publishers; $20).

Rail Ventures: The Comprehensive Planning Guide to Rail Travel in the United States & Canada, by Jack Swanson (Wayfinder Press; $12.95).

The Rockies: Canada's Magnificent Wilderness, by Ben Gadd (Beautiful America Publishing Company; $24.95).

Vancouver Guide, by Terri Wershler (Chronicle Books; $10.95).

History and Culture

Canadian Folklore, by Edith Fowke (Oxford University Press; $9.95).

Contours of Canadian Thought, by A. B. McKillop (University of Toronto Press; $13.95).

France and England in North America, **in 2 volumes,** by Francis Parkman (Library of America; $32.50 per volume).

The Penguin History of Canada, by Kenneth McNaught (Penguin Books; $8.95).

A Reader's Guide to Canadian History, **in 2 volumes,** edited by D. A. Muise (University of Toronto Press; $14.95 per volume).

Sweet Promises: A Reader in Indian-White Relations in Canada, edited by J. R. Miller (University of Toronto Press; $24.95).

Literature

Anne Hébert: Selected Poems (Bookslinger; $10).

Black Robe, by Brian Moore (Fawcett Books; $4.99).

The Enthusiasms of Robertson Davies, by Robertson Davies; edited by Judith Skelton Grant (Penguin; $9.95).

Friend of My Youth, by Alice Munro (Penguin; $8.95).

Home Sweet Home: My Canadian Album, by Mordecai Richler (Random House; $16.95).

The Oxford Book of Canadian Ghost Stories, edited by Alberto Manguel (Oxford University Press; $15.95).

The Oxford Book of Canadian Short Stories in English, edited by Margaret Atwood (Oxford University Press; $27.95).

The Oxford Illustrated Literary Guide to Canada, by Albert and Theresa Moritz (Oxford University Press; $39.95).

Surfacing, by Margaret Atwood (Fawcett Books; $4.95).

In addition, *Culturgrams* is a handy series of pamphlets that provides a good sampling of information on the people, cultures, sights, and bargains to be found in over 90 countries around the world. Each four-page, newsletter-size leaflet covers one country, and Canada is included in the series. The topics included range from customs and courtesies to lifestyles and demographics. These fact-filled pamphlets are published by the David M. Kennedy Center for International Studies at Brigham Young University; for an order form contact the group c/o Publication Services (280 HRCB, Provo, UT 84602; phone: 801-378-6528). When ordering from 1 to 5 *Culturgrams* the price is $1 each; 6 to 49 pamphlets cost 50¢ each; for larger quantities, the price per copy goes down proportionately.

MAGAZINES: As sampling the regional fare is likely to be one of the highlights of any visit, you will find reading about local edibles worthwhile either before you go or after you return. *Gourmet,* a magazine specializing in food, frequently carries mouthwatering articles on food and restaurants in Canada, although its scope is much broader. It is available at newsstands nationwide for $2.50 an issue, or as a subscription for $18 a year from *Gourmet* (PO Box 53789, Boulder, CO 80322; phone: 800-365-2454).

There are numerous additional magazines for every special interest available; check at your library information desk for a directory of such publications, or look over the selection offered at a well-stocked newsstand.

NEWSLETTERS: Throughout GETTING READY TO GO we have mentioned specific newsletters which our readers may be interested in consulting for further information. One of the very best sources of detailed travel information is *Consumer Reports Travel Letter.* Published monthly by Consumers Union (PO Box 53629, Boulder, CO 80322-3629; phone: 800-234-1970), it offers comprehensive coverage of the travel scene on a wide variety of fronts. A year's subscription costs $37; 2 years, $57.

In addition, the following travel newsletters provide useful up-to-date information on travel services and bargains:

> *Entree* (PO Box 5148, Santa Barbara, CA 93150; phone: 805-969-5848). This newsletter caters to a sophisticated, discriminating traveler with the means to explore the places mentioned. Subscribers have access to a 24-hour hotline providing information on restaurants and accommodations around the world. Monthly; a year's subscription costs $59.

> *The Hideaway Report* (Harper Assocs., PO Box 50, Sun Valley, ID 83353; phone: 208-622-3193). This monthly source highlights retreats — including Canadian idylls — for sophisticated travelers. A year's subscription costs $90.

> *Romantic Hideaways* (217 E. 86th St., Suite 258, New York, NY 10028; phone: 212-969-8682). This newsletter leans toward those special places made for those traveling in twos. A year's subscription for this monthly publication costs $65.

> *Travel Smart* (Communications House, 40 Beechdale Rd., Dobbs Ferry, NY 10522; phone: 914-693-8300 in New York; 800-327-3633 elsewhere in the US). This monthly covers a wide variety of trips and travel discounts. A year's subscription costs $44.

COMPUTER SERVICES: Anyone who owns a personal computer and a modem can subscribe to a database service providing everything from airline schedules and fares to restaurant listings. Two such services to try:

> *CompuServe* (5000 Arlington Center Blvd., Columbus, OH 43220; phone: 800-848-8199 or 614-457-8600). It costs $39.95 to join, plus hourly usage fees of $6 to $12.50.

> *Prodigy Services* (445 Hamilton Ave., White Plains, NY 10601; phone: 800-822-6922 or 914-993-8000). A month's subscription costs $12.95, plus variable phone charges.

■ **Note:** Before using any computer bulletin-board services, be sure to take precautions to prevent downloading of a computer "virus." First install one of the programs designed to screen out such nuisances.

Weights and Measures

 When traveling in Canada, you'll find that just about every quantity, whether it is distance, length, weight, or capacity, will be expressed in unfamiliar terms. In fact, this is true for travel almost everywhere in the world, since the US is one of the last countries to make its way to the metric system. Your trip to Vancouver may serve to familiarize you with what may one day be the weights and measures at your grocery store.

There are some specific things to keep in mind during your trip. Fruits and vegetables at a market generally are recorded in kilos (kilograms), as are your luggage at the airport and your body weight. (This latter is particularly pleasing to people of significant size who, instead of weighing 220 pounds, hit the scales at a mere 100 kilos.) A kilo equals 2.2 pounds and 1 pound is .45 of a kilo. Body temperature usually is measured in degrees centigrade or Celsius rather than on the Fahrenheit scale, so that a normal body temperature is 37C, not 98.6F, and freezing is 0 degrees C rather than 32F.

Gasoline is sold by the liter (approximately 3.8 to a 1 gallon). Tire pressure gauges and other equipment measure in kilograms per square centimeter rather than pounds per square inch. Highway signs are written in kilometers rather than miles (1 mile equals 1.6 km; 1 km equals .62 mile). And speed limits are in kilometers per hour, so think twice before hitting the gas when you see a speed limit of 100. That means 62 miles per hour.

The tables and conversion factors listed below should give you all the information you will need to understand any transaction, road sign, or map you encounter during your travels.

CONVERSION TABLES METRIC TO US MEASUREMENTS		
Multiply:	**by:**	**to convert to:**
LENGTH		
millimeters	.04	inches
meters	3.3	feet
meters	1.1	yards
kilometers	.6	miles
CAPACITY		
liters	2.11	pints (liquid)
liters	1.06	quarts (liquid)
liters	.26	gallons (liquid)
WEIGHT		
grams	.04	ounces (avoir.)
kilograms	2.2	pounds (avoir.)
US TO METRIC MEASUREMENTS		
LENGTH		
inches	25.0	millimeters
feet	.3	meters
yards	.9	meters
miles	1.6	kilometers
CAPACITY		
pints	.47	liters
quarts	.95	liters
gallons	3.8	liters
WEIGHT		
ounces	28.0	grams
pounds	.45	kilograms
TEMPERATURE $°F = (°C \times 9/5) + 32$ $°C = (°F - 32) \times 5/9$		

APPROXIMATE EQUIVALENTS		
Metric Unit	**Abbreviation**	**US Equivalent**
LENGTH		
meter	m	39.37 inches
kilometer	km	.62 mile
millimeter	mm	.04 inch
CAPACITY		
liter	l	1.057 quarts
WEIGHT		
gram	g	.035 ounce
kilogram	kg	2.2 pounds
metric ton	MT	1.1 tons
ENERGY		
kilowatt	kw	1.34 horsepower

Cameras and Equipment

 Vacations are everybody's favorite time for taking pictures and home movies. After all, most of us want to remember the places we visit — and show them off to others. Here are a few suggestions to help you get the best results from your travel photography or videography. For more information see *A Shutterbug's Vancouver* in DIVERSIONS.

BEFORE THE TRIP

If you're taking your camera or camcorder out after a long period in mothballs, or have just bought a new one, check it thoroughly before you leave to prevent unexpected breakdowns or disappointing pictures.

1. Still cameras should be cleaned carefully and thoroughly, inside and out. If using a camcorder, run a head cleaner through it. You also may want to have your camcorder professionally serviced (opening the casing yourself will violate the manufacturer's warranty). Always use filters to protect your lens while traveling.
2. Check the batteries for your camera's light meter and flash, and take along extras just in case yours wear out during the trip. For camcorders, bring along extra Nickel-Cadmium (Ni-Cad) batteries; if you use rechargeable batteries, a recharger will cut down on the extras.
3. Using all the settings and features, shoot at least one test roll of film or one videocassette, using the type you plan to take along with you.

EQUIPMENT TO TAKE ALONG

Keep your gear light and compact. Items that are too heavy or bulky to be carried comfortably on a full-day excursion will likely remain in your hotel room.

1. Invest in a broad camera or camcorder strap if you now have a thin one. It will make carrying the camera much more comfortable.
2. A sturdy canvas, vinyl, or leather camera or camcorder bag, preferably with padded pockets (not an airline bag), will keep your equipment organized and easy to find. If you will be doing much shooting around the water, a waterproof case is best.
3. For cleaning, bring along a camel's hair brush that retracts into a rubber squeeze bulb. Also take plenty of lens tissue, soft cloths, and plastic bags to protect equipment from dust and moisture.

FILM AND TAPES: If you are concerned about airport security X-rays damaging rolls of undeveloped still film (X-rays do not affect processed film) or tapes, store them in one of the lead-lined bags sold in camera shops. This possibility is not as much of a threat as it used to be, however. In both the US and Canada, incidents of X-ray damage to unprocessed film (exposed or unexposed) are few because low-dosage X-ray equipment is used virtually everywhere. If you're traveling without a protective bag, you may want to ask to have your photo equipment inspected by hand. One type of film that should never be subjected to X-rays is the very high speed ASA 1000 film; there are lead-lined bags made especially for it — and, in the event that you are refused a hand inspection, this is the only way to save your film. The walk-through metal detector devices at airports do not affect film, though the film cartridges may set them off.

You should have no problem finding film or tapes in Vancouver. When buying film, tapes, or photo accessories the best rule of thumb is to stick to name brands with which you are familiar. The availability of film processing labs and equipment repair shops will vary.

THE CITY

VANCOUVER

In Vancouver, life is dominated by the elements — the sea, the mountains, and the weather that the two brew up between them. Pale buildings gleam in the marine air like opals set against varied hues of green — the green of the sea and the darker, truer green of the fir-covered slopes east of the city. The skyline is high-rise steel and glass, with snow-capped mountains for a backdrop. Around almost any corner is a glimpse of water, usually streaked by the white wake of an oceangoing freighter or dotted by white triangles of sailboats trailing colorful spinnakers.

Tucked into the southwestern corner of British Columbia, Canada's Pacific province, Vancouver is just about as close to the sea as it can be without leaving continental Canada. Downtown Vancouver sits on a peninsula bounded by English Bay to the west, the Fraser River to the south, and Burrard Inlet to the north. Across Burrard Inlet is the more securely land-locked residential suburb of North Vancouver. Flanking its lovely neighborhoods are the tall peaks of the Coastal Range — Grouse Mountain, Mt. Seymour, and Hollyburn. These 3,000-to-4,000-foot peaks do more than provide a magnificent background to the city; by capturing the storms that sweep in from the sea and down from the Alaskan panhandle, they create Vancouver's foggy, rainy climate, the gardener's delight and the sun worshiper's despair.

The city is caught between the towering mountains and the omnipresent sea; it would be tempting to say after a glimpse at the map that the mountains almost seem to be pushing the city into the waiting fingers of the sea, except that most residents embrace the surrounding elements and there is no hint of hostility in the relationship. They've *come* to Vancouver for the sea and the mountains, and those fingers of Pacific Ocean fill their leisure time with a diversity of activities unavailable anywhere else in Canada.

The sea, mountains, and moderate climate were prime forces in the city's development as part of Canada. A few thousand miles lie between Vancouver and Canada's other major cities, Toronto and Montreal. (Vancouver, with just over 1.6 million residents in its metropolitan area, is Canada's third-largest city and home to half of British Columbia's population.) The sense of remoteness is further augmented by the Rocky Mountains, 400 miles (644 km) east of Vancouver, a psychological as well as physical barrier that isolates the city from eastern, urban Canada. Toronto and Montreal are 5 and 6 hours away by air. As a result, the city more resembles the US West Coast than the rest of Canada (the US border is only 30 miles/48 km south; San Francisco is 2 hours away by air). It is as if the bonds of sea and mountain, which the city shares with the entire American Pacific coast, are stronger than the weight of culture and politics it shares with the rest of Canada.

The impact of the sea on life in Vancouver is enormous. The city has an excellent natural harbor that is active year-round. Wheat, timber, lumber, oil, and manufactured goods flow through the port in a steady stream, providing a crucial economic and transportation link with the rest of the world and maintaining an especially active trade relationship with Japan. Ships transport grain and lumber from Vancouver, and return with cars, appliances, and other Japanese consumer goods. The many rivers that flow from the Coastal Range into the sea along the Vancouver coast make the area prime salmon country. Salmon is offered everywhere — smoked, fresh, or frozen and packed to travel. It's part of the menu in many of the city's restaurants, from salmon sushi to salmon Wellington. And those who fish in Vancouver may very well see it face-to-face.

When residents aren't on the sea or in it, they spend a good deal of their time over it. Because the city stretches over peninsulas and islands, most people have to cross water at least twice a day on one of the city's 20 bridges. And everywhere are seagulls — vying with pigeons for a place in the sun (or rain) on apartment ledges; scrambling after scraps at hamburger drive-ins; and battling with ducks and swans in the ponds of Stanley Park.

Still, with a population of just over 1.5 million residents in its metropolitan area, Vancouver is medium-size by many standards. And while in the aggressively new high-rise office buildings there is a pulse of money and youth and drive, the residents of the city seem to favor a balance between work and leisure. Below the high-rises, people stroll along the waterfront development at the foot of Granville Street, and linger over lunch on the grass (when it's dry) at Stanley Park.

Vancouver offers almost an embarrassment of riches for recreational activity, from boating and sailing out of Burrard Inlet or English Bay to skiing on Grouse Mountain. The thousand acres of Stanley Park offer miles of walking and biking trails through silent woodlands and over rolling lawns; cricket, tennis, lawn bowling, and putting; and less active sports, such as bird, water, and people watching.

The city itself is very much the product of the 20th century. The residents' interest and concern with the environment are reflected in the cleanliness of downtown streets. The newness of the city is reflected in its slick-as-glass skyline, a forest of high-rise buildings pricking the sky. The city's historic buildings are predominantly in the older sections of town — Gastown, where the city started, and Chinatown. Residential areas consist of nicely laid out streets with apartment buildings in the west end on the southern shore of English Bay; large, spectacular homes in Shaughnessy and Kerrisdale, south of downtown; sprawling contemporary homes in the southwestern suburbs of Richmond and Burnaby, as well as in West Vancouver, on the north shore, where residents enjoy the highest per capita wealth in Canada.

The Indians who have lived here for at least 3,000 years fished salmon and whale and traded furs with the white men, who first entered the area in 1791, when Spanish explorer José Narváez met with Musqueam Indian braves who paddled out to English Bay to greet him. British Captain George Vancouver surveyed Burrard Inlet the next year, and Simon Fraser, a Vermont-born explorer and fur trader, reached the Pacific from an inland route in 1808. But the European settlers who are usually credited with the city's early development are three Englishmen — John Morton, William Hailstone, and Samuel Brighouse, "the three greenhorns." Only in their 20s when they arrived in 1862, the young entrepreneurs found an uninhabited land, filled with nothing more than a stand of tall trees stretching from the mountains to the sea. Their grand plan — to clear a parcel of the vast 150-acre wilderness in what is now Vancouver's west end and build a brick factory — was derided as sheer folly, thus their nickname; but the "greenhorns" had the last laugh. (When the *Canadian Pacific Railway* was looking for a site for the West Coast terminus of its national rail route, the greenhorns donated a third of their own land in a successful effort to spur the *CPR* to choose it as part of the development. The railroad moved in, the value of the property soared many times its original cost, and folly turned to fortune.)

There was no permanent white settlement here until 1867, when a talkative publican named "Gassy" Jack Deighton built a saloon and set up business near a very small sawmill where liquor was forbidden. A community grew up around the establishment, and two more saloons opened to serve the thirsty lumberjacks. The town lacked refinement, but it was certainly lively. Occasional sprees turned into community bashes that closed down the mill for days at a time. The area was so rich in natural resources, however, that the town kept growing. In 1886, with a population of 2,500 and 350 wooden buildings, it was incorporated as a city and named Vancouver. To celebrate, the new city's leaders ordered a brand-new fire wagon, but Vancouver burned down a month later in the Great Fire of June 13, 1886 — just weeks before the wagon arrived. All in all, it was an ironic turn of events: The fire had been deliberately set by city planners to clear the land, but it raged out of control and 20 people lost their lives. But the flames did level the city; though the project didn't go exactly as planned, the land was, in fact, cleared.

The city was soon rebuilt and began to thrive with the construction of the transcontinental railroad. A large influx of Chinese workers also came with the railroad, and thus began a number of ugly incidents between whites and the Chinese. When the city forcibly deported the Chinese from work camps to Victoria on Vancouver Island, the provincial government stepped in with constables to restore order. The deportation so outraged provincial officials that the city's charter was revoked for a period of time. As a result of such rabid racism, Vancouver's Chinese community segregated itself in Chinatown and established something of a parallel community.

The *Canadian Pacific Railway* finally arrived in 1887, and Vancouver began to flourish. That same year the city's first hotel, the *Vancouver,* opened its doors, and the *Hudson's Bay Company* launched the city's first department store. (Now known as *The Bay,* it still is open for business.) Within the next few years several hotels and department stores were established.

In the 20th century, Vancouver has grown by leaps and bounds. The opening of the Panama Canal in 1914 strengthened the city by providing easy access to Europe for grain shipments from the western prairies. During US Prohibition, shipping took a new turn, as rum-runners plied the coast for intrepid entrepreneurs who smuggled spirits southward. Today the situation is somewhat reversed. Because of lower liquor prices in the US, Vancouver residents often stock up before crossing the border from Washington State at Blaine.

Metropolitan Vancouver includes Burnaby, Richmond, New Westminster, Delta, and Surrey as well as North and West Vancouver. Although its roots were predominantly British, the city now flowers with newcomers from all over the world. Today nearly half the metropolitan area's residents are of non-British descent. Vancouver's East Indian population is one of Canada's largest and most vibrant, but the fastest growth has come from Pacific Rim countries, especially Hong Kong. (Canada has a favorable immigration policy for well-to-do Hong Kong Chinese, and Vancouver has been their destination of choice with the approach of their homeland's reversion to the People's Republic of China in 1997.) There are newspapers and magazines which cater to these ethnic communities; there's even a radio station. But the most tangible benefit by far has been the sea change in the tastes and smells of the city's food: The ethnic restaurants are among the best on the continent; dim sum served in Vancouver's Chinatown rivals the savories served on restaurant row in Kowloon; and exotic goods and groceries abound.

In spite of the variety, however, Vancouver's original Scottish-English heritage is almost always apparent. "Labor" and "honor" are spelled with a "u" here; the final two letters of words like "theater" and "center" are transposed; the locals "queue up," and are almost universally polite.

Vancouver has all the accoutrements of a major city — a symphony orchestra, an opera company, and several dance companies. The shopping is good here. West Vancouver's *Park Royal Shopping Centre* was the first strip shopping mall in Canada. Malls have since become all the rage in the city, with 17 sizable ones at last count. There is ongoing restoration of original downtown buildings, which now house boutiques, restaurants, art and filmmaking studios, antiques stores, and galleries on South Granville Street, Asian crafts stores and vegetable markets in Chinatown, and delis, boutiques, and specialty stores in Gastown. But when visitors have had their fill of shopping, they should head for the place in which Vancouverites spend most of their free time — the great outdoors.

Called by many an Occidental pearl set in a silver sea, the city's lush parks and gardens are its luster. Leisure activity focuses year-round on these green spaces. And from virtually any point in the city, it's a matter of minutes to the sandy beaches or rocky bays. Many people own boats and go sailing and fishing. During the summer, folks swim in English Bay (every *New Year's Day* hundreds of hardy souls brave a dip in the cold depths, in an annual ritual called the *Polar Bear Swim*).

Vancouver's skiers head for the mountains in wintertime. Grouse, Cypress, and Seymour mountains, approximately 20 minutes away, provide challenging slopes and equipment rentals. The world-famous Whistler/Blackcomb ski area is only 90 minutes from downtown.

In many ways, Vancouver has a typical West Coast atmosphere, with its high priority on outdoor activities, and its slow-paced, low-key feel. Though business does get done in Vancouver, the pace is less hectic than that of eastern urban centers. Standing shoulder to shoulder with the wilderness, Vancouver — with its mix of races and nationalities, skyscrapers and ski runs — offers a variety of delights to the discerning visitor.

VANCOUVER AT-A-GLANCE

SEEING THE CITY: Grouse Mountain, rising 3,700 feet above sea level in North Vancouver, commands a spectacular view of the city and the surrounding coastal area. Take the *Grouse Mountain Skyride,* an aerial tramway that runs from the parking lot to the summit, and enjoy panoramic views along the way. Open daily. Admission charge. At the top of Capilano Rd. on Nancy Greene Way in North Vancouver (phone: 984-0661).

More than 550 feet above the harbor, *The Lookout!* at Harbour Centre offers a range of waterfront activities. This viewing deck and orientation center for visitors is a great place to watch the cruise ships, freighters, sailboats, and seaplanes go by. Staff members are on hand to point out special sights. After enjoying the breathtaking city scene, see the center's 12-minute slide show, "One in a World, Vancouver," then stop for a snack at the cappuccino bar. 555 W. Hastings St. (phone: 689-0421).

Perched atop Little Mountain, the highest natural elevation in the city, Queen Elizabeth Park affords spectacular views within the city limits; and if you want to look even farther, there are telescopes to brings the mountains into clear sight. Cambie and 33rd Sts.

The drive from the airport along tree-lined Granville Street, with the North Shore mountains in the background, is also a wonderful introduction to this beautiful city.

SPECIAL PLACES: Walking is the best way to get a feel for certain sections of Vancouver, including Gastown, Chinatown, the Granville Island complex, Canada Place, and Stanley Park. And the best way to get from one neighborhood to another is to use the city's efficient *Skytrain,* which serves most of the areas listed below (for more information see *Sources and Resources*). Other of the area's attractions lie in the suburbs and outlying districts, to which it is most convenient to drive. Regardless of how you go, while wending your way through the city don't be surprised if you come upon a movie in the making. Filmmaking is big business here: The city is third only to Los Angeles and New York in the number of North American TV and film productions. So it's not unusual to come upon a block lined with fake palm trees, or to see a summer park covered with snow, as filmmakers change reality to suit a script.

Note: Although Vancouver's crime rate is relatively low for a city its size, this is a major metropolis with all that this implies. Car break-ins and thefts are not uncommon, particularly involving rental cars and vehicles with out-of-town license plates. As a precaution, don't leave valuables in your car, and be sure to lock the doors.

DOWNTOWN

Chinatown – The second-largest Chinese quarter in North America (only San Francisco's is larger or more energetic) encompasses a fair-size piece of downtown. Centered on Pender Street between Gore and Carrall Streets, this area has been the nucleus of the Chinese community for almost a century, first as a self-imposed ghetto in which the Chinese protected themselves from discrimination and physical abuse, today as a vibrant commercial community. Restaurants offer authentic Cantonese, Mandarin, and Shanghai cooking as well as Chinese-Canadian, which is virtually indistinguishable from Chinese-American. The stores range from large import emporia to holes in the wall, with mah-jongg sets, jade and ivory carvings, dried lychee nuts, and dozens of other intriguing items. The groceries feature smoked duck, bok choy, ginger root, and squid. At the Chinese newspaper office, the latest edition is posted in the window. Herbalists promise cures with roots and leaves and powdered bones. On Pender Street you can buy a cricket cage for $1 or a cloisonné vase for $100. There are also jade figurines of Kuan Yin, the goddess of mercy, and soapstone Foo dogs that guard domestic temples. Some highlights are the world's thinnest office building (Pender and Carrall Sts.); the Dr. Sun Yat-sen Classical Chinese Garden (578 Carrall St.; also see *Glorious Gardens* in DIVERSIONS); the Kuomintang Building (529 Gore St.); the Chinese Cultural Centre (50 E. Pender St.); and Wong's Benevolent Society (121-125 E. Pender St.), exemplary of the balcony style of the area. Two good places to eat are *Yen Lock* (67 E. Pender St.; phone: 683-8589) and *Sun Tung Lock,* a seafood restaurant (127 E. Pender St.). Both offer appetizing dim sum and other Cantonese specialties. (See *Eating Out.*)

Stanley Park – Surrounded by the sea on three sides, this city park is one of the most beautiful in the world. Located at the foot of West Georgia Street, the park has 1,000 acres bespeckled with tall evergreens, gardens, lakes, lagoons, 50 miles of trails, tennis courts, a miniature golf course, bowling greens, restaurants, coffee shops, snack bars, a zoo, and the *Vancouver Aquarium* (see below). Residents use the park for hiking, jogging, biking, concerts, picnicking, and simple relaxing. The seawall flanks the water for 5 miles and makes a lovely walk. Open daily. Some admission charges. (Also see *Walk 1: Stanley Park* in DIRECTIONS.)

Vancouver Aquarium – With over 9,000 aquatic inhabitants, this is Canada's largest and most famous aquarium. Attractions include the H. R. MacMillan Gallery of Whales, the Marine Mammal Center, and IMAQ, the Arctic Sea display. Popular exhibitions are the Amazon Gallery and the British Columbia Hall of Fish, displaying local sea life. There are public feedings of sharks, sea otters, and harbor seals. The gift shop features local craftwork. Open daily. Admission charge. In Stanley Park (phone: 682-1118).

Gastown – Bounded by Water, Alexander, Columbia, and Cordova Streets, and named for "Gassy" Jack Deighton, first citizen and saloonkeeper, this is where Vancouver began as a rowdy mill town. Later it was the city's Skid Row and, still later, home of the drug culture. Today it is a living example of successful urban renewal. Extensive renovation has transformed many of the warehouses into antiques stores, boutiques, galleries, and restaurants with lovely brick façades and gaslight fixtures. *The Landing* (at the Cordova St. entrance to Gastown) is an upscale shopping center. The world's first steam clock is at Cambie and Water Streets. *Umberto Al Porto* (321 Water St.; phone: 683-8376) has homemade pasta and a harbor view from the upstairs lounge (see *Eating Out*). The *Water Street Café* (300 Water St.; phone: 689-2832) is also a popular eating spot featuring a relaxing atmosphere and innovative menu. (Also see *Walk 2: Gastown* in DIRECTIONS.)

Granville Island Market – Just under the south end of the Granville Bridge, this large indoor market has become the prime gathering spot for those in search of the freshest seafood and produce. You can get salmon packed to go, and a number of the stalls sell snacking food that can be consumed while watching the tugboats glide to and fro. Take any Granville Street bus and change at Broadway at Fir Street for the No. 51. Two independent ferry services, *Granville Island Ferries* and the *Aquabus,* run daily between Vancouver's West End and the Island. Granville Island itself is growing in importance each day — the complex is now home to two theaters, galleries, assorted shops, a number of restaurants, and *Granville Island Brewing* (phone: 738-9463), which offers a behind-the-scenes tour at no charge.

Robson Street – Although originally christened Robson Street, this 3-block area west of Burrard Street took on a Germanic air in the 1960s; to promote its ethnic flavor, it was renamed Robsonstrasse, a soubriquet that lasted for about a decade. The original street name was restored and a few of the old-time businesses remain: The *Heidelberg House* restaurant (No. 1164; phone: 684-0817) offers hearty, dependable cooking, and you can still buy knockwurst in bulk. But the street where shopkeepers once knew their customers by name is now primarily a haven for shops with well-known names such as *Ralph Lauren, Rodier Paris,* and *Ferragamo;* locals consider it on a par with Los Angeles's Rodeo Drive. *Skytrain* exit: Burrard. (Also see *Shopping* in DIVERSIONS.)

Robson Square – This innovative complex designed by Arthur Erickson (he also designed the Canadian Embassy in Washington, DC, and the San Diego Convention Center) houses the provincial government offices, the courthouse, and shopping facilities in a multilevel galleria. Among the attractions are a skating rink and a theater. Robson St. at Hornby St.

Canada Place – Built for *EXPO '86,* this building is known for its ship-like appearance and five sails on the roof. It houses the Trade and Convention Centre, the *Pan Pacific* hotel, and *CN IMAX* (Canadian National Image Maximum) *Theatre.* The special IMAX process, designed and developed in Canada, dramatically increases the frame size of regular 35-mm film tenfold. You'll feel as if you're in the picture. Admission charge for the daily screenings. 999 Canada Pl., at the north end of Howe St. (phone: 682-6422). (Also see *Walk 4: Canada Place* in DIRECTIONS.)

Vancouver Art Gallery – Francis Rattenbury, the designer of the regal *Empress* hotel and the Parliament Buildings in Victoria on Vancouver Island, built the Old Court House at Georgia and Hornby Streets in 1906; since 1980 it has been home to the city's major art gallery. The BC Centennial Fountain, at the front of the sandstone and granite structure, celebrates the mainland's union with Vancouver Island in 1866. Of the four exhibition halls, one is devoted to the works of Victoria artist Emily Carr, whose early 1900s paintings of forests and totems are renowned. Changing exhibits include works from the permanent collection and traveling shows from other galleries. The stone steps on the building's south side are a popular gathering spot at lunchtime. Open daily (except October to May, when it's closed Tuesdays). Admission charge, except Thursday evenings. 750 Hornby St. (phone: 682-4668). *Skytrain* exit: Burrard.

Science World – With hands-on, interactive exhibits, photographic artifacts, bugs and beaver lodges, lightning bolts and laser beams, and live demonstrations of scientific phenomena, all in a welcoming "please touch" atmosphere, this museum is for children of all ages. Housed in a 17-story geodesic dome, a legacy of *EXPO '86,* it contains the *Omnimax Theatre,* which features "sense-surround" films projected on the world's largest domed screen. The museum stands out at night like a star-studded sphere. Open daily. Admission charge. 1455 Quebec St. (phone: 687-7832). *Skytrain* exit: Main St. (Also see *Memorable Museums* in DIVERSIONS.)

Orpheum Theatre – What was once targeted for demolition is now a National Historic Site and home to the *Vancouver Symphony Orchestra* and to performances as varied as kids' shows and rock concerts. A small group of determined citizens succeeded in keeping this 1927 landmark with its soaring dome, ornamental arches, and crystal chandeliers from being destroyed. Free guided tours can be pre-booked. 844 Granville St.; the entrance is on Seymour and Smithe Sts. (phone: 665-3031).

Hotel Vancouver – Like the *Château Frontenac* in Quebec City, no skyline picture of Vancouver is complete without the appearance of the green copper roof, gargoyles, and French Renaissance design of this grande dame of Vancouver hotels. Yet its history is a Western one of boom and bust. The first building, a wooden structure, was erected in 1887, only to be replaced in 1916 by a 14-story Italian villa–style structure. A third version, begun in 1928, was halted because of the Depression and then rushed to completion in time to host England's King George VI during the royal visit of May 1939. During World War II, the hotel, in disrepair, was taken over by the Canadian government and for a time was used as a hostel for returning veterans; it was razed in 1949 and totally rebuilt. Thankfully, its original owners, *Canadian Pacific Railway,* have restored the hotel to its former glory, offering Old World elegance in this thoroughly modern city. A large model of Captain George Vancouver's sailing ship, the *Discovery,* is on permanent display in the lobby. 900 W. Georgia St. (phone: 684-3131). *Skytrain* exit: Burrard.

Birk's Clock – Meeting under the clock at *Birk's* jewelry store was a tradition for generations of downtown-bound Vancouverites who, for the short period that the four-sided, stone façade timepiece was put in storage, could be found milling about Granville Street, lost without their timely landmark. One of the few freestanding clocks that remain in the province (first erected in 1906 at Hastings and Granville Streets and moved to its present corner 6 years later), it was removed while the original store was being replaced by the *Vancouver Centre* (and a new *Birk's*), but it is back and ticking — you can set your watch by it. Granville and Georgia Sts. *Skytrain* exit: Granville.

The Bay – The area around Georgia and Granville was bush when, in 1893, the first local offshoot of the prestigious fur trading Hudson's Bay Company opened. The company had received its Royal Charter to trade in the northern wilderness in 1670. The last remnants of the original structure were demolished in 1926 and the current store, with its trademark Corinthian columns, replaced it. Now known simply as *The Bay,* the department store underwent interior renovations in the 1970s and today connects with the underground *Vancouver Centre* mall. Granville and Georgia Sts. *Skytrain* exit: Granville.

Christ Church Cathedral – The oldest surviving church in Vancouver (since 1929 it has served as the cathedral of the Anglican diocese of New Westminster), its construction began in 1889. A granite basement was the first segment, and so the church was called the Root House. The Anglican church, with its stained glass windows and Douglas fir beams and roof, took 6 years to complete. After heated public controversy halted a 1974 attempt to replace the cathedral with a modern tower, it was designated a historic landmark. On the east wall (opposite the door) the *Royal Empire Society* erected a tablet, "To commemorate the life and work of the Intrepid Explorer [Captain] James Cook (1728–1779)." 690 Burrard St., corner of Georgia St. *Skytrain* exit: Burrard.

Cathedral Place – Next to Christ Church Cathedral — thus its name — this soaring complex, primarily an office building with shops on its main level, is also home to the *Canadian Craft Museum* (phone: 687-8266). Displayed here are exhibits of international, historical and Canadian contemporary artworks. (Also see *Memorable Museums* in DIVERSIONS.) Formerly the site of the Georgia Medical-Dental Building, Cathedral Place's new façade boasts full-size replicas of the original carved stone nurses that for more than 60 years graced the old medical center. 639 Hornby St. *Skytrain* exit: Burrard.

Cathedral of Our Lady of the Holy Rosary – When this Gothic Revival Roman Catholic parish church was completed in 1900 its spire dominated the city skyline. And despite the coming of loftier buildings, it still is impressive. The church was the first in the city (1916) to be designated as a cathedral, 13 years before the Anglican Christ Church achieved that status. Dunsmuir and Richards Sts. *Skytrain* exit: Granville.

BC Place – From a concert featuring Sting to BC *Lions* football games to trade shows and tractor pulls, this stadium, beneath its pillowy-looking, air-supported dome (the world's largest), has been a major activity center for locals and visitors alike since 1986. It is the permanent site of the *BC Sports Hall of Fame* (phone: 687-5520), which celebrates over a century of sporting achievement by the province's athletes, with medals and memorabilia from *Olympic Games*. The *Hall of Fame,* now in its final phase of construction, will be the most modern of its kind in Canada when it is completed, with such high-tech innovations as computerized "track races," "soccer games," and "wall climbing." Before the stadium stands a statue of Terry Fox, the gallant one-legged runner from nearby Port Coquitlam, whose determination to help conquer cancer, the disease that felled him, won the hearts of millions. 1 Robson St. at Beatty St. (phone: 669-2300). *Skytrain* exit: Stadium.

Westcoast Transmission Building – People who saw this structure being built in the 1960s likened it to an oversize redwood tree, with the central core representing the trunk, and its 12 suspension cables supporting the expansive canopy. Now familiar to TV viewers the world over as the headquarters for "MacGyver's" Phoenix Foundation, it was at the time one of the only buildings in the world to be built from the top down. The result: The parking garage has no columns and the large plaza on street level is actually under the square-shaped transmission building itself. Being here is not unlike being under one of those 300-foot giant firs, its branches rising above. 1333 W. Georgia St.

Burrard Bridge – Opened in 1932 to carry traffic to the city's burgeoning south side, this six-lane connection to suburbia is more than a traffic route. Over a dozen sculpted lions, along with busts of explorers Captain Vancouver and Captain Burrard, were built as part of the design. The inscription "By Sea and Land We Prosper" greets commuters and visitors alike. At the north end of the bridge, on the west side of the street, is a cement statue by Edward Apt titled *A Girl Waiting For a Bus.*

Harbour Centre – For years this was *Eaton's* department store, one of the city's largest. The current structure, in part a reconstruction of that emporium, now also includes 21 floors of offices, a shopping mall, and the downtown branch of Simon Fraser University. A pair of outdoor glass elevators offers a view of the city as they whiz visitors to *Lookout!* an observation deck topped by a revolving restaurant. The flying-saucer-shape top has become one of the most recognized features of downtown Vancouver. 555 W. Hastings St. (phone: 689-0421). *Skytrain* exit: Waterfront. (Also see *Walk 3: Historic Hastings* in DIRECTIONS.)

Dominion Building – When this 13-story building was completed in 1908, it was considered the tallest structure in the British Empire and the most modern office building in Canada. The red-brick building has been cleaned and refurbished and much of its marble, ornate tilework, and woodwork are still in place. 207 W. Hastings St. (Also see *Walk 3: Historic Hastings* in DIRECTIONS.)

Vancouver Police Centennial Museum – Located in the old coroner's building and the former morgue with its "storage" drawers and minutely detailed crime exhibit of a woman murdered in a rooming house, this is no ordinary house of constabulary collectibles. (The refrigerated crypts are kept in operating condition in case of a crisis.) There's a well-equipped autopsy room with a mannequin that bears an uncanny likeness to the legendary swashbuckling movie star Errol Flynn, who died suddenly while in Vancouver. The story of the force's first century is told through diplays of police badges, weapons, and a variety of artifacts, including marked cards, counterfeit currency, and opium paraphernalia. Close to Gastown and Chinatown. Open daily. Admission charge. 240 E. Cordova St. (phone: 665-3346).

Marine Building – Perhaps the city's most beloved heritage building, this Art Deco "wedding cake" structure with its small but lavishly ornate lobby was erected in 1929, just in time to be hard hit by the Depression. Vancouver's first "skyscraper" managed to survive bad times and threats of a wrecking ball and today, thanks to its city-sanctioned landmark status, is untouchable. Its precise carvings and stone mass were meant to suggest, according to its architects, "some giant crag rising from the sea, clinging with sea flora and fauna, tinted in sea green and touched by gold." It now houses *The Imperial* (phone: 688-8191; see *Eating Out*), one of the city's best Chinese restaurants, and two small eateries, as well as the eclectic gift shop, *Tangram Designs* (phone: 263-1231). Stand across the street for a better look at the terra cotta trim. 355 Burrard St., corner of Hastings St. *Skytrain* exit: Waterfront. (Also see *Walk 3: Historic Hastings* in DIRECTIONS.)

Portal Park – The breathing space of choice in downtown Vancouver features a relief map on its floor beneath a glass dome that illustrates the city's relationship to its Pacific Rim neighbors. There are four arched portals, with stained glass inserts on stone pillars. Curved stone benches overlook the busiest harbor in Canada. W. Hastings St. at the foot of Thurlow St. *Skytrain* exit: Waterfront. (Also see *Walk 3: Historic Hastings* in DIRECTIONS.)

Sam Kee Building – *Ripley's Believe It or Not* and the *Guinness Book of Records* call this the world's narrowest commercial building: The structure, built in 1913, is 4 feet, 11 inches wide. When Pender Street was widened in 1912, the city expropriated most of the commercial property, leaving only this strip. Undaunted, importer-exporter Chang Toy built a long, narrow, steel-frame building (there was no Sam Kee; that was the name of Chang's business). Six bay windows added 2½ feet to the upstairs width and a 10-foot-wide basement extended to the edge of the street. The upstairs once served as living quarters for Chinese families and the basement as public baths; today the building houses offices. 8 W. Pender St., corner of Carrall St.

Dr. Sun Yat Sen Classical Garden and Park – Completed for *EXPO '86,* this is the first such garden in North America. A calligraphic inscription at the entrance translates to "Garden of Ease," a most apt description of this tranquil oasis in the midst of bustling Chinatown. Symbolic of the Ming Dynasty (1368–1644), it is a sublime mix of pavilions, ponds, plants, and rocks. Artisans from China's Jiangsu province transformed the onetime parking lot using only traditional methods and tools. The adjacent park blends stones, rockeries, and running water to create a peaceful atmosphere. Both were named for the first President of the Republic of China, who visited Vancouver's Chinatown prior to his country's 1911 revolution. The garden is open daily, 10 AM to 7:30 PM, May through August; 10 AM to 4:30 PM, September through April. Admission charge to the garden. (Also see *Parks and Gardens* in DIVERSIONS.) Both are located behind the Chinese Community Centre, 250 E. Pender St. (phone: 687-0729; for the garden, 662-3207).

St. James Anglican Church – This Gothic-style heritage structure, with its slightly Byzantine interior, was designed in the late 1930s by architect Adrian Gilbert Scott; he had recently built a church in Cairo and the edifice reflects his interest in things Egyptian. Constructed of reinforced concrete, it replaced a church built in 1881 and destroyed in a fire 5 years later. An air space, measuring 2 feet between the inner and outer walls, adds depth to the windows and arches. Cordova and Gore Sts.

Gastown Steam Clock – The world's first steam-power timepiece is fueled by the vapor rising beneath city streets. It whistles and puffs on the quarter hour and serenades with Westminster chimes each hour. Its creator, Ray Saunders, will fill you in on the details from his eponymous clock shop around the corner (123 Cambie St.; phone: 669-3525). The landmark is a favorite with TV and film production crews. Cambie and Water Sts.

Vanterm – The best (and most comfortable) way to get a window on the world of the busiest port along the West Coast of North America is to visit this shipping terminal. The terminal windows are wide and clean. Open during business hours. No admission charge. Ample parking. Located at the foot of Clark Dr. (phone: 666-1629).

BEYOND DOWNTOWN AND THE SUBURBS

Van Dusen Botanical Gardens – Gardening is such a passion in Vancouver that it has been called the city's religion. If that's the case, Van Dusen must be the community's cathedral. Its 55 acres of formal gardens and lakes are given over to displays of native and exotic plants. The fountain at the entrance is a gift from the *Swedish Society* and depicts the contribution of Swedish Canadians to the economic and cultural life of British Columbia. Open daily. Admission charge. 37th Ave. and Oak St. (phone: 266-7194). Also see *Parks and Gardens* in DIVERSIONS.

Simon Fraser University – Sitting atop Burnaby Mountain, this campus commands beautiful views of the city and the surrounding coastal areas. Most of its striking modern buildings were designed by Vancouver architect Arthur Erickson. Hourly tours of the campus are conducted during July and August and on weekends the rest of the year (no charge). The campus theater has frequent programs that may interest visitors. Open daily. No admission charge. In Burnaby on Burnaby Mountain (phone: 291-3111). Also see *Quintessential Vancouver* in DIVERSIONS.

Bloedel Conservatory – Under this ultramodern dome, some 350 exotic plants and flowers thrive in simulated desert, rain forest, and tropical environments. There are also 50 varieties of birds from throughout the world. Located in Queen Elizabeth Park, a spectacular place of lush gardens and plantings that was once a rock quarry. Open daily. Admission charge. Cambie and 33rd Sts. (phone: 872-5513).

Nitobe Memorial Gardens – This traditional Japanese garden on the University of BC campus is a serene, tranquil setting for contemplation. Though the gardens are small, they encourage lingering. There's a tea house for ceremonial occasions. Open daily from April to early October; otherwise, closed on weekends. Admission charge. NW Marine Dr. (phone: 228-3928).

Lighthouse Park – Eight miles of trails lead through a virgin forest, one of the most beautiful in the southwestern corner of British Columbia. The park is named for the 60-foot Point Atkinson Lighthouse, to which a short, half-mile hiking trail leads. It ends at a rocky bluff overlooking the beautiful Georgia Strait. Open daily. No admission charge. 5 miles (8 km) west of Lions Gate Bridge on Marine Dr., West Vancouver.

Grouse Mountain – In addition to the *Skyride* and stunning views of the city from the summit (see *Seeing the City,* above), this 4,100-foot mountain — only 20 minutes from downtown — has good ski runs with four chair lifts, a chalet, a lounge, rentals, and a variety of slopes. In summertime its many paths are great for hiking. Another attraction is the *Theatre in the Sky,* which shows a multi-image presentation about the history of Vancouver on three large screens and several television monitors. The *Grouse Nest* dining room serves lunch and dinner and has excellent views. Open daily. Admission charge. At the top of Capilano Rd. in North Vancouver (phone: 984-0661).

Capilano Suspension Bridge – One of the world's longest suspension foot bridges, it hangs 230 feet above the Capilano River and stretches 450 feet across the canyon. The original bridge was erected in 1889; the bridge that stands now was built in 1956. Those who walk across the bridge will feel it move under their feet. There's a gift shop and totem pole park. Open daily until dark, with illumination in July and August until 10:30 PM. Admission charge. 3735 Capilano Rd., North Vancouver (phone: 985-7474).

Capilano Salmon Hatchery – A working fish farm built to increase the declining salmon run in the Capilano River, which so far has been extremely effective. Visitors can observe salmon in glass tanks and study diagrams that describe the life cycle of this amazing fish. Open daily. No admission charge. 4500 Capilano Park Rd., North Vancouver (phone: 987-1411).

Cypress Provincial Park – This mountain park overlooking the city has meadows, lakes, and forests spanning 7,037 acres of the North Shore mountains. Hiking, snowshoeing, and cross-country and downhill skiing are favorite activities here. Open daily (phone: 929-1291).

Burnaby Village Museum – Life in the Vancouver area from 1890 to 1925, complete with village smithy, bandstand, chapel, school, and log cabins, is depicted at this living museum with its costumed interpreters. Some of the structures were moved from other locations, and some, like the chapel, were erected for the museum (although its pews date from 1905). There's a bakery, a general store, a drugstore with red-and-green globes in the window, a theater showing silent movies, and a Chinese herbalist. An ice cream parlor and an occasional vaudeville show at the bandstand add to the charm. At *Christmas,* the scene is lighted in festive splendor. Call for schedules. Closed January through March; open daily April through May, 11 AM to 4:30 PM; June through *Labour Day,* 10 AM to 5 PM; September and *Thanksgiving* weekend (October 9 to 11), 11 AM to 4:30 PM; and for part of December for *Heritage Christmas,* 1:30 to 9:30 PM. Admission charge. 6501 Deer Lake Ave., Burnaby (phone: 293-6501).

Museum of Anthropology – An award-winning glass and concrete structure on a cliff, the University of British Columbia's museum overlooks mountains and sea on the Point Grey campus. Designed by renowned Vancouver architect Arthur Erickson, the museum lays claim to the world's finest collection of Northwest Indian art. Erickson's most arresting innovation is the 45-foot-high glass enclosure in the Great Hall behind which stands a magnificent collection of Haida and Kwagiutl totem poles and other carvings. Holdings include woodcarvings, ancient house posts, bentwood boxes, dishes, and bowls, as well as art and artifacts from around the world. The large cedar entry doors were carved by 'Ksan craftsmen (Native Americans from the Hazelton area). Open Tuesdays, 11 AM to 9 PM; Wednesdays to Sundays, 11 AM to 5 PM; closed Mondays. Admission charge. 6393 NW Marine Dr. (phone: 822-3825).

H.R. MacMillan Planetarium – Astronomy and laser shows on a 60-foot dome with high-tech projection and sound equipment bring the universe down to earth. There are also family matinees and music-oriented laser light shows. Programs change frequently; be sure to make reservations in advance. Closed Mondays, except holidays. Admission charge. 1100 Chestnut St., Vanier Park (phone: 736-4431 or 736-3656 for taped information).

Gordon Southam Observatory – The first public observatory in western Canada houses a number of telescopes, some of which are from time to time taken out for public use outside the facility. Visitors are invited to "Shoot the Moon" when the moon is full; for a small fee per camera, shutterbugs can attach their 35mm SLRs to the telescopes and indulge in lunar photography. The observatory, which is in the same complex as the *MacMillan Planetarium,* is open weekdays. It also is open weekends and holidays, depending on the weather and availability of volunteers, so call ahead to check. Bring the kids. No admission charge. 1100 Chestnut St., Vanier Park (phone: 738-2855).

Vancouver Museum – Canada's largest civic museum and one of Vancouver's oldest cultural organizations, its charming permanent display includes reconstructed rooms and settings from the first days of the settlement through the Edwardian era. There are special traveling exhibits, along with lectures and films. A gift shop and the *Vanier Room* restaurant (phone: 736-6336), with one of the finest views of sea and mountains, add to the ambience. Ample free parking. Also located in the *MacMillan Planetarium* complex. Open daily in summer; closed Mondays off-season. Admission charge, except first Thursday of each month from 5 to 9 PM. 1100 Chestnut St., Vanier Park (phone: 736-7736).

Maritime Museum – Not far from the three attractions above, this is the place for those with a fascination for the sea, home to such artifacts as pieces from the SS *Beaver,* which went aground off Prospect Point in 1888, that tell the story of the Port of Vancouver. Here, too, is the *St. Roch,* the RCMP Arctic patrol and supply vessel which, in 1928, was the first ship to circumnavigate the North American continent by traversing the treacherous Northwest Passage. Down at the museum's Heritage Harbour is its revolving display of local and international historic vessels. Open daily. Admission charge. 1905 Ogden Ave., Vanier Park, 1 block from the planetarium (phone: 736-4431).

English Bay Beach – No major city (with the exception of Sydney) has so many fine beaches (11), and this one has special events as well. Since the turn of the century, English Bay Beach has attracted swimmers and sun worshipers and, in more recent years, windsurfers. The summer venue for the *Vancouver Sea Festival,* it was here, too, that the annual *Polar Bear Swim* got its start on *New Year's Day,* 1919. Today hardy souls, often numbering in the hundreds, take the plunge into the frigid waters. Avid strollers can get here by going west on Robson Street to Denman Street. Turn left on Denman and continue to Beach Avenue.

Hastings Mills Store – This 1865 building, which was part of Captain Stamp's thriving little mill town at the foot of Dunlevy Street on Burrard Inlet, is considered the oldest building in Vancouver, one of the few to survive the Great Fire of 1886. It served as the first post office on the inlet and as the settlement's first library and community center. More than 60 years ago, the *Native Daughters of BC* repaired and restored the landmark and had it moved by barge to Pioneer Park. In addition to artifacts of the era, the museum has a dramatic drawing of the fire by the city's first archivist. Open daily June to September and weekends only the rest of the year. Call for schedules. Donation suggested. 1575 Alma Rd. at Point Grey Rd. (phone: 228-1213).

Lynn Canyon Ecology Centre – A not-to-be-missed experience for nature lovers, this popular place has areas devoted to plant, animal, and human life; kids love the puppets, puzzles, and drawing area. Few nature centers are so aptly located: Forested Lynn Canyon Park has extensive hiking trails, a picnic site, and a swaying, cable-hung suspension bridge that spans the roaring white water of Lynn Canyon creek. In summer there are guided walks through the park; there's also a cafeteria. Open daily, 10 AM to 5 PM; closed weekends in December and January. In Lynn Valley Park, North Vancouver at 3633 Park Rd. (phone: 987-5922). Motorists: Go east on Hastings Street to Cassiar Street. Cross the Second Narrows Bridge and take the fifth exit, Lynn Valley Road. Turn right onto Peters Road and then right again into the park. Pedestrians: Take the *SeaBus* to North Vancouver, then *BC Transit.* Call *BC Transit* (phone: 261-5100) for the best route from your point of departure.

FARTHER OUT

Reifel Bird Sanctuary – Home and nesting ground of about 230 species of swans, geese, and ducks, this wild bird sanctuary has footpaths and observation towers. The 850-acre site is open daily. Admission charge. Take Highway 99 south to the Ladner exit, then River Rd. west; cross the Westham Island Bridge and continue to the end of the road (phone: 946-6980).

Vancouver Game Farm – Lions and tigers and bears, monkeys, zebras, and giraffes, are among the 80 species from all over the world that inhabit these 120 acres of farmland. Visitors can amble around the grounds or tour by car. The amiable elephants are available for rides during the summer. There also are picnic facilities and a gift shop. Open daily. Admission charge. 5048 264th St., Aldergrove (phone: 261-0225).

Fort Langley National Historic Park – Built in 1827 as the Hudson's Bay Company's fort, this park includes the original company store and restored gates, palisades, officers' quarters, and shops. The fort is historically interesting because it predates Vancouver by a number of years. Open daily. Admission charge. 30 miles (48 km) east in Fort Langley (phone: 888-4424).

Royal Hudson Steam Train – A must for train buffs, this is a journey into the past aboard a genuine steam engine. Day trips aboard the *Royal Hudson Steam Engine 2860* leave from North Vancouver, follow Howe Sound, with its magnificent ocean and mountain views, and proceed up the coast to the logging community of Squamish, which is probably the least interesting part of the journey. The train is replete with a bar car and several refurbished passenger cars. The round trip takes a good 6 hours, including a lunch stop in Squamish. Another — perhaps better — way both to see Howe Sound and to ride the train is to take a combination boat-train day trip that transports travelers one way on the train and then returns them via the MV *Britannia*, Canada's largest sightseeing vessel. Trips are made from May 21 to September 24, Wednesdays through Sundays. Reservations necessary. Tickets and details from *Harbour Ferries*, at the north foot of Denman St. (phone: 687-3245 or 687-9558).

■ **EXTRA SPECIAL:** Just a 90-minute ferry ride through the spectacular Gulf Islands is Vancouver Island, 24 miles across the Strait of Georgia from the mainland. Some 285 miles (456 km) in length, it is Canada's largest Pacific island and quite spectacular. Actually the top of a partially submerged mountain system, much of the island is heavily forested and mountainous. This is most dramatically apparent in the Pacific Rim National Park on the western coast. Here seals, sea lions, and shore birds inhabit 250 square miles of craggy headlands, white sandy beaches, interior lakes, and estuaries. There are campgrounds in the park and accommodations nearby.

From the terminal at Swartz Bay, it's a 45-minute drive to Victoria, the provincial capital. Victoria is beautifully situated on the shores of the Juan de Fuca Strait, surrounded by sea, with snow-capped mountains forming an impressive backdrop. This is the most English community on the continent, a haven of Sunday afternoon games of lawn bowling, well-loved gardens, and proper English afternoon tea. The wealth of its 300,000 residents is reflected in the lovely residential districts of fine homes and carefully tended gardens. The main attractions are the dignified Parliament Buildings and the magnificent and justifiably renowned Butchart Gardens (open daily; admission charge; phone: 652-5256, or 652-4422 during business hours) — 50 acres developed from an old quarry with six gardens, including the Sunken Lake with its fountains, an English rose garden, the lush Italian gardens, and a delicate Japanese garden. At night the gardens are all illuminated. There's a restaurant, coffee shop, and gift shop, and live entertainment during July and August.

Shops in Victoria offer good values in woolens, china, crystal, jade, antiques, and handicrafts. Visitors planning an overnight stay should reserve a room at the *Empress* (phone: 384-8111), the castle by the sea that is the grande dame of Canadian Pacific hotels. A $45-million restoration in 1989 has fully recaptured this place's original charm and elegance, right down to its leafy palms in exotic Oriental urns. For something smaller and a bit out of town, try the charming *Oak Bay Beach* hotel (1175 Beach Dr.; phone: 598-4556).

SOURCES AND RESOURCES

TOURIST INFORMATION: For general information, brochures, and maps, contact the Vancouver Travel InfoCentre (1055 Dunsmuir St.; phone: 683-2000). The office is conveniently located just down the street from the *Hyatt Regency* hotel. City street maps are available at most newsstands and department stores.

For maps and general information on Victoria, contact Tourism Victoria (812 Wharf St.; phone: 382-2127) across from the *Empress* hotel.

Local Coverage – The *Province,* morning daily and the only Sunday paper; the *Sun,* morning daily except Sundays. *Vancouver* and *Western Living* are monthly magazines concerned with West Coast lifestyle; another monthly, *Where Vancouver,* includes maps and information on shopping and entertainment.

Food – *Vancouver* contains short items on some of the city's restaurants, and the *Sun* and *Province* both have regular restaurant reviews. *Vancouver Gastronomique* ($9.95) describes a full range of dining options.

 TELEPHONE: The area code for Vancouver is 604.

 CURRENCY: All prices are quoted in US dollars unless otherwise indicated. **Sales Tax** – British Columbia has a provincial sales tax of 6%. In addition, a 7% federal tax, called the Goods and Services Tax (GST), is levied on most purchases. In many cases, visitors can receive refunds of both the provincial and federal taxes. Stores that deal with tourists generally carry British Columbia tax rebate forms. For GST rebate information, see *Duty-Free Shopping and Goods and Services Tax* in GETTING READY TO GO.

 GETTING AROUND: Airport Transportation – Both the *Airport Express* and *Perimeter Transportation* run a minibus service leaving downtown from 5:45 AM to 11 PM, with stops at major downtown hotels. For information, call 273-9023.

Bus – The *BC Transit* bus system covers most of Greater Vancouver with extensive downtown service. During off-peak hours (from 9:30 AM to 3 PM and after 6 PM, Mondays through Fridays, and all day on weekends) you can travel throughout the system's three zones using all conveyances (bus, *Skytrain,* and *SeaBus* — see below for latter two) on a single, exact fare. Service is greatly reduced after midnight. For information, call 261-5100. The booklet, *Discover Vancouver on Transit,* is available at most information outlets and major bus stations. It gives easy-to-follow routes to attractions throughout the Greater Vancouver area.

Car Rental – For information on renting a car, see "Car Rental" in *On Arrival,* GETTING READY TO GO.

Ferry – *SeaBus* is a ferry system that links the North Shore with downtown Vancouver. The *Burrard Otter* and the *Burrard Beaver* shuttle passengers between the North Shore's *Lonsdale Quay Market* and *Skytrain*'s Waterfront station at the foot of Granville Street downtown. Ferries depart every 15 minutes from the downtown terminal at the *CP Rail* station and from the North Vancouver terminal at the foot of Lonsdale. Each can carry as many as 400 people at a time. For schedule and fares, call *BC Transit* (phone: 261-5100).

For information on service to Vancouver Island, contact *BC Ferries* (phone: 669-1211), which sail to Victoria and Nanaimo, farther north on the island. *Royal Sealink Express* (phone: 687-6925) has two catamaran passenger ferries that run between downtown Vancouver and downtown Victoria, a 2½-hour trip one way. *Nanaimo Express* (phone: 687-6925), a 296-seat catamaran, operates daily between the *Seabus* terminal in Vancouver and Inner Harbour in Nanaimo on Vancouver Island; the trip is 65 minutes one way.

Sightseeing Tours – *Gray Line* (phone: 681-8687) operates tours from most of the downtown hotels; in summer, colorful British doubledeckers join the fleet. *Trolley Tours* (phone: 255-2444) has old-style trolleys that stop at 17 attractions on their 90-minute, narrated circuit. You can make as many stops as you wish along the route, then pick up the next trolley.

Skytrain – This automated light rapid transit (*ALRT*) system makes ten convenient stops in the city, and serves the suburbs of Burnaby, New Westminster, and Surrey. It is part of *BC Transit*'s efficient transportation system that also includes mass transit buses and the *SeaBus* ferry (phone: 261-5100).

Taxi – Major companies are *Advance* (phone: 876-5555); *Black Top Cabs* (phone: 681-2181); *Maclure's* (phone: 731-9211); and *Yellow Cab* (phone: 681-3311). Taxi stands are located throughout the city and at most hotels. Hailing cabs in the street is difficult. Almost any fare within the city will be under $10; a trip to the airport from downtown runs about $15.

 LOCAL SERVICES: For additional information about local services, call the Vancouver Board of Trade (phone: 681-2111).

    Baby-sitting – *A Baby Sitter Everytime* (phone: 689-2888).

    Computer Rentals – *Ability Computer Rentals,* 1250-789 W. Pender St. (phone: 681-7032).

Dry Cleaner – *Valetor,* on the concourse level of *The Bay* (phone: 681-6211) and other locations.

Limousine – *Classic Limousine Service* (phone: 669-5466); *Star Limousine Service* (phone: 875-9466); *Take 4 Limousine Service* (phone: 299-4444).

Mechanic – *AMG,* 110 W. 4th Ave. (phone: 877-1331).

Medical Emergency – *Associated House Call Physician Services* (phone: 434-1000).

National/International Courier – *Federal Express* (phone: 273-1544); *Purolator Couriers* (phone: 270-1000).

Photocopies – *Zippy Print,* 1147 Melville St. (phone: 683-8488) and other locations.

Post Office – Main branch, 349 W. Georgia St. (phone: 662-5725).

Professional Photography – *Campbell Studios* (2580 Burrard St.; phone: 736-0261); *CustomColor* (1114 Robson St.; phone: 669-1574); *Dunne & Rundell Cameras* (891 Granville St.; phone: 681-9254).

Secretary/Stenographer – *Accutype Secretarial Services,* 207-1425 Marine Dr., West Vancouver (phone: 926-1985).

Translator – *Berlitz,* 830 W. Pender St. (phone: 685-9331).

Traveler's Checks – *American Express* (1201-1166 Alberni St.; phone: 687-2641). For refunds or to report lost or stolen traveler's checks, call 800-221-7282. *Thomas Cook* (*Pacific Centre,* 617 Granville St.; phone: 687-6111). For refunds or to report lost or stolen traveler's checks, call *MasterCard Travel Check Refund Center* at 800-223-7373.

Typewriter Rental – *Polson,* 458 W. Broadway (phone: 879-0631).

Western Union/Telex – Many locations around the city (phone: 800-321-2933); *Unitel Communications* (175 W. Cordova St.; phone: 681-4231).

Other – *Classy Formal Wear* (1026 Robson St.; phone: 684-4317) has tuxedos for rent or for sale.

 SPECIAL EVENTS: For exact dates, check with the Vancouver Travel InfoCentre (see *Tourist Information*). At the *Polar Bear Swim,* held every *New Year's Day* since 1919, hardy souls of all ages dip into the Pacific at English Bay.

The *Chinese New Year* is celebrated in a colorful, rollicking way every year (this year's festivities will be held from January 19 to *Chinese New Year's Day,* January 23), with a parade, lion dances, and firecrackers in Chinatown. Occidentals get into the act at the *Chinese New Year Fair*, where entertainment, food, demonstrations, and a trade show and sale is held for 3 days at the Pacific Showmart Building on the Pacific National Exhibition Grounds. The last night of the celebration extends into the wee hours. City malls and parks hold special events, too.

In May, the annual *Children's Festival* — considered one of the best of its kind in North America — features a lively program of puppet shows, mime, dancers, singers, and plays — all performed under colorful tents in Vanier Park.

During the *Canadian International Dragon Boat Festival* in June, ornately decorated boats propelled by up to 4 dozen oarsmen race down False Creek for the honor of representing Canada at the world championships in Hong Kong. Dragon boat races commemorate a 3,000-year-old legend of a poet/statesman who drowned himself. As part of the ceremony to mark his death, people toss bamboo-wrapped sticky rice into the waters to feed the fish so that they will not bother the body of the drowned man.

In late June, the annual *Vancouver International Jazz Festival* attracts such greats as Dizzy Gillespie, along with thousands of jazz buffs, to indoor and outdoor venues throughout the city and to a 3-day open-air spectacular at the Plaza of Nations. Days later the city celebrates *Canada Day* (July 1) with picnics, fireworks, and a star-packed musical show at Canada Place.

Another *Canada Day* event is the *Steveston Salmon Festival*, the largest 1-day community festival in Canada. Organizers serve up 1,700 pounds of salmon and 3,000 plates of chow mein. Events range from the *King of the Fraser* fishing competition to a chowder cook-off. Also celebrated as part of the *Canada Day* festivities is the annual *International Outboard Grand Prix*, a 3-day competition held at Barnet Marine Park on the inlet off Barnet Highway. Formula One boats and modified hydrofoils powered by 300hp engines compete at speeds of up to 130 mph. The competition is part of a US-Canada circuit.

The *Vancouver Sea Festival* is one of the best summer celebrations on the continent. For 3 days in mid-July the city is a feast of salmon barbecues and seafood, with parades, concerts, and sports events. The *Symphony of Fire* is an international fireworks competition synchronized to music. Best views are from the water and several boat charters are available (for information about charters contact your hotel concierge or Tourism Vancouver; phone: 604-683-2000). Contestants from around the world come to compete in the madcap *Bathtub Races*, which occur a week after the pyrotechnics. "Sailors" in wild getups race their modified "bathtubs" in the waters between Nanaimo on Vancouver Island and the city. The intrepid bathtubbers land before news cameras and hundreds of spectators at Kitsilano Beach.

Mid-July also brings the *Vancouver Folk Music Festival*, a long weekend filled with performances by musicians from all over North America; there are workshops and jam sessions as well.

Old Broadway musicals get a new life in Stanley Park during July and August when *Theatre Under the Stars* presents nightly shows at *Malkin Bowl*, weather permitting; also during July and August, *Bard on the Beach*, with magnificent costumes, sparse sets, and fine actors, presents Shakespeare in a place of spectacular views of sunsets against the backdrop of North Shore mountains at Vanier Park.

Held on a weekend in early August, the *Abbotsford International Air Show* features aerobatics and aircraft displays by everything from Piper Cubs to 747s. It takes place at the Abbotsford Airport, 45 miles (72 km) east of Vancouver. For information, call 859-9211. Every year in late August, a grand parade through downtown Vancouver kicks off the *Pacific National Exhibition*, featuring concerts by renowned artists, logging sports exhibitions, livestock and agricultural displays, horse races, food fairs, and a good midway. For information, call 253-2311.

Local restaurants and ethnic groups provide samplings of their specialties at the annual *Taste of Nations Food Fair* at Plaza of Nations on the *EXPO '86* site in August. The same month, Granville Island is the home of the yearly *International Comedy Festival;* the area's three theaters and several outdoor stages showcase the best in humor from around the world. And in late August, viewing stands are erected and the roads around *BC Place* converted to a 2-km circuit for the *Molson Indy 500,* which attracts the biggest names in non–Formula One racing.

In September, legion halls, bingo parlors, and church basements are just a few of the sites frequented by avid theatergoers during the annual *Fringe Festival* in the Mt. Pleasant area. Offbeat plays are the norm, although some performers use the format to showcase their classical talents. Hundreds of productions and dozens of plays are mounted during this marathon day-and-night theaterfest. September also marks the *International Film Festival,* where accomplished producers from Europe, the Far East, and the US screen their best. There's also a special segment featuring Canadian films.

In December, the *Christmas Carol Ship,* with a troupe of carolers on board, leads a flotilla of ships, all lit up for *Christmas,* around Vancouver Harbour evenings during a 10-day period before the 25th. More than a dozen boat charter companies offer holiday harbor cruises, but book well in advance, as this local favorite is usually sold out early. For information on participating charter companies, call 683-2000.

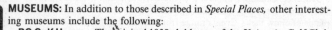

MUSEUMS: In addition to those described in *Special Places,* other interesting museums include the following:

BC Golf House – The original 1930 clubhouse of the *University Golf Club,* located just behind the 17th tee, houses a small museum commemorating golf throughout the province. Closed Mondays. No admission charge. 2545 Blanca St. (phone: 222-4699).

BC Sugar Museum – Sugar refining shaped the economic history of British Columbia, and the first refinery opened more than a century ago. Displays vividly trace the province's sweet history through letters, photos, and artifacts. One exhibit is of sugar-making equipment dating back to 1715. Guided tours can be arranged Mondays through Fridays from 9 AM to 4 PM. No admission charge. The museum is located at the BC Sugar Refinery at the foot of Rogers St. (phone: 253-1131).

Canadian Museum of Flight and Transportation – Set in a park with picnic tables and benches, this place displays biplanes, gliders, and heritage aircraft along with support vehicles. Taped guided tours are available. Gift shop. Open mid-May through mid-October. Call for hours. Admission charge. Follow Highway 99 south to White Rock/Crescent Beach, exit 13527. Crescent Beach Rd., Surrey (phone: 535-1115).

SS *Samson V* – This steam-powered paddlewheeler plied the Fraser River from 1937 to 1980. Her history, and that of her sister ships dating back to early settler days, is told by way of pictures and memorabilia. She is moored on the Fraser, 1 block from the New Westminster *Skytrain* station alongside the *Westminster Quay Public Market.* Open weekends and holidays (some additional openings in summer; call for schedules). Admission by donation. 810 Front St., New Westminster (phone: 521-7656).

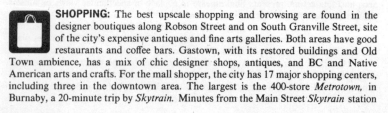

SHOPPING: The best upscale shopping and browsing are found in the designer boutiques along Robson Street and on South Granville Street, site of the city's expensive antiques and fine arts galleries. Both areas have good restaurants and coffee bars. Gastown, with its restored buildings and Old Town ambience, has a mix of chic designer shops, antiques, and BC and Native American arts and crafts. For the mall shopper, the city has 17 major shopping centers, including three in the downtown area. The largest is the 400-store *Metrotown,* in Burnaby, a 20-minute trip by *Skytrain.* Minutes from the Main Street *Skytrain* station is an experience of another kind: the *Vancouver Flea Market.* With over 350 stalls and huge crowds to match, it is the fair-weather choice of weekend and holiday shoppers. Just look for the red barn (703 Terminal Ave.; phone: 685-0666). The following are some of the city's favorite shopping haunts.

Alfred Sung – The Canadian designer's regular line of women's formal wear and children's fashions as well as his popular sports fashions. 1143 Robson St. (phone: 687-2153).

Angel's – A favorite stop for visiting actors and musicians, who buy from the rack or custom-order hand-painted, one-of-a-kind shirts, jackets, and other wearable art, including infantswear. Check out the full line of specially created fabric paints for do-it-yourselfers. 1293 Robson St. (phone: 681-0947).

Atkinson's – Exclusive lines of linen, crystal, china, silver, teddy bears, French perfume, and evening bags. 3057 Granville St. (phone: 736-3378).

Bacci – Designer fashions and shoes from Europe attract the wealthy children of former flower children. 2788 Granville St. (phone: 732-7317).

Bakers Dozen Two and Bakers Dozen – The first has artifacts and furniture of western Canadiana and handcrafted pond boats from Nova Scotia, the second, a half block away, has toy collectibles, including a remarkable selection of Dinky Toy cars and trucks. *Bakers Dozen Two,* 3520 Main St. (phone: 879-3348); *Bakers Dozen,* 3467 Main St. (phone: 879-3348).

Birk's – Canada's most prestigious jeweler for over a century, it likens itself to *Tiffany's,* right down to the blue boxes. Several locations, but its most prominent one is at the *Birk's* clock. 710 Granville St. (phone: 669-3333).

Boboli – Italian-designed clothing for men and women. 2776 Granville St. (phone: 736-3458).

Book Warehouse – A profusion of discounted books with some great bargains and complimentary coffee. Open 7 days a week at several locations. Main location, 1150 Robson St. (phone: 685-5711).

Bratz – For chic kids: high-style European fashions, accessories, and shoes, plus a hair salon. 2828 Granville St. (phone: 734-4344).

Canadian Impressions – Cowichan-style sweaters and other Canadian woolen knits and BC jade. 321 Water St. (phone: 689-9024).

Chanel Boutique – A wide selection of shoes and accessories from the legendary Paris label. 755 Burrard St. (phone: 682-0522).

Cheena BC Ltd. – For those who want to take home a taste of Vancouver, this salmon specialty shop features BC smoked salmon packed for travel. 667 Howe St. (phone: 684-5374).

The Chief's Mask – An Indian-owned and -operated bookstore, this spot carries classics and the most recent books and other publications about the First Nations (Native Americans). 72 Water St. (phone: 687-4100).

Crafthouse – One-of-a-kind arts and crafts from the best of BC's artists and craftspeople, all members of the *Crafts Association of BC.* 1386 Cartwright St. (phone: 687-7270).

Crystal Ark – Behind *Kids Only Market* (see below) is this storehouse of New Age energy: natural crystals and gemstones from around the world, including crystal balls, geodes, and rock clusters. Jewelry is made on the premises. 1496 Cartwright St., Granville Island (phone: 681-8900).

Deeler's Antiques – One of the largest importers of antique furniture in town. 832 *North Park Royal Mall,* West Vancouver (phone: 922-0213).

Derek Simpkins Gallery of Tribal Art – Collectors of Northwest Coast art congregate at this gallery, which specializes in the works of Robert Davidson, Joe David, and Richard Hunt. 2329 Granville St. (phone: 732-4555).

Duthie Books – Every title you can imagine housed in spacious downtown quarters that include the *Paperback Cellar*. Other locations, too, but this is the main one. Out-of-print searches a specialty. 919 Robson St. (phone: 684-4496).

Edinburgh Tartan Shop – You can check out the design of your clan at this specialty shop offering woolens, cashmere, plaids, kilts, and other fine goods associated with Scotland. 375 Water St. (phone: 681-8889).

Edward Chapman – For over a century this has been *the* place for men's imported classic British woolens. 833 W. Pender (phone: 685-6207). Women are catered to at *Edward Chapman Ladies Shop*, 750 W. Pender St. (phone: 688-6711) and *Westin Bayshore Inn* (1601 W. Georgia St.; phone: 685-6734).

Ferragamo – The only Canadian location of this international designer of women's shoes and handbags and men's footwear and accessories. 918 Robson St. (phone: 669-4495).

Flag Shop – Flag-wavers of every ilk never had such a choice. There's a good selection, too, of crests and pins. 1755 W. 4th Ave. at Burrard St. (phone: 736-8161).

Frances Hill – Canadian clothing with an emphasis on sweaters, parkas, and coats that put fashion into cold-weather wear. 151 Water St. (phone: 685-1828).

Frankie Robinson Oriental Gallery – Japanese and Chinese chests and modern folk-art pieces. 3055 Granville St. (phone: 734-6568).

Gabriel Gallery – The showcase for new and established BC artists, sculptors, and potters. 1033 Cambie St. (phone: 687-3384).

Gallery of BC Ceramics – Over 60 potters, each with a singular, distinctive talent, are represented at this Granville Island gallery. 1359 Cartwright St. (phone: 669-5645).

Games People – From backgammon to computer chess, for games people love to play. Downtown branch at 157 Water St. (phone: 685-5825), plus other locations.

Garden Antiques – The specialty is antique garden tools, old jardinières, garden ornaments, and other things botanical, plus a selection of Victorian garden and verandah furniture. 3518 Main St. (phone: 876-2311).

Granville Antique Gallery – Collectors of fine old china rely on this shop for Doulton, Dresden, Capo di Monte, Meissen, and other high-quality pieces. 3025 Granville St. (phone: 736-7407).

Heritage Canada – Authentic native arts, including carvings, large totem poles, moccasins, mukluks, and hand-knit Cowichan sweaters, are featured at two locations. 356 Water St. (phone: 669-6375) and *Vancouver Centre Mall* (phone: 669-2447).

Hill's Indian Crafts – Masks, rattles, bentwood boxes, baskets, beadwork, native-design jewelry, Haida argillite (lava-like stone) sculptures, Cowichan sweaters, and totem poles make this shop as interesting as any museum. 165 Water St. (phone: 685-4249).

Holt Renfrew – The former Canadian fur company is now a trendsetter in men's and women's fashions. Opposite the entrance to the *Four Seasons* hotel in *Pacific Centre*. 633 Granville St. (phone: 681-3121).

Images for a Canadian Heritage – This charming shop specializes in Inuit sculptures, Indian woodcarvings, limited-edition prints, and original art. 164 Water St. (phone: 685-7046).

Inuit Gallery – One of Canada's most highly regarded emporia of Inuit masterworks and Northwest Coast Indian art. 345 Water St. (phone: 688-7323).

Jade World – For a fascinating behind-the-scenes look at jade, from rough stone to sculpture and jewelry, check out the factory and carving studio (on the premises) before entering here. 1696 W. 1st Ave. (phone: 733-7212).

Kids Only Market – Play areas and live entertainment add fun to shopping in a unique, kids-are-welcome setting. Twenty-two shops are clustered in this sprawling, colorful area that caters to the younger set with clothing, toys, and games. On Granville Island at 1496 Cartwright St. (phone: 689-8447).

Leona Lattimer Gallery – Traditionally carved silver jewelry, Inuit soapstone scupltures, cedar bentwood boxes, bowls, blankets adorned with button designs, and masks, all displayed in a gallery-like setting in a simulated cedar longhouse. 1590 W. 2nd Ave. (phone: 732-4556).

Leone's – Socialites and celebrities shop here for European fashions by such designers as Gianni Versace, Giorgio Armani, and Christian LaCroix. High-style accessories, too. Then relax over in-house cappuccino. At *Sinclair Centre,* 757 W. Hastings St. (phone: 683-1133).

London Shop – With classic fashions for women, this small boutique has long been a favorite with locals. At the *Westin Bayshore,* 1601 W. Georgia St. (phone: 682-1136).

Mammoth Enterprises – Designer Richard Marcus has an unusual and pleasing collection of jewelry and sculptures created from mastodon tusks. Available at *Birk's* and at some hotel gift shops or, by appointment, from the artist's studio. 320-380 W. 1st Ave. (phone: 872-2115).

Mari Boutique – Japanese-designed clothes and shoes for men and women. 2439 Granville St. (phone: 732-8668).

Martha Sturdy – Latest designs from the well-known Canadian jeweler. 3065 Granville St. (phone: 737-0037).

Mondo Uomo – Menswear designed by Gianni Versace, Valentino, and Ferré. 2709 Granville St. (phone: 734-6555).

Murchie's – This ultimate in coffee and tea outlets began blending imported coffees in 1894. Today they dispense over 90 varieties and carry all the accessories to make and serve their brews. 970 Robson St. (phone: 662-3776).

My Fair Lady – Exclusively sold at this shop are the works of Dorothy Grant, a Haida artist whose highly sought-after designs are inspired by ceremonial Indian clothing and symbols. Her wool and cashmere coats, suits, and jackets are embellished with Haida crests, ravens, eagles, bears, and killer whales. The motifs are designed by her husband, the noted Haida artist Robert Davidson. 101-65 Richmond St., New Westminster (phone: 527-7577).

Neto Leather – Canada's largest selection of fashionable leatherwear, including their Kidz Kollection line of children's leather fashions. 347 Water St. (phone: 682-6424).

Pappas Furs – Creations of leading designers have made this furrier one of Canada's best-known for three generations. Call for limo service. 449 Hamilton St. (phone: 681-6391).

Peter Fox Shoes – Unique designs combined with astonishing comfort in Italian-made footwear make this charmingly frescoed Gastown boutique a popular spot. 303 W. Cordova St. (phone: 662-3040).

Pipe Den – Best known for its custom-blended tobaccos, it also has a wide selection of pipes and will even re-condition your old favorite. 714 W. Hastings St. (phone: 688-5023).

Purdy's Chocolates – A decades-long favorite with Vancouver sweet tooths, this chocolatier has branches in most malls, including the downtown *Pacific Centre* (phone: 681-7814).

Railway World – Everything for the train buff, from models to engineers' caps to books of railway lore. 150 Water St. (phone: 681-4811).

Sergio Bustamante – The noted Mexican artist now has a Vancouver address. Fantasy-tinged sculptures, many in papier-mâché, complement his one-of-a-kind silver and gold jewelry. 1130 Mainland St. (phone: 684-1340).

The Source – A great mix of antiques and collectibles, including old British pub items. 929 Main St. (phone: 684-9914).

Starbuck's – There are over a dozen of these trendy Seattle-based coffeehouses selling fresh-roasted blends and the best cappuccino in town. Two of the larger outlets are catercorner to each other at Robson and Thurlow Streets. 1099 Robson St. (phone: 685-1099) and 1100 Robson St. (phone: 688-5125).

Toni Cavelti – This European craftsman creates distinctive jewelry in gold and silver. 565 W. Georgia St. (phone: 681-3481).

Uno Langmann Antiques & Art – A superb selection of art and antiques, including 18th- and 19th-century furniture and some Northwest Coast Indian works. 2117 Granville St. (phone: 736-8825).

Vancouver Antique Centre – About 15 shops in a historic building offer an eclectic selection of antiques and collectibles. 422 Richards St. (phone: 669-0089).

Vancouver Pen Shop – The largest pen selection in the Canadian west, it has supplies for calligraphers of all levels. 512 W. Hastings St. (phone: 681-1612).

La Vie En Rose – Upscale lingerie, lace, and embroidery. 1101 Robson St. (phone: 684-5600).

Zonda Nellis – The designer, whose handwoven garments are found in elite stores in major US cities, lives in Vancouver. Check out her chic line of men's sweaters. 2203 Granville St. (phone: 736-5668).

BEST DISCOUNT SHOPS

If you're one of those — like us — who believes that the eighth deadly sin is buying retail, Vancouver offers these inexpensive outlets.

Millar & Coe – With well over 1,000 patterns of fine china and hundreds of designs in crystal, all at discount prices, this store has been a must for collectors and gift-givers since 1912. 419 W. Hastings St. (phone: 685-3322).

Sample Room – Designer clothing for men and women at discount prices. 1000 Mainland St. (phone: 685-8485).

Shoes By Folio – High-quality shoes and sandals for men and women at discount prices. 1005 Mainland St. (phone: 689-7110).

SPORTS: With its emphasis on the great outdoors — and in spite of its not always sunny skies — Vancouver is a great sports town for both participants and spectators.

Baseball – The *Canadians,* the triple A farm team of the Chicago *White Sox,* fill the stands at *Nat Bailey Stadium.* 4601 Ontario St. (phone: 872-5232).

Bicycling – The line-divided Stanley Park seawall is a favorite among cyclists of all levels. The more energetic continue on past the *Expo '86* lands and around False Creek. Rent 1- to 5-speed bikes, mountain bikes, or tandems from *Stanley Park Bike Rentals.* Two outlets: Denman and Georgia Sts. (phone: 688-5141) or closer to the park entrance at 676 Chilco St. (phone: 681-5581).

Fishing – Vancouver offers easy access to both freshwater and deep-sea fishing. There's fishing in the Capilano River, where trout, steelhead, and Dolly Varden are caught, and in any of the bays surrounding the city. The main catch is salmon. Fishing charter companies include *Westin Bayshore Yacht Charter* (1601 W. Georgia St.; phone: 682-3377 or 682-4811) and *Granville Island Boat Rentals* (dockside at Granville Island; phone: 682-6287 or 988-8811).

Football – The BC *Lions,* Vancouver's contenders in the Canadian Football League, take on all comers at the city's domed *BC Place Stadium,* 777 Pacific Blvd. S. (phone: 669-2300).

Golf – Several private golf courses have exchange privileges with major courses throughout North America and there are over a dozen public links in the Greater Vancouver area. The *University Golf Club* (5185 University Blvd.; phone: 224-1818) is considered one of the best public courses in Canada. *Gleneagles* (6190 Marine Dr., West Vancouver; phone: 921-7353) and *Mayfair Lakes* (5400 No. 7 Rd., Richmond; phone: 276-0505) also rank high.

Hockey – The National Hockey League's Vancouver *Canucks* defend the ice at *Pacific Coliseum* in Exhibition Park (phone: 280-4444).

Horse Racing – The horses run at Exhibition Park, on the Pacific National Exhibition grounds, from April through October. For information and reservations, call 254-1631.

Jogging – Stanley Park has an almost 5-mile-long seawall that circles around the beautiful park. Jogging along the 1-mile West Vancouver seawall also is popular.

Motor Racing – Catch national and international race car action at *Westwood Motorsport Park,* 12 miles (19 km) from downtown, from March to September (phone: 464-9378). The *Molson Indy 500* brings name drivers to race on the temporary 2-km circuit around *BC Place* in late August.

Sailing – There are several yacht clubs, including the venerable *Royal Vancouver Yacht Club* (3811 Point Grey Rd.; phone: 224-1344). Among the boat charter outfits are *Admiralty Yachts* (Granville Island; phone: 685-7371) and *Island Boat Charters* (Granville Island; phone: 688-6625).

Skiing – Grouse, Seymour, and Cypress mountains have splendid slopes overlooking the city. Some of the finest skiing in North America is at Whistler and Blackcomb mountains, about 1½-hour's drive from Vancouver. Dozens of ski packages are available, ranging from 1-day jaunts to week-long ski-ins. The Vancouver Travel InfoCentre has full details (phone: 683-2000). Also see *Downhill Skiing* in DIVERSIONS.

Soccer – The Canadian Soccer League's Vancouver *86ers,* who hold the North American professional sports record for consecutive victories, play from May through September. *Swangard Stadium* in Burnaby (phone: 435-7121).

Tennis – The city maintains an extensive number of municipal courts. Most popular are those in Stanley Park.

 THEATER: Vancouver hosts a number of professional, semi-professional, and amateur theater companies and is a big source of acting and technical talent for the film and TV industry. In summer, the two most popular theaters are outdoors: Stanley Park's long-running *Theatre Under the Stars* (phone: 687-0174), with its revival of big Broadway musicals at *Malkin Bowl,* and *Bard on the Beach,* Shakespeare at Vanier Park (phone: 325-5955). Small companies, with loyal followings, mount productions throughout the season on a variety of stages. The daily papers and the weekly *Georgia Straight* have comprehensive listings and reviews. Also call the *Arts Hotline* (phone: 684-2787). Among the companies that regularly garner awards nominations are the innovative *Pink Ink* (phone: 872-1861) and the socially conscious *Tamahnous Theatre* (phone: 688-8399).

Arts Club (Granville Island; phone: 688-3273) presents Broadway shows as well as homegrown productions that often go on tour. The evening view from the main stage theater lounge over False Creek is worth the price of admission. *Firehall Arts Centre* (280 E. Cordova St.; phone: 689-0926), once home to the first motorized fire department in North America, now produces three plays a year. It stages a contemporary dance series and the annual *Dancing on the Edge Festival. Orpheum* (Smithe and Seymour Sts.; phone: 665-3050), the old (1928) theater palace, is where the *Vancouver Symphony Orchestra* plays; it's also the venue for a variety of touring theatrical and musical events. *Metro Theatre* (1370 SW Marine Dr.; phone: 266-7191), an amateur company that has found its stride in British farce, Agatha Christie–type mysteries, and full-scale musicals, plays to lively crowds. *Queen Elizabeth Theatre* (Hamilton St. at Georgia St.; phone: 665-3050) is the stage of choice for touring Broadway shows and Canadian companies. The 2,800-seat house is home base for the *Vancouver Opera* (see below) and has an active program of dance performances, featuring the *Joffrey Ballet, Royal Winnipeg Ballet,* and the province's own troupe, *Ballet BC* (phone: 669-5954). One of the top improv troupes in the country, *Theatre Sports League* (751 Thurlow St.; phone: 688-7013), performs in a less-than-glamorous setting at *Back Alley Theatre. Playhouse Theatre Company* (Hamilton St. at Dunsmuir St.; phone: 873-3311) offers a diverse six-play season: drama, comedy, and satire in classics, new Canadian plays, and Broadway and West End hits. Sharing the boards at *Waterfront Theatre* on Granville Island (phone: 685-6127) are *New Play Centre,* with works by local playwrights, and the *Carousel Theatre,* for the young and young at heart.

 MUSIC: The hills (and streets) are alive with such noon-hour chamber music concerts as *Out for Lunch,* or *Lunch and Listen,* performed at various sites by the *Ramcoff Concert Society* (phone: 986-6838). The *Coastal Jazz and Blues Society* (phone: 688-0706) presents indoor and outdoor programs of jazz. The *Vancouver Symphony Orchestra* (phone: 684-9100) takes to the great outdoors each summer with performances in parks, on barges, and from time to time, like the von Trapp family, atop mountains. Street musicians strum, whistle, and sing at the drop of a coin at Granville Island and other crowded places.

Vancouver Opera (1132 Hamilton St.; phone: 682-2871) presents four productions from its standard 20-work repertoire (with some occasional surprises) during its October to May season at the *Queen Elizabeth Theatre.* Schedules are available at the box office (see address above). Renowned for his innovative programming, *Vancouver Symphony Orchestra* music director Sergiu Comissiona is at the podium for 12 weeks a year (guest conductors appear the rest of the season) at the acoustically acclaimed *Orpheum Theatre* (601 Smythe St.; phone: 684-9100; see also *Special Places*). Fondly known as the "Cultch," *Vancouver East Cultural Centre* (1895 Venables St.; phone: 254-9678), a converted church in the East End, is the site for a wide variety of musical events from chamber music to jazz and doo-wop to percussion and Old World music. A good reference point for citywide musical events is the *Canadian Music Centre* (phone: 734-4622). Rock concerts frequently take place at *BC Place,* the *Pacific Coliseum,* the *Orpheum, 86 Street Music Hall,* and sometimes at the *Queen Elizabeth Theatre.* Jazz lovers flock to hear local and visiting artists at the *Monterey* at *Pacific Palisades* (1277 Robson St.; phone: 688-0461). The *Commodore Ballroom* (870 Granville St.; phone: 681-7838) holds 1,000 people and is more a concert than dance hall, although the swing and sway set still sashays on its 1930s spring-loaded floor. Reggae, jazz, blues, and rock, too. Since it opened for *EXPO '86, 86 Street Music and Dance Hall* (Plaza of Nations, 750 Pacific Blvd. S.; phone: 683-8687) has become a hot spot (850 capacity) for new and old music, with touring acts, including major recording artists, as well as local talent. Local and visiting musicians jam and play Dixieland, swing, and big-band music at the *Hot Jazz Society* (2120 Main St.; phone: 873-4131). The best of touring and local music acts are part of the reason why patrons queue up to get into *Richards on Richards* (1036 Richards St.; phone: 687-6794).

 NIGHTCLUBS AND NIGHTLIFE: Vancouver has an eclectic after-hours scene offering something for everyone. For games players there's bingo with a difference at *Starship on Main* (2655 Main St.; phone: 879-8930), the world's first electronic bingo parlor, where you can play on computer screens. There are licensed gambling tables at several alcohol-free casinos, with proceeds from blackjack, roulette, and *sic bo* (a variation on a Chinese dice game) going to charities. The downtown locations are *Royal Diamond Casino* (1195 Richards St.; phone: 685-2340) and the *Great Canadian Casino* in the *Holiday Inn* (2477 Heather St.; phone: 872-5543). *The Town Pump* (66 Water St.; phone: 683-6695), a restaurant and cabaret, is a casual, sprawling, Gastown club that features some of the city's best live music acts. Among the favorite watering holes are lounges at upscale hotels such as the *Gerard Bar* at *Le Meridien* (845 Burrard St.; phone: 682-5511); *Bacchus Lounge* at the *Wedgewood* (845 Hornby St.; phone: 689-7777); and the *Garden Lounge* at the *Four Seasons* (791 W. Georgia St.; phone: 689-9333). *Pelican Bay Bar* in the *Granville Island* hotel (1253 Johnston St.; phone: 683-7373) is popular with yuppies and baby boomers who want to schmooze. The city is no slouch in the humor department, either. Its two comedy clubs — *Yuk Yuks* (Plaza of Nations, 750 Pacific Blvd. S.; phone: 687-5233) and *Punchlines* (15 Water St.; phone: 684-3015) — are among the best in the country. Reservations are recommended at both.

BEST IN TOWN

CHECKING IN: Those looking for budget and mid-range accommodations have always been well served here, but in recent years the luxury category has been enhanced, mainly with the addition of four hotels — the *Pan Pacific, Le Meridien, Four Seasons,* and *Waterfront Centre.* Expect to pay $130 and up per night for a double room listed as expensive; $75 to $130 in the moderate range and from $55 to $75 in the inexpensive category. Many of these hotels offer special weekend and off-season packages at lower rates, often with added bonuses like dining vouchers.

For bed and breakfast accommodations contact *A Home Away From Home B & B Agency Ltd.* (1441 Howard Ave., Burnaby, BC V5B 3S2; phone: 294-1760; fax: 294-0799); *Best Canadian Bed and Breakfast Network* (1090 W. King Edward Ave., Vancouver, BC V6H 1Z4; phone: 738-7207); *Canada-West Accommodations Bed and Breakfast Reservation Service* (PO Box 86607, North Vancouver, BC V4L 4L2; phone: 929-1424; fax: 685-3400); *Copes Choice B & B Accommodations* (864 E. 14th St., North Vancouver, BC V7L 2P5; phone: 987-8988); *Old English B & B Registry* (PO Box 86818, North Vancouver, BC V7L 4L3; phone: 986-5069); *Town & Country B & B* (PO Box 46544 Station G, Vancouver, BC V6R 4G8; phone: 731-5942); *Vancouver B & B Limited* (4390 Frances St., Vancouver, BC V5C 2R3; phone: 298-8815; fax: 298-5917); *Westway Accommodation Registry* (PO Box 48950 Bentall Centre, Vancouver, BC V7X 1A8; phone: 273-8293; fax: 278-6745). Hostelers should contact the *Canadian Hostelling Association — BC Region* (1515 Discovery St., Vancouver, BC V6R 4K5; phone: 224-3208; fax: 224-4852). All telephone numbers are in the 604 area code unless otherwise indicated.

Coast Plaza – The primary attractions at this West End property are a proximity to the beach activity at English Bay and a 2-block stroll from the delights of Stanley Park. Some rooms come with a complete kitchen for an additional $10 per day. The 267-room facility is topped by *Humphrey's* restaurant on the 35th floor and is the home of *Shamper's* nightclub. There's a garden patio and a shopping complex on the lower level. A complimentary mini-van takes guests downtown. 1733 Comox St. (phone: 688-7711 or 800-663-1144; fax: 688-5934). Expensive.

Delta Place – This lovely downtown hostelry in the financial district has 197 well-appointed rooms. Amenities include individually designed rooms and suites, marble bathrooms, a main dining room, the *Clipper Lounge,* a health club, a swimming pool, squash and racquetball courts, and a library. 645 Howe St. (phone: 687-1122; 800-877-1133 in the US; 800-268-1133 in Canada; fax: 643-7267). Expensive.

Four Seasons – Set in the center of the city, this leading establishment soars above *Pacific Centre.* Everything is located right here or just an enclosed walk away. There are 3 restaurants, including the elegant *Chartwell* (see *Eating Out)* and the more casual *Seasons' Cafe.* The *Garden Lounge,* with its piano bar, is a favorite meeting spot. The 385 rooms and suites have spectacular city and mountain views. There also is an indoor and an outdoor pool, and an exercise room. 791 W. Georgia St. (phone: 689-9333; 800-332-3442 in the US; 800-268-6282 in Canada; fax: 684-4555). Expensive.

Hyatt Regency – Quite lively, the city's biggest hostelry sits atop the *Royal Centre* shopping mall. There are lots of luxurious touches in the 646 rooms; pluses include an outdoor heated pool, a sauna, exercise rooms, and 3 restaurants. *Fish and Co.,* the hotel's seafood eatery, is always busy. There are several lounges, too. 655 Burrard St. (phone: 687-6543 or 800-233-1234; fax: 689-3707). Expensive.

Le Meridien – One of the luxury hotels in town, it's gracious, appealing, and entirely satisfying. Although the rooms tend to be on the smallish side, they are exceptionally well decorated. Marble bathrooms are sumptuous, and corner rooms that end with the number 26 have especially good views. There's a substantial health and beauty center, plus a swimming pool and sundeck located in *La Grande Residence,* the adjacent residential tower. Super service and extremely personal attention for a property with almost 400 rooms. Dining spots include *Café Fleuri,* with its *Chocoholic Bar* and weekly international buffets (see *Eating Out*), and the elegant *Le Club. Gerard Lounge,* with its separate entrance, is popular with visiting movie stars and crews. 845 Burrard St. (phone: 682-5511 or 800-543-4300; fax: 682-5513). Expensive.

Pan Pacific – Right on the harbor at Canada Place, this place provides a view of harbor activity nearly as spectacular as the harbor views from many Hong Kong hotels. A member of the Leading Hotels of the World group, it blends artfully with its location; the design includes a pier-like wing jutting into the water. There are 507 luxurious rooms and suites, including some classed as ultra-deluxe (with special amenities such as a private concierge). The 3 restaurants here include one with casual dining and a harbor view, another with Japanese food, and the more formal *Five Sails* (see *Eating Out*), with continental fare and panoramas of both the water and the North Shore mountains. Another highlight is the fitness club, with squash and racquetball courts, a sauna, and aerobics classes. 999 Canada Place (phone: 662-8111; 800-937-1515 in the US; 800-663-1515 in Canada; fax: 685-8690). Expensive.

Ramada Renaissance – Overlooking the harbor, this 19-story establishment has 412 rooms and 20 suites. Topped by *Vistas on the Bay,* a revolving restaurant that serves West Coast fare, it is also home to *Dynasty,* one of the city's top Chinese restaurants (see *Eating Out* for both). There's an indoor pool and weight room. 1133 W. Hastings St. (phone: 689-9211; 800-228-9898 in the US; 800-268-8998 in Canada; fax: 691-2791). Expensive.

Vancouver – Operated by *Canadian Pacific,* this property has long been a landmark on the downtown skyline. Stately, comfortable, and elegant throughout, there are 508 rooms and suites, all of which have been restored to their original elegance in a multimillion-dollar face-lift. Its Royal Suite on the 14th floor is reserved for visits by members of the House of Windsor. But it is not without its informal touches. *The Roof* is a favorite weekend restaurant stop, with good food, entertainment, dancing Tuesdays through Saturdays, and a nice view. A health club, with outdoor deck and glass-enclosed pool, is a new addition. 900 W. Georgia St. (phone: 684-3131; 800-828-7447 in the US; fax: 662-1937). Expensive.

Waterfront Centre – Connected to Canada Place on the harbor, the newest of Vancouver's high-rises affords spectacular views of sea and mountains from most of its 489 rooms and from its outdoor pool and deck. There's a well-equipped fitness center, a shopping complex with a food court on the lower level, a dining room, and *Herons Lounge,* with patio dining. Many rooms are set aside for nonsmokers. 900 Canada Pl. Way (phone: 691-1991; 800-828-7447 in the US; 800-268-9411 in Canada; fax: 691-1991). Expensive.

Westin Bayshore Inn – It's in the heart of the city, but the ocean is at the doorstep; in fact, yacht owners can moor their vessels at the hotel dock. The late Howard Hughes once rented the top floors for a brief stay. There are 329 bright, well-decorated rooms and suites, with an additional 190 in the newer tower, a selection of elegant shops in the lobby, Beefeater-costumed doormen, a health club with indoor pool, an outdoor pool, a *Trader Vic's* restaurant (see *Eating Out*), and the *Garden* restaurant on the lobby level. 1601 W. Georgia St. (phone: 682-3377 or 800-228-3000; fax: 687-3102). Expensive.

Georgian Court – Many of the 180 rooms afford magnificent panoramic views, and if you intend to go to any of the sporting events or trade shows at *BC Place,* this is your best bet. One of the city's finest dining rooms, the *William Tell* (see *Eating Out*), is located here, along with the more casual, sports-oriented *Rigney's Bar and Grill.* Of the 12 floors, 4 are designated for nonsmokers. 773 Beatty St. (phone: 682-5555 or 800-663-1155; fax: 682-8830). Expensive to moderate.

Granville Island – Situated near the city's popular covered market, this waterfront hostelry has a total of 54 rooms and suites. Also within are a popular nightspot and the *Pelican Bay* restaurant (see *Eating Out*); outside are many seawall pathways, some of which lead to the island's restaurants, shops, and theaters. 1253 Johnston St. (phone: 683-7373 or 800-663-1840; fax: 683-3061). Expensive to moderate.

Wedgewood – Right across from the Robson Square complex, this intimate place with European ambience and Old World charm has 94 attractively decorated rooms. A fireplace in the piano lounge makes it especially inviting on rainy nights. There also is a lovely dining room which is popular for Sunday brunch. 845 Hornby St. (phone: 689-7777 or 800-663-0666; fax: 688-3074). Expensive to moderate.

Delta Pacific – Convenient to the airport, this inn is just 20 minutes from downtown. Facilities include covered tennis and squash courts, pools, patios, saunas, and a conference center; there's also a creative center and playground for children. Rooms are modern, spacious, and comfortable. A courtesy bus will meet guests at the airport. 10251 St. Edward's Dr., Richmond (phone: 278-9611; 800-877-1133 in the US; 800-268-1133 in Canada; fax: 276-1121). Moderate.

Georgia – The *Beatles* once stayed here, and if that's not enough, there's also plenty of Old World charm. Though the rooms are air conditioned, fresh-air fans will find that the windows here can be opened. There's a charming British pub, *George V,* downstairs and a streetside restaurant, *Night Court,* is busy at lunchtime and open to the wee hours. 801 W. Georgia St. (phone: 682-5566 or 800-663-1111; fax: 682-8192). Moderate.

Holiday Inn Downtown – Accommodations here offer good value. The 210 rooms are quiet, comfortable, and attractive; there's an indoor pool, a restaurant, bistro, and lounge with live entertainment on weekends. Close to Robson Square Law Courts complex. 1110 Howe St. (phone: 684-2151 or 800-465-4329; fax: 684-4736). Moderate.

O'Doul's – This link in the Best Western chain has 130 rooms and suites, a popular restaurant and lounge, an indoor pool, Jacuzzi, and exercise room. It's an easy walk to Stanley Park and close to shopping. 1300 Robson St. (phone: 684-8461 or 800-663-5491; fax: 684-8326). Moderate.

Pacific Palisades – Located on Robson Street, where some of the best shopping in Vancouver is found, this is an all-suites hotel with harbor, mountain, and bay views; amenities include a coffee shop and dining area, a business center, and a fitness center with an indoor pool. Also here is the *Monterey Lounge,* a jazz bar. Some of the 233 units have kitchen facilities. 1277 Robson St. (phone: 688-0416 or 800-663-1815; fax: 688-4374). Moderate.

Parkhill – A $3.5-million renovation has upgraded the 192 studios, suites, and public rooms with new carpets and air conditioning. In addition to a dining room, there's a Japanese restaurant and a lounge. 1160 Davie St. (phone: 685-1311). Moderate.

Park Royal – This small, quiet 30-room hostelry is nestled below the mountains on the banks of the Capilano River, across the Lion's Gate Bridge, 20 minutes from downtown. Beaches, golf, and ski lifts are nearby, as is the *Park Royal Shopping Centre.* There's a lovely terrace, surrounded by flowers and trees, where lunch, cocktails, and light evening meals are served. The *Tudor Dining Room's* Sunday brunch is quite popular among the locals, as is the cozy pub. 540 Clyde St. at Sixth Ave., West Vancouver (phone: 926-5511; fax: 926-6082). Moderate.

Sheraton Landmark – Along with *Cloud Nine,* the city's first revolving rooftop restaurant, this place has 358 rooms, 9 nonsmoking floors, a lobby café, and 2 lounges. 1400 Robson St. (phone: 687-0511 or 800-325-3535; fax: 687-2801). Moderate.

Westbrook – Once host to many of the international participants at *Expo '86,* it boasts 200 studio suites, each with a queen-size bed, separate sitting area, and a kitchenette. Other features include *Page's Café,* a sports complex (with indoor pool, whirlpool bath, sauna, and weight room), and a good location. 1234 Hornby St. (phone: 688-1234 or 800-663-1234; fax: 689-1762). Moderate.

Barclay – Situated in the heart of the West End within strolling distance of most of the attractions of the city core, this small European-style property has 61 rooms and 24 suites. *Barclay's,* the house restaurant, has reasonable prices. 1348 Robson St. (phone: 688-8850; fax: 688-2534). Inexpensive.

Sylvia – Just a stone's throw from the Pacific Ocean, this 9-story, 111-unit West End hostelry offers great value and is right across the street from Stanley Park. The ivy-covered building also has housekeeping suites; its restaurant and bistro are popular among locals. Make reservations in advance, particularly in summer. 1154 Gilford St. (phone: 681-9321). Inexpensive.

EATING OUT: Once upon a time, not so very long ago, the so-called Liverpool of the Pacific had a menu to match. In old "meat-and-potatoes" Vancouver, *Hy's Encore* (now closed) was the destination of choice, with occasional forays into Chinatown for sweet-and-sour ribs. On very special occasions — anniversaries and graduations — there might be a lofty visit to *The Roof* or to the cosmopolitan *William Tell.* But today the city is in the midst of a restaurant boom, and joining the above-mentioned notables are first-rate seafood and ethnic dining spots. These, added to its already good supply of French and Italian restaurants, steakhouses, and numerous high-quality Chinatown spots, give the city a wide range of cuisines from which to choose. Expect to pay $60 and up for dinner for two in the very expensive range; $45 to $60 in the expensive range; $30 to $45 in the moderate range; and under $30 (in some cases way under) in the inexpensive category. Prices do not include drinks, wine, or tip. All telephone numbers are in the 604 area code.

Five Sails – Located beneath the landmark sails in the *Pan Pacific* hotel, the views of mountain and harbor are spectacular and the Pacific Rim cuisine (ahi ahi tuna, smoked Thai snapper), innovative. Rack of lamb is cooked to pink perfection. Open daily for dinner. Reservations advised. Major credit cards accepted. In the *Pan Pacific Hotel* — on the upper lobby level, 999 Canada Pl. (phone: 662-8111, ext. 4290). Very expensive.

Il Barino – A popular place for lovers of northern Italian fare. The menu (edible flower salads, pasta, roasted eggplant) is a mix of country and sophistication and the presentation is always picture perfect. Open weekdays for lunch; Mondays through Saturdays for dinner. Reservations advised. Major credit cards accepted. 1116 Mainland St. (phone: 687-1116). Expensive.

Beijing – This place boasts northern and southern Chinese food at its best, with Szechuan, Shanghai, and Cantonese specialties. Seafood selections are plentiful and popular, and lunches offer Shanghai and Cantonese dim sum, noodles, and daily specials. Good service and regal atmosphere. Open daily. Reservations advised. Major credit cards accepted. 865 Hornby St. (phone: 688-7788). Expensive.

Bianco Nero – Touches of whimsy separate this classy dining spot from the more formal, predictable ones in town. On each table in this black-on-white establishment sits a single exotic bird of paradise; red poppies in black vases are atop white Romanesque pillars. The fare is traditional pasta and meat dishes, but its extensive wine list is a favorite of theatergoers (the *Vancouver Playhouse* and *Queen Elizabeth* are nearby). The chocolate mousse served in a flowered bowl, sprinkled with Oreo cookie crumbs and topped with a fresh carnation, is particularly fine. For a more intimate evening, come after curtain time. Open weekdays for lunch; Mondays through Saturdays for dinner. Reservations advised. Major credit cards accepted. 475 W. Georgia St. (phone: 682-6376). Expensive.

La Brochette – For almost 15 years this small, exclusive place in Gastown has been a showcase for the time-tested creations prepared atop the 17th-century grill of chef/owner Dagobert Niemann. The best place in town for traditional French cuisine. Open for dinner Tuesdays through Saturdays, or by special arrangement with the chef. Closed most of July and August. Reservations necessary. Major credit cards accepted. 52 Alexander St. (phone: 684-0631). Expensive.

Café Fleuri – This *Meridien* hotel dining room is a good place to see TV and movie stars, especially on Thursdays and Fridays when its decadent *Chocoholic Bar* opens with over 20 chocolatey selections that range from crêpes to fondue to pizza. Main menu favorites include grilled BC salmon with tequila lime butter and grilled calf's liver with tarragon whiskey sauce. Celebrities and visitors alike come back for more at the seafood buffet on Fridays and Saturdays. There is a different theme buffet each week and the Sunday buffet accompanied by jazz is especially popular. Open daily from 6:30 AM to 10 PM. Reservations advised. Major credit cards accepted. 845 Burrard St., near Robson St. (phone: 682-5511). Expensive.

Cannery – This dockside place, with its weathered woods, old brass, and nautical artifacts, looks as if it has been around for a very long time, but actually it's just about 20 years old. The seafood and the views of the harbor and mountains make this a favorite spot in town. Open Mondays through Fridays for lunch; dinner daily. Reservations necessary. Major credit cards accepted. 2205 Commissioner St., about a 10-minute drive from city center (phone: 254-9606). Expensive.

Chartwell – The formal dining room in the *Four Seasons* hotel offers elegant surroundings, superior service, and food that's fresh, local, and natural. Have a look at the award-winning wine list. Open daily for dinner; lunch weekdays. Reservations advised. Major credit cards accepted. 791 Georgia St. (phone: 689-9333). Expensive.

Le Crocodile – Chef-owner Michel Jacob continues to win the hearts and palates of Vancouverites and critics alike with his world class French culinary talents. The freshest of seafood, lamb, and fowl are complemented by delectable sauces and graceful presentation. Impressive service, with consistent attention to detail. Lunch served Mondays through Fridays; dinner Mondays through Saturdays. Reservations necessary. Major credit cards accepted. 909 Burrard St., entrance off Smithe St. (phone: 669-4298). Expensive.

Dynasty – Located in the *Ramada Renaissance* hotel, this dining place features Cantonese food and French service in sleek surroundings. Dinner daily; open for lunch Mondays through Fridays. Reservations advised. Major credit cards accepted. 1133 W. Hastings St. (phone: 689-9211). Expensive.

Le Gavroche – Set in a charming West End house, it offers an interesting — and changing — menu. The game dishes are particularly notable, and the seasonal specialties all are good bets. Desserts are geared to send a weight watcher back to the drawing board. Closed Sundays. Reservations necessary. Major credit cards accepted. 1616 Alberni St. (phone: 685-3924). Expensive.

Hermitage – Chef-owner Herve Martin has cooked for royalty (he was *Pan Pacific*'s chef when Prince Charles and Princess Diana visited for a week in 1986 and he was at one time the personal chef to King Leopold of Belgium) and adds a special finesse to his creations in this charming place. The menu changes weekly to feature the distinct foods of different regions of France. The wine list includes a special collection from his brother-in-law's vineyard in Burgundy. Open weekdays for lunch; Mondays through Saturdays for dinner. Reservations advised. Major credit cards accepted. 115-1025 Robson St. (phone: 689-3237). Expensive.

Hy's Mansion – This turn-of-the-century mansion, with its huge fireplaces, wood-paneled walls, and pre-Raphaelite stained glass window halfway up the grand staircase is *Hy's* other place for red meat (see below for *Hy's Encore*). It has a large and varied menu, but the emphasis is on steaks — charbroiled, grilled, flambéed, and sauced. Open daily for dinner. Reservations advised. Major credit cards accepted. 1523 Davie St. (phone: 689-1111). Expensive.

Imperial – This spacious, 320-seat Chinese seafood spot commands a harbor view; the opulent decor features crystal chandeliers and jade carvings. Hong Kong–trained chef Wei Sing Chow prepares creative Cantonese seafood specialties. Dim sum are served at lunch. Open daily. Reservations advised. Major credit cards accepted. 355 Burrard St. (phone: 688-8191). Expensive.

Mulvaney's – The charming decor — all bright and airy with lots of greenery — is enhanced by the view of the busy False Creek waterfront. Specialties include seafood and cajun cooking; there's dancing Thursdays through Saturdays. Open daily from 5:30 PM. Reservations advised. Major credit cards accepted. Granville Island, next to *Arts Club Theatre* (phone: 685-6571). Expensive.

Trader Vic's – This Polynesian place of tropical delights in the *Westin Bayshore* has long been a favorite with Vancouverites and visitors, thanks, in part, to the incomparable views of mountains and harbor. Try the Bongo Bongo soup (puréed spinach and oyster) to start. Open weekdays for lunch, daily for dinner. Reservations advised. Major credit cards accepted. 1601 W. Georgia St. (phone: 682-3377). Expensive.

Umberto's and Il Giardino di Umberto – What began as an Italian eatery in an old yellow house, a heritage building (1896) known as the Leslye House, has grown into two adjacent dining spots. The original *Umberto's* (1380 Hornby St.; phone: 687-6316) serves traditional northern Italian food nightly and *Il Giardino di Umberto* (1382 Hornby St.; phone: 669-2422) serves equally delicious wild fowl and game. Umberto Menghi, the affable and energetic proprietor, divides his evenings among these places and *Settebello* and *Umberto al Porto* (below). Reservations necessary, even for lunch. Major credit cards accepted. Expensive.

Villa del Lupo – Located in a renovated house near trendy Yaletown and not far from the *Queen Elizabeth Theatre* and *BC Place*, this elegant Italian dining room has a mouth-watering menu that lives up to expectations. Try the fresh Dungeness crab cakes as an appetizer, the best in town. It has all the typical pasta dishes, some unique salads (with odd but delicious combinations like goat cheese and prawns), and rich desserts. Open weekdays for lunch, daily for dinner. Reservations advised. Major credit cards accepted. 869 Hamilton St. (phone: 688-7436). Expensive.

Vistas on the Bay – Revolving atop the *Ramada Renaissance* is one of the best places for Vancouver dining. Like the views, the menu is ever-changing, taking advantage of local seafood and produce. The crab and avocado appetizer is a meal in itself. Open daily for breakfast, lunch, and dinner. Sunday brunch — served from 10:30 AM to 2 PM — is a must. Reservations advised. Major credit cards accepted. 1133 W. Hastings (phone: 689-9211). Expensive.

William Tell – Known as "the special occasion place," this dining spot serves haute cuisine in a luxurious atmosphere of traditional elegance. The delicious fare draws heavily on local delicacies, complemented by the chef's contemporary touch. Open daily. Reservations advised. Major credit cards accepted. 765 Beatty St. (phone: 688-3504). Expensive.

Zeffirelli's – The dark wood paneling and paintings in this lovely little second-story find overlooking bustling Robson Street provide a pleasant backdrop for the hearty Italian favorites and lighter fare (like sage-and-sherry chicken livers on toast) offered here. Add to that a robust wine list and you'll find that this bit of Italy is worth the climb upstairs. Open 11 AM to 11 PM weekdays, 5:30 to 11 PM weekends. Reservations advised. Major credit cards accepted. 1136 Robson St. (phone: 687-0655). Expensive.

Amorous Oyster – A creative little seafood bistro with an ever-changing blackboard menu. Located just a 10-minute cab ride from downtown, it's known for its excellent service. Open weekdays for lunch and daily for dinner. Reservations advised. Major credit cards accepted. 3236 Oak St. (phone: 732-5916). Expensive to moderate.

Bishop's – John Bishop is a true perfectionist and the output of his kitchen wins wide applause for its superior presentation and taste. While the place is small and located in residential Kitsilano, it is well worth the 10-minute taxi ride from downtown. Open for lunch Mondays through Fridays; dinner daily. Reservations advised. Major credit cards accepted. 2183 W. 4th Ave. (phone: 738-2025). Expensive to moderate.

Bridges – In a bright yellow building on a highly visible corner of Granville Island, this place offers a prize view of marine activities, the city skyline, and the bustle that makes the island such a lively spot. Seating is on numerous levels to take advantage of the view, and the menu of mostly seafood changes every day. A wine bar and pub fill the lower floor, and a wide deck is popular for fair-weather dining. Open daily. Reservations necessary for the upstairs dining room. Major credit cards accepted. 1696 Duranleau St. (phone: 687-4400). Expensive to moderate.

Caffè de' Medici – Classic fixtures, paintings, and attractive furnishings make this Italian eatery look as if it has been part of the scene for years. In reality, it's part of the modern *Galleria* complex near the central corner of Burrard and Robson Streets. The pasta is outstanding, and the chef is known for handling seafood with care. Open for lunch Mondays through Fridays; dinner daily. Reservations advised. Major credit cards accepted. 1025 Robson St. (phone: 669-9322). Expensive to moderate.

Delilah's – Famous with locals for serving the best martinis in town, this place blends modern comfort with 1930s Art Deco. Prix fixe menu with two- or five-course dinners. Open for dinner daily; Sunday brunch. Since reservations are not accepted (and it's a very popular place), try to get here early and remember that it's worth the wait. Visa, MasterCard, and Diners Club accepted. 1906 Haro St. (phone: 687-3424). Expensive to moderate.

English Bay Café – Once a beachfront fish-and-chips shop, this is now an elegant eatery with a fabulous ocean view. The lower-level bistro offers casual dining, and on warm evenings dinner is also served on the outdoor deck. Specialties in the dining room include rack of lamb, fresh seafood, pasta, and chicken. Sunday brunch also is served. Open daily. Reservations necessary. Major credit cards accepted. 1795 Beach Ave. (phone: 669-2225). Expensive to moderate.

Fish House – Operated by the same folks who created the *Cannery*, this Stanley Park mainstay in a landmark building with a view of English Bay offers a wide selection of local and imported seafood — from lobster to seafood pizza. Try the Killer Shrimp from Lord Stanley's Oyster Bar. And save room for dessert. The deep-dish fruit pies are great diet-breakers. The atmosphere is cozy and the service friendly. Open daily. Reservations advised. Major credit cards accepted. West end of Beach Ave., near the Stanley Park tennis courts (phone: 681-7275). Expensive to moderate.

Hy's Encore – For over 30 years, this has been the unchallenged leader among steakhouses. With its dark wood paneling, brass fixtures, and oils of faux-ancestors in gilt frames, it has a gentlemen's club look that seems just right for your red-meat meal. Restaurateur Hy Aisanstatt of Calgary opened the first *Hy's* in 1955. It's an easy walk from downtown hotels. Open weekdays for lunch; daily for dinner. Reservations advised. Major credit cards accepted. 637 Hornby St. (phone: 683-7671). Expensive to moderate.

Joe Fortes' Seafood & Chop House – In Vancouver's early days, Mr. Fortes was a well-loved character who lived on the beach and taught many youngsters to swim. Named in his honor, this attractive place, decorated with mahogany, brass, and greenery, is a favorite with young executives. Open daily. Reservations advised. Major credit cards accepted. 777 Thurlow St. (phone: 669-1940). Expensive to moderate.

A Kettle of Fish – The type of seafood place that people are always searching for — committed to serving *really* fresh seafood, not the ubiquitous "fresh frozen" kind. It has a convivial greenhouse feeling with skylights, lots of plants, and objects that would be at home in an English garden. The menu changes daily, as the owner never knows just what's going to be fresh. Open daily. Reservations advised. Major credit cards accepted. 900 Pacific St. (phone: 682-6661). Expensive to moderate.

Noodle Makers – In a town filled with some of the best Chinese food found anywhere, diners say the lemon chicken in this former noodle factory at the edge of Gastown is the best in town. The center of the room has a pond, where brilliantly colored koi are fed at the sound of a gong each evening. Open weekdays for lunch; daily for dinner. Reservations advised for six or more. Major credit cards accepted. 122 Powell St. (phone: 683-9196). Expensive to moderate.

Pelican Bay – Nesting on the east side of burgeoning Granville Island is a waterside eatery that's part of the *Granville Island* hotel. The menu is continental, with a slant toward seafood, and the view of houseboats, barges, and birds is very picturesque. Open daily. Reservations advised. Major credit cards accepted. 1253 Johnston St. (phone: 683-7373). Expensive to moderate.

Prow – An aptly named place, it sits on the northeastern corner of Canada Place, surrounded on three sides by the waters of Vancouver harbor. The entire range of maritime activity can be observed from most tables: seaplanes, tugs, freighters, and the occasional seal all contribute to the scene. The food is creatively prepared, and the handling of vegetables an added plus. Open daily; no lunch served on

Saturdays. Reservations advised. Major credit cards accepted. 999 Canada Place (phone: 684-1339). Expensive to moderate.

Quilicum – The only place in town featuring authentic dishes of Indians native to Canada's Northwest Coast. Try the salmon cooked over alderwood and garnished with cedar. Patrons sit at tatami-like tables, and Indian artwork (for sale) lines the dining room walls. Open daily. Reservations advised. Major credit cards accepted. 1724 Davie St. (phone: 681-7044). Expensive to moderate.

Raintree – Specializing in the freshest of Northwest Coast cooking, a style that focuses on the hearty and healthy, everything at this place is good. To top it off, there is an award-winning wine list and a million-dollar view of Coal Harbour and the North Shore mountains. Live jazz and blues in the lounge Thursday, Friday, and Saturday evenings. Lunch Mondays through Fridays; dinner nightly; Sunday brunch. Reservations advised. Major credit cards accepted. Complimentary underground parking. 1630 Alberni St. (phone: 688-5570). Expensive to moderate.

Tanpopo – The catchy name of this establishment is a variation of *Tampopo,* a 1987 Japanese movie about the search for a perfect bowl of noodles. Black and gray decor is simple and pleasing. Try the daily specials, such as herring roe on kelp or yellowtail tuna (*hamachi*). Open daily. Reservations advised on weekends. Major credit cards accepted. 1795 Pendrell St. (phone: 681-7777). Expensive to moderate.

Bandi's – Located in a nice little clapboard house, it has an atmosphere that one might expect to find in a country inn — in Hungary. The food is hearty and very tasty, the soup delicious, and the homemade peasant bread addictive. Open for lunch Mondays through Fridays; dinner daily. Reservations necessary. Major credit cards accepted. 1427 Howe St. (phone: 685-3391). Moderate.

Barbara-Jo's – Home cooking with a southern US flair in cozy, down-home surroundings is an unlikely theme for this high-stepping, modern western city, but this place is so good it would do well in Atlanta. Try the crab cakes or the grilled quail with roasted-corn salsa, but save room for a square of warm gingerbread with caramel pecan sauce. Open for lunch Fridays only; Tuesdays through Saturdays for dinner. Reservations advised. Major credit cards accepted. 2549 Cambie St. (phone: 874-4663). Moderate.

Café de Paris – The music, the decor — marble-topped tables and brass fixtures — and the French waiters all lend an authentic Gallic mood to this convivial bistro. The café has a menu that caters to various appetites, and it is a popular stop after a stroll in nearby Stanley Park. Closed Sundays. Reservations necessary. Major credit cards accepted. 751 Denman St. (phone: 687-1418). Moderate.

Café Splash – Tucked into a corner of a waterside apartment complex, the two main features here are a good view of Granville Island water activities and the superior efforts of a talented chef. The menu offers a variety of grilled seafood, steaks, veal, chicken, duck, and pheasant. There is alfresco dining during the summer. Open Mondays through Fridays for lunch, daily for dinner, and Sundays for brunch. Reservations advised. Major credit cards accepted. 1600 Howe St. (phone: 682-5600). Moderate.

Chili Club – Bing Thom, the creator of the Canada Pavilion for *Expo '86,* designed this glass-and-chrome Thai establishment on the waterfront at False Creek. Upstairs, there's a glassed-in bar with a sweeping view. The cool sea colors of green, blue, and white contrast smartly with the spicy dishes, enhanced with herbs and spices flown in weekly from Thailand. Try the pork satay with peanut sauce, *tom kah kai* (chicken soup with coconut milk), exotic seafood, and tasty tidbits that also appear on the menu in the *Club's* Hong Kong outlets. Open Mondays through Saturdays 11 AM to 11 PM, Sundays 5 to 11 PM. Reservations advised. Major credit cards accepted. 1000 Beach Ave., east of the Aquatic Centre (phone: 681-6000). Moderate.

Cin Cin – Climb up a romantic staircase for the sights, sounds, smells, and tastes of the Mediterranean. The decor is simple and elegant, not overdone, as is the fare cooked over an alderwood grill. Try the salmon served in almond peppercorn crust with merlot sauce. Open daily for dinner. Reservations advised. Major credit cards accepted. 1154 Robson St., upstairs (phone: 688-7338). Moderate.

La Cote d'Azur – Vancouver's oldest French dining spot is situated in a vintage house with a huge fireplace, candles, and fresh flowers that set a romantic tone for leisurely dining. The menu offers classic French food prepared with the freshest ingredients, and includes traditional favorites plus changing daily specialties. A comprehensive wine cellar and friendly service add the final touches to a memorable meal. Closed Sundays and for lunch on Mondays and Saturdays. Reservations advised. Major credit cards accepted. 1216 Robson St. (phone: 685-2629). Moderate.

India Village – When locals think of the best in Indian food in town, this spot heads the list. Noted for its traditional curries that range from subtle to fiery hot, this Gastown place marinates its tandoori chicken in yogurt and spices for 24 hours before baking in a clay oven. Vegetarians rave about *kafta malai,* a mix of ground vegetables rolled into balls, deep fried, and served in a spicy, rich curry sauce. Open daily 11:30 AM to 11 PM. Reservations advised on weekends. Major credit cards accepted. 308 Water St. (phone: 681-0678). Moderate.

Kamei Sushi – Many city sushi fans feel that this is the leading spot for the Japanese delicacy. Diners may sit at the counter to watch the chefs artfully construct the various dishes, or in the dining room. The non-sushi items on the menu also are very good. Open daily. Reservations advised. Major credit cards accepted. 811 Thurlow St. (phone: 684-4823). Branches at 1414 W. Broadway (phone: 732-0112) and 601 W. Broadway (phone: 876-3388) provide both more room and a higher level of energy. Moderate.

The Keg – The original of what is now an international chain. The fare is hearty, with an emphasis on steaks, plus a few seafood dishes. There's also a salad bar. It's good family value, although some people find the joviality a little taxing. Open daily. Reservations advised. Major credit cards accepted. Three locations: *The Keg,* on Granville Island (phone: 685-4735), *Keg Coal Harbour* (phone: 682-5608), and the *Keg Downtown* (phone: 685-4388). Moderate.

Koji – Although the chef for whom this place was named no longer works here, other sushi experts have stepped up to his counter and continue to turn out superior dishes. The decor is attractive and there's a nice view of the downtown cityscape. Lunch Mondays through Fridays, dinner daily. Reservations advised. Major credit cards accepted. 601 W. Broadway (phone: 876-9267) and 630 Hornby St., downtown (phone: 685-7355). Moderate.

Milestones – Boasting a fantastic view of English Bay, this is a casual spot where a big appetite is needed to handle the huge portions. A six-page menu offers everything from breakfast entrées to gourmet burgers, hot dogs, pasta, and the best curly fries in town. Almost always packed full with locals. Open daily from 11 AM weekdays, 10 AM weekends. No reservations. Major credit cards accepted. 1210 Denman St. (phone: 662-3431). Moderate.

Monterey – This dining spot offers the complete sensory experience — innovative meals in beautiful surroundings. The menu focuses on fresh British Columbian items prepared by one of Canada's top chefs; dishes are accented by edible flowers and herbs grown in the restaurant's own garden. Open daily. Reservations advised. Major credit cards accepted. 1277 Robson St. (phone: 688-0461). Moderate.

El Patio – With its sunny Mediterranean atmosphere and menu to match, this is the ideal escape on a rainy day. It's even better in balmy weather when *tapas* are served on the outdoor patio. The menu is a mix of Spanish, Greek, and Italian cooking. It's a popular spot for people before or after events at the nearby *Queen Elizabeth Theatre* and *BC Place*. Open weekdays for lunch; Mondays through Saturdays for dinner. Reservations advised. Major credit cards accepted. 891 Cambie St., at Smithe St. (phone: 681-9149). Moderate.

Prospect Point Café – Nearby Prospect Point has one of the best views in Stanley Park, and it is shared by this café. An inventive menu offering West Coast food — salmon, scallops, and salads — and an imaginative decor increase its appeal. Outdoor dining is offered in good weather. Open daily. Reservations advised. Major credit cards accepted. Stanley Park (phone: 669-2737). Moderate.

Santa Fe Café – Fresh, innovative Southwest-California dishes are prepared in this open-air kitchen. Open for lunch Mondays through Fridays; dinner daily. Reservations advised. Major credit cards accepted. 1688 W. 4th Ave. (phone: 738-8777). Moderate.

Sawasdee Thai – Vancouver's original Thai dining spot, its two locations offer wonderful, spicy cooking at very reasonable prices. There are four different levels of hot dishes. Lunch served Mondays through Fridays; dinner Mondays through Saturdays. Reservations advised. Visa and MasterCard accepted. 2145 Granville St. (phone: 737-8222) and 4250 Main St. (phone: 876-4030). Moderate.

Settebello – The accomplished restaurateur Umberto Menghi, who owns four fine dining rooms in this city and one in San Francisco (called *Umberto's*), is the guiding light at this avant-garde pizza palace. Toppings that in other places would be extraordinary (duck, cajun chicken, smoked salmon, calamari) are commonplace at this second-story spot. Noise alert: This is not a place for quiet conversation. Open daily 11:30 AM to 10:30 PM. Reservations advised. Major credit cards accepted. 1131 Robson St. (phone: 681-7377). Moderate.

Umberto al Porto – Homemade pasta and an array of Italian specialties are served at this Gastown establishment. The upper level offers a terrific view of the harbor and the distant mountains. Located in one of Gastown's most attractive buildings, it's close to most of the area's best shops. Open Mondays through Fridays for lunch; Mondays through Saturdays for dinner. Reservations advised. Major credit cards accepted. 321 Water St. (phone: 683-8376). Moderate.

Vassilis Taverna – At this family-run spot, a favorite with Grecophiles, all the usual favorites are offered, along with a few interesting adaptations. The Greek salad and roast chicken are special treats. Open daily. Reservations advised. Major credit cards accepted. 2884 W. Broadway (phone: 733-3231). Moderate.

Isadora's – A special children's menu and a small play area, along with a casual, relaxed atmosphere, make this Granville Island restaurant a big hit with families. Nutrition is high on the agenda and fresh seafood and produce, from the nearby market, shape the daily specials. Try the salmon on bannock for an unusual treat. Open weekdays for breakfast, lunch, and dinner; weekends for brunch and dinner. Reservations advised for six or more. Major credit cards accepted. 1540 Old Bridge St., Granville Island, next to the *Waterfront Theatre* (phone: 681-8816). Moderate to inexpensive.

Afghan Horsemen – Off the beaten track, diners may sit at tables or on the floor, Afghani-style, while enjoying their meals. The Horsemen's Platter provides a way for a couple to sample the best of Afghani food. Open for lunch weekdays; dinner Mondays through Saturdays. Reservations advised on weekends. Major credit cards accepted. 445 W. Broadway (phone: 873-5923). Inexpensive.

Naam – The last survivor of the era when West Fourth Avenue was this city's

Haight-Ashbury. Not a lot has changed since opening day in 1968, when the first flower child "dug" the mismatched furniture and crockery, great food, and friendly vibes. Besides curiosity seekers, it attracts more than its share of vegetarians and night owls with its low prices, large portions, and made-from-scratch house specialties (bee-pollen cookies, dandelion tea, and Morrocan stew, for example) served 24 hours a day. There's even live music on weekends. The beer list includes products from 10 cottage breweries. Open daily. Reservations advised for parties over six. Major credit cards accepted. 2724 W. Fourth Ave. (phone: 738-7151). Inexpensive.

The Only (Seafood Café) – Firmly ensconced in the steambath and pawnshop district, this longtime institution serves some of the freshest seafood around. Inside are a few booths, a serpentine counter, dozens of gas burners, and huge frying pans. The menu includes clams, oysters, salmon, and sole. Every few minutes someone will truck a cartload of salmon through the place. (Mind your jacket!) No frills, no sauces, no appetizers, no liquor, no restrooms, no parking, no reservations, no credit cards accepted. Just incredibly fresh seafood. Closed Sundays. 20 E. Hastings St. (phone: 681-6546). Inexpensive.

Pink Pearl – Just about the most authentic Chinese food this side of Taiwan. The Sunday morning dim sum brunch is crowded, chaotic, noisy, and absolutely irresistible. The fresh local crab in black bean sauce is reason in itself to visit Vancouver. If you have time for only one Asian meal, make this your stop. Open daily. Reservations advised. Major credit cards accepted. 1132 E. Hastings St. (phone: 253-4316). Inexpensive.

DIVERSIONS

DIVERSIONS

For the Experience

Quintessential Vancouver

 On Fridays the exodus from downtown begins in mid-afternoon, earlier if the day is sunny (an all too infrequent forecast), or there's a long weekend ahead. A quick glance at the snarled traffic would lead you to believe that the automobile is the lifeline of this thoroughly modern city. Ah, but wait. A few hours later these same commuter cars — depending on the season — are metamorphosed into transporters of mountain bikes, skis, snowboards, and gardening tools, and stuffed in the trunks are rackets of all kinds and sizes, hiking boots, picnic baskets, frisbees (and the ubiquitous rain slickers). Now you're getting closer to what Vancouver is all about: the great outdoors. Whether it's to mountains, sea, or parks, or just to backyards or apartment balconies, people in this city love to be outside. Fresh air is the city's elixir, preferably dry, although wet weather is seldom a deterrent. Following are a few of Vancouver's varied outdoor (and indoor) experiences. Bring your umbrella — and enjoy.

BURNABY MOUNTAIN AND SIMON FRASER UNIVERSITY: At 1,200 feet, Burnaby Mountain is almost twice as high as Mount Royal in Montreal and can be a bit of an ear-popper, but the 360° view of the city and its environs is well worth it. Up here — on a day when the port city is not smeared in marmalade haze — you'll appreciate why world travelers consider this the most magnificent natural harbor in the world. (Some say only Hobart, Australia, and Rio de Janeiro compare.) Before heading back down, stay awhile and admire the buildings and grounds of Simon Fraser University.

Not all futuristic concrete and tempered glass, SFU is one of Vancouver's most stunning green spaces. If you come in the spring chances are the deep pink and brilliant crimson rhododendrons will be in bloom. At the academic quadrangle, go to a bridge crossing a still pond for a view of the downtown skyline against a mountain backdrop, or watch the goldfish swim around a single, solid boulder — placed as aesthetically as in a Japanese garden. Relax on a grassy mound; on a clear day you'll see the North Shore mountains, Burrard Inlet, the Pacific Ocean, and the Fraser River (named for the same explorer and fur trader who gave the university its name). In all directions is the patchwork of bedroom communities, stitched together with car-clogged roads, and the trademark green roof of the *Vancouver* hotel, the soul of downtown (see *Vancouver's Best Hotels*). To reach this peaceful peak from downtown, drive east on Hastings Street about 6 miles (10 km), then turn left at Sperling Avenue, then left again at Curtis Street, which becomes Gaglardi Way and leads directly to the university grounds. Weekdays in July and August student-led guided tours leave from the academic quadrangle every hour on the half hour from 10:30 AM to 3:30 PM. Alternate times during the week and on weekends can be arranged (contact Community Relations, SFU; phone: 604-291-3210).

A DAY AT KITSILANO BEACH: Of all Vancouver's city beaches (there are 11), Kits, on English Bay, is the most hedonistic. Indeed, no other beach in Canada has so much to offer. There is *Showboat* (an outdoor stage in the shape of a Mississippi showboat), a seawater pool, and more people body building, volleyball playing, and frisbee throwing per square foot than anywhere else in the country. (Don't mention ozone holes to these sun-loving types with their perfect tans and toned bodies.) Latter-day Tarzans hang out on a strip of worn-out grass near the asphalt path in front of the Kits Tower concession stand. But the always-crowded pool deck is where the serious workout types congregate, the super-athletes who do laps in the pool one day, ocean swims the next. The basketball courts go nonstop on weekends, with sweaty players in pick-up games.

But Kits is not just for the young and fit. Lots of regular folks get here early, grab a log, and stay late. The logs — huge timbers washed ashore from the sea, which are used as tables, back rests, and benches — give the beach its real character. The view from the sand is of an active harbor, ocean liners, sailboats, tugs, and freighters, with a backdrop of North Shore mountains and city high-rises whose windows gleam orange in the sun. In summer, it seems everyone in town is here, buying fish 'n' chips at the concession stand and staking out a spot to watch the incredible, rosy, golden sunset. Kits has its quiet moments, too. Office workers jog off the day's frustrations, people walk their dogs, young couples push toddlers in strollers, and seniors walk slowly by, all absorbing the day's fading rays. On Mondays, Wednesdays, and Fridays in the summer, locals and visitors alike meet at 7:30 PM for the 2-hour free song-and-dance show at the *Kitsilano Showboat.* In 1935, the show became an annual event; through the years it has given such homegrown performers as Mimi Hines and Yvonne de Carlo their starts. To get here cross Burrard Street Bridge and follow Cornwall Street to the water. And don't forget the sunscreen.

DIM SUM AT THE PINK PEARL: For lovers of Oriental food, *this* is Vancouver's most natural setting. Indeed, frequent visitors to the Orient say that the only difference between here and places in Hong Kong are its Sunday opening hours: 9:30 AM to 3 PM here; 4 AM to 4 PM in Hong Kong. This experience will stack up with anything you've done in Chinatowns in New York, Toronto, or San Francisco. Steam carts are wheeled with incredible dexterity by solemnly efficient servers, most of them from northern China. The decor — with lots of lucky red and gold, combined with calming pinks and celadon — is cheerfully attractive. Rosewood chairs are upholstered in red silk embroidered with symbols denoting long life. The tables are round, designed for easy conversation, as they are in most Chinese homes, and the open layout of the large, 700-seat dining room provides a surprising portion of privacy. Now for the food. The seafood is merely out of this world: Try *har gow,* a delectable steamed shrimp dumpling; fried shrimp dumplings; prawns in batter; and seafood dumplings with Chinese mushrooms and green onions. Take only a sampling of each, because after that there's ribs with plum sauce, steamed crêpes with beef filling, and pork dumplings with wonton wrap. Vegetarians will want to wait for the carts jammed with peanut- and chive-filled dumplings, or *chiu chow* — a vegetable combination with bamboo shoots and crunchy vegetables, like Chinese broccoli — steamed right at the table.

The trick here is to be quick and decisive. Though the steam carts — stacked with bamboo containers, each with its saucer of three or four portions — are always coming, some may be filled with treats that you've just had. Just say no to a dish if you don't want it; the delicacies that you've noticed at the table next to you will be coming your way soon. The server stamps a card on the table and tallies up the total (it's always reasonable) at the end of your feast. Pots of Chinese tea are kept filled and hot. There's a dinner menu, too, where diners can choose lobster, crab, prawns, and sometimes even eel from the fish tank at the entrance. Dessert lovers will want to know that the ubiquitous yellow tarts are not a sweet lemon confection but a bland egg custard. (Also see *Vancouver's Best Victuals.*)

A RIDE ON THE ROYAL HUDSON: The visit up Howe Sound, a deep fjord that extends about 30 miles (40 km) into the coastal mountains, serves up the most dramatic scenery in the surrounding area. And what better way to enjoy the view than from aboard this huge steam engine, which once pulled trains across Canada. Tracks parallel Route 99, a quintessentially Canadian road carved into the almost sheer cliffs, with breathtaking views of mountains and the turquoise waters of the sound between Horseshoe Bay and Squamish, an old logging town. *Royal Hudson No. 2860* earns its place in national rail history by association: Its sister engine, *No. 2850,* carried King George VI and Queen Elizabeth (the Queen Mum) across the country during the 1939 Royal Visit and was one of the gleaming, showy exhibits at the *New York World Fair* (1939–1940). Subsequently, all Hudsons were designated "Royal." The current one ran the rails until 1957; it was the engine chosen to be restored and has been doing the Howe Sound run for almost 20 years.

From the moment the little engine chugs away from the city center through the tunnel beneath the Lions Gate Bridge at 10 AM, the scenery begins to unfold. The bridge itself was built in 1938 by Britain's Guinness family to unite the North Shore with the city, and boost their posh British Properties development. The train crosses the Capilano River, skirts Ambleside Beach, and heads north toward Horseshoe Bay, curving around each bay and inlet. On some of these turns you'll be able to get good photographs of the engine and front cars from the caboose. Then snap away for the next 2 hours. Ships and sailboats dot the seascapes on one side; Ice Age scars accent the sheer rock cliffs. One of six tunnels hacked into the wall of rock is the 4,200-foot-long one near Horseshoe Bay. About noon you'll be in Squamish, which means "Mother of the Wind" in Coast Salish — and you'll soon discover the reason for its name: It's definitely a windy spot, but there's nothing notable about the town. From here a bus will take you to Shannon Falls, where, according to Indian legend, the province's third-largest waterfall was created by a serpent slithering down the cliffs. In winter, when the water freezes in a snake-like trail, you'll get the picture. Here, a looming granite monolith known as the Stawamus Chief, second in size only to the Rock of Gibraltar, resembles a sleeping Indian; seen through binoculars, images from Jonathan Swift's *Gulliver's Travels* may seem more appropriate, as climbers from all over the world dot the massive landscape, making their way up some of the 280 known routes on this rock and its satellites. Beyond the falls is an abandoned, sprawling, 6-story building, once home to the biggest copper mine in the British Commonwealth. Today it's the site of the *BC Museum of Mining* (admission charge; open daily 10 AM to 5 PM; last tour begins at 4 PM; phone: 604-688-8735), where visitors can take an hour-long guided tour aboard a mining train through the tunnels. There are demonstrations of mining equipment and a walk through the old copper smelting plant. The train departs Squamish at 2 PM and arrives at North Vancouver station 2 hours later. Those wanting to combine rail and sea might want to take a one-way trip on the train and return aboard the MV *Britannia.* The 150-foot vessel sails from Squamish with up to 500 people on board and serves a barbecue salmon lunch (price not included). But be patient; this is one *slow* boat. For train reservations, call *BC Rail* at 604-631-3500; for boat reservations, call 604-688-7246. The season for both train and ferry runs from late May through September.

CHEERING THE CANUCKS: Ice hockey is *the* Canadian game — fast, sometimes furious, at times like ballet. For the uninitiated it may seem more like wrestling on ice, but they miss the point: Those rambunctious sweater-pulling confrontations between beefy enforcers only adds to the excitement, heightens the "He shoots — He scores" action of the precision passers and shooters. The best time to book is Sunday afternoon, when the scene at *Pacific Coliseum* is very much a family affair. Ardent fans of all ages arrive with their faces painted in the club's black and gold colors; one longtime spectator cheers with a rafter-filling "air-raid" siren; and a pair of blonde, self-appointed pep-squadders dash from section to section leading chants. At intermission try the fresh sushi or the old standbys — hotdogs, nachos, and piping hot chocolate. Beer drinkers drowning their sorrows (in its 22 years the team has never won the coveted *Stanley Cup*) retire to the *Beer Garden* below the arena's main concourse. Although a sold-out sign usually is posted well in advance, the club often holds back tickets for sale on game day, so check with your hotel concierge, or with *Ticketmaster* (phone: 604-280-4444). As with many arenas, the best seats, close to the ice, are the reds, although many seats in the lower blues of this column-free arena offer great views. (Upper blues are referred to as the "nosebleed" section.)

AN AFTERNOON ON GRANVILLE ISLAND: If Kits is where Vancouverites go to play, this is where they go to shop. Every weekend they come here in droves in search of the best in fruit, flowers, and fish. Although you can have lunch or a snack, sip cappuccino while sitting on stone steps and log pilings watching street musicians, or gazing out at small boats plying the waters of False Creek, this is not just another pretty place. Here you can buy the freshest seafood at an extensive marine market, or at the country-style market find organically raised chickens, the best red meat, vegetables, fruit, and fresh bread. There are candle makers, potters, weavers, and glassblowers, too, and a sea village of houseboats for those who call the island port home. For years this onetime sandbar was a busy industrial site, but by the late 1960s it had deteriorated to a mix of light industries and abandoned, rusting warehouses and factories. The federal government's plan to create an urban park with a mix of markets, crafts, and light industry worked very well. Theaters and restaurants followed, and now it is one of the most enormously successful, imaginative, waterfront redevelopment programs in North America. A place that has become a weekend ritual for people here, the leisure mood also slips into weekdays for those not confined by work schedules. It has also become the venue of choice for organizers of special events, including the international *Dragon Boat Races* and outdoor symphony concerts. On your visit, stop across from the bus stop in front of the *Arts Club Theatre* at the Granville Island Information Centre (phone: 604-666-5784) for an audiovisual presentation, daily itineraries, and free maps. Parking is free but you'll find buses are easier (call *BC Transit;* phone: 604-261-5200).

TEA WITH THE EMPRESS: The British Empire may be dead, but you'd never know it at the *Empress* hotel in Victoria, British Columbia, a fairy-tale–castle monument to imperial England. Victoria, with its subtropical climate, seems like a lifetime away from the freezing winters of the rest of Canada. But to walk past the precise, formal gardens and into the *Empress*'s rambling lobbies is to retreat even farther from the real world, to another place in another time. The hotel looks like an English country home, but on a scale far more vast. There are columns and coffered ceilings, polished floors, and soaring windows that frame elegant salons. The *Empress* was built in 1908, when ladies wore whalebone corsets and gentlemen carried walking sticks, and even today, contemporary attire seems a bit out of place. The very British tradition of afternoon tea is carried on here to perfection. Steaming tea is served in fragile bone-china cups and is accompanied by dainty cucumber sandwiches, fresh berries, buttery scones, sweet Devonshire cream, and an array of tempting crumpets and cakes. Anyone who is anyone in Victoria makes at least an occasional appearance for tea; so, too, should you. While sitting in one of the gracious salons, making genteel conversation between sips of tea and nibbles of cake, the problems of the 20th century seem not merely distant, but nonexistent. This is surely Canada's most agreeable time warp. There are four daily sittings in summer, but one really should book ahead.

THE WONDERS OF WHISTLER RESORT: Not far from downtown (due north 70 miles/120 km via Rte. 99), a slow-going coastal road that affords beautiful views of the fjord at Howe Sound winds to not only the — arguably — best skiing in North America but to one of the most restful, scenic resorts anywhere. Once an attraction only to ski aficionados, this was — and still is — where world class skiers train on the longest and most challenging runs on the continent. But though Whistler remains synonymous with "the world's best skiing," the mountain has been "discovered" by those more into après-ski — très après. On a Saturday in July the mountain roads near neck-craning, 7,160-foot-high Whistler and its neighbor, 7,494-foot Blackcomb, are as busy as they are in January. Outdoor enthusiasts come for the crystal-clear mountain air; the perfume of the old-growth forests of towering Douglas firs; or a bone-soothing sauna; some spend the night at any one of 60 hotels and browse the more than 100 upscale boutiques and eateries of Whistler Village, with food that ranges from the best buffalo burgers to continental cuisine, from burritos to sushi.

In winter, sunrises cast blue-green shadows on the snow-white, mile-high, undulating hills, which in late afternoon have a backdrop of lemon-yellow sky. In summer, these same rugged peaks are draped in varying tones of verdure that shade to azure, then purple as the day turns to dusk. In addition to the spectacular scenery, there's something for everyone: skiing and snowboarding on Horstman Glacier, the north face of Blackcomb; the best in fishing, hiking, birding, and mountain bike trails; and a par 72, 6,397-yard Arnold Palmer–designed golf course with nine lakes and two winding creeks (open May to September; phone: 604-932-3928). Year-round, after sunsets, there are music festivals — from alpenhorns, to classics, to red-hot jazz, to rock 'n' roll. The hills are alive with the sound of schussing — and a whole lot more.

If you'd rather not drive, there's the train (*BC Rail;* phone: 604-984-5246) or bus from downtown (*Maverick Coach Lines;* phone: 604-255-1171). There is also a bus service from Vancouver International Airport (*Perimeter Bus Service;* phone: 604-261-2299). For more information contact the *Whistler Activity and Information Centre* (phone: 604-932-2394) or *Whistler Resort Association,* 4010 Whistler Way, Whistler, BC V0N 1B4 (phone: 604-932-3928).

Vancouver's Best Hotels

 Say "room with a view" in this city and you've practically said it all. The best of hotels here emphasize bringing the outdoors in, either through decor or panoramic vistas of sea and mountains or, more often, both. Perhaps it's because of the often dull or wet weather, but architects and interior designers are big on natural light and airiness, combining plants, flowers, and innovative furnishings with cheery color schemes. And although sometimes almost 21st century in their outward appearance (except for the *Empress* and the *Vancouver,* the grandest of them all), these outstanding hotels have not neglected Old World comfort.

EMPRESS: The Edwardian myth of imperial majesty is embodied in this hotel at the western edge of the empire. Opened in 1908, this charming anachronism sets standards for service that have, amazingly, been maintained for nearly a century. The effect of being somewhere in the United Kingdom is inescapable: double-deck London buses unload at the front door, and the "Upstairs/Downstairs" mood continues through high-ceilinged public rooms with the hushed echo of greatness. The service standard is reminiscent of the military: If something doesn't move, polish it; if it does, salute (or in this case, curtsy). There are 482 guestrooms, many with priceless views of Victoria and the harbor. Don't miss afternoon tea, which includes scones, Devonshire cream, crumpets, cucumber sandwiches, and large dollops of ceremony. Everyone who is anyone in Victoria comes here to see and be seen, to gossip, and to revel in the ambience of an era past (also see *Quintessential Vancouver*). Facilities include 3 bars, a dining room, a pool, and an exercise room. Information: *The Empress,* 721 Government St., Victoria, BC V8W 1W5 (phone: 604-384-8111 or 800-268-9411).

LE MERIDIEN: At this stylish member of the French-owned chain the emphasis is on service — right down to the complimentary umbrella hanging in the closet (in Vancouver, rain is, if not on the horizon, in the forecast) and the nightly weather report and delicious French chocolates from the downstairs *Chocoholic Bar* on the pillow. Headquarters for Hollywood North, producers and filmmakers who shoot TV series and feature films here, it offers terraces with peek-a-boo mountain views. Indeed, it's *the* choice for both movie makers and movie watchers: The list of 200 in-room movie selections is the most extensive in the city. The 397 rooms, with their pale apricot walls, cheery chintzes, fresh flowers, and tall windows are awash in natural light. *Le Spa* is a fully equipped fitness center with a swimming pool and a beauty center and, next to the spa, *La Grande Résidence* tower is a 162-apartment complex available to guests who stay 30 days or longer. There are 2 restaurants: *Café Fleuri,* with its soft-pink walls and floral napery and the airiness of a charming gazebo, and the more formal *Le Club,* an intimate dining room. The *Gerard Lounge,* an oasis for the film-industry crowd, has its own canopied entrance and a fireplace. Information: *Le Méridien,* 845 Burrard St., Vancouver, BC V6Z 2K6 (phone: 604-682-5511).

PAN PACIFIC: All of the public rooms and the 504 rooms and suites in this $100-million structure overlooking Burrard Inlet are paneled in light bird's-eye maple and furnished in earth tones to match the surrounding natural environment, and every room has a view — mountains, sea, Stanley Park, and the lights of downtown — through one-way glass. There are several high-quality shops and 3 fine restaurants, including *Suntory* and the *Five Sails,* and Friday evenings classical music fanciers congregate at *Café Pacifica* to get Puccini with their pasta. Here the Milan-trained tenor/chef Enrico Balestra presides over the Italian Opera Buffet where, in the midst of dishing out fettuccine alfredo or chicken *parmigiano,* he might burst into Lanza's repertoire and, with his accompanist, perform arias from favorite operas. It's just a couple of escalator rides away from the Vancouver Trade and Convention Centre and the Cruise Ship Terminal. Information: *Pan Pacific,* 999 Canada Pl., Vancouver, BC V6C 3B5 (phone: 604-689-9211).

VANCOUVER: Ethel Ferguson, a longtime, loyal housekeeper, knew it could never last. In the 1960s, the grand old hostelry where she had spent so much of her life began changing with the times: New owners called for "regulation" furnishings; gilt edgings on the ceiling were painted over; mahogany walls wallpapered; orange-and-blue deep-pile carpeting installed. But Ethel was not fazed. While the full-scale modernization was taking place, she squirreled away Chippendale and mahogany pieces in various nooks and crannies in the 508-room château, in the hopes that common sense would once again prevail. And sure enough, not that long ago, she had her wish. Thanks to Ethel's pack-rat penchant, *Canadian Pacific,* determined to restore the place to its past glory, had enough furniture to decorate 35 rooms of the 12th floor.

And today, in a city of spanking-new towers, this place of griffins and gargoyles reigns supreme. Although it was completed back in 1939, in time for the Royal Visit of King George VI and Queen Elizabeth (the Queen Mum), it has the feel of the Victorians: The 1939 Pacific Ballroom has been restored with ceiling medallions, trompe l'oeil fabric wreaths, and massive chandeliers. But expect the new with the old: There is a fully equipped fitness center, a glass-domed indoor pool, a Jacuzzi, a wading pool, and an outdoor deck with southern exposure. There are 2 restaurants: *Griffins* and *The Roof,* the 15th-floor "Panorama Roof," as it was known for decades, where debutantes and other socialite shoppers still stop for afternoon tea. The large model in the lobby of Captain Vancouver's sailing ship *Discovery* has little stained glass windows in the captain's quarters and ten tiny cannon. Restoration of the hotel is ongoing, but unobtrusive. Ethel would be pleased. Information: *Vancouver,* 900 W. Georgia St., Vancouver, BC V6C 2W6 (phone: 604-684-3131).

WATERFRONT CENTRE: Wrapped in reflective blue glass, this 3-year-old, 23-story tower looks the part of its stylized symbol — a blue heron. But that is only part of the story here. A work of art itself on the outside, it has some of the best works of emerging avant-garde artists from Canadian and Pacific Rim countries inside. Its US contribution is in the lobby — fossilized limestone from the Texas hills frames the front desk and elevators. (Look closely at the stone and you will see remnants of ancient shells.) Many of the 489 rooms have outdoor terraces; most have splendid views. The fully equipped fitness club has a heated outdoor pool with a lounge area that looks out over the harbor. *Herons* restaurant, with its Texas mesquite wood floors and open kitchen with rotisserie, serves from breakfast through dinner; in good weather there's also patio dining; and nightly piano music is offered in the lounge. An enclosed walkway leads from an area of exclusive shops and a food court to the Trade and Convention Centre. Minutes away is Gastown and the *SeaBus* to the North Shore. Another *Canadian Pacific* hotel, its opening in 1991 marked the 100th anniversary of the first sailing to the Orient of the company's *Empress* ships from this harbor. Information: *Waterfront Centre,* 900 Canada Pl. Way, Vancouver, BC V6C 3K2 (phone: 604-691-1991).

WESTIN BAYSHORE: For years no place could touch this one for sheer luxury. Shortly after the tower opened in 1961, eccentric billionaire Howard Hughes and his entourage moved into the top 2 floors, considering it the perfect blend of posh and privacy. They stayed for 6 months. And no wonder: Its excellent location at the water's edge, with Stanley Park as a neighbor and the North Shore mountains seemingly a stone's throw away, is an ideal setting; also here are special touches, such as its trademark doormen in distinctive Beefeater costumes, an indoor health club, and a marina that can charter a boat for 5 hours or 5 days, or moor your own craft if you arrive by sea. There's also a dock for private seaplanes. At the trellised *Garden* restaurant, chef Heinz Lenger likes to experiment with sauces and exotic fruits. (Try his three-pepper-blackened fish with kumquat sauce.) The South Seas flavor of *Trader Vic's* is still here, but there's an emphasis on Asian cuisine and seafood now. Lounges are adjacent to both restaurants, and lobby-level shops include such noted clothiers as *Edward Chapman* (phone: 604-685-6734) and *The London Shop* (phone: 604-682-1136). A courtesy bus shuttles uptown every half hour during the day. Information: *Westin Bayshore,* 1601 W. Georgia St., Vancouver, BC V6G 2V4 (phone: 604-682-3377).

Vancouver's Best Victuals

It used to be red meat or seafood, take your pick. But no more. Few cities offer up such an eclectic mix, making dining out such a matter of mood. Do you fancy hearty or nouvelle? Will it be antique silver or ivory chopsticks? Whatever, you're sure to delight in making your selection in this emerging cosmopolitan city. Any of the following will provide a memorable dining experience.

DYNASTY: This relative newcomer has taken the city by storm to become what is arguably its foremost Cantonese dining room. Its symbol, the "flying devil of Dunhuang," which represents "mankind's best and most beautiful," could not have been more aptly chosen. The room itself feels like a Chinese pavilion with its rosewood furniture, wall niches with vases from ancient dynasties, silk-wrapped walls, soft lighting, and a series of short partitions that lend an air of privacy. But it's the food that brings diners back. A TV celebrity in Hong Kong, where he cooked for luminaries from

Queen Elizabeth to Elizabeth Taylor, Lam Kam Shing brought most of his woks, pots, and hard-to-get ingredients from home; specialties include braised abalone or shark's fin with crab sauce. But Lam doesn't concentrate solely on Cantonese cuisine. Once a month he features a food festival, with dishes from Taiwan, Vietnam, the province of Szechuan, or, on a whimsical note, Italy. His Italian-spiced pasta is unquestionably Oriental, as is his "traditional Western" *Christmas* dinner. Information: *Dynasty,* at the *Ramada Renaissance,* 1133 W. Hastings St. (phone: 604-689-9211).

HERMITAGE: This elegant little French place has been developing a loyal following since 1988; Herve Martin, onetime chef to Belgian royalty, is very much an on-scene host. Originally from Burgundy, Martin's gastronomic tastes lean in that direction. So does his wine list, which includes seven selections with the Domaine de Chamilly label from his brother-in-law's Burgundy vineyards. The 60-seat dining room itself has a charming warmth, with dark wood, a burgundy and forest-green color scheme, iron antiques, a bit of brick, and patterned curtains. The menu changes each week to focus on specialties of different regions of his homeland. Look for the dish he created for Queen Sophia of Spain: wonton with shrimp-and-lobster bisque and vanilla-bean sauce. Or try one developed for duck lovers who fear too much fat: duck breast with armagnac sauce and his own version of cracklings. There is no printed dessert menu; except for the usual apple tart and *crème caramel,* he makes grand finales that fit his mood of the day. Try the chocolate-and-pistachio mousse with Grand Marnier *crème anglaise,* or lime-and-raspberry mousse with a blackberry *coulis.* Martin also markets a line of jams, jellies, vinegars, pickles, and sauces. Information: *Hermitage,* 115-1025 Robson St. (phone: 604-689-3237).

NOODLEMAKERS: A pair of brilliantly colored benevolent warriors are carved on the heavy entrance doors of this onetime noodle factory at the edge of Gastown. Inside, four sculpted idols are at the ready, as is the festive lion hanging from the ceiling, about to start a spirit-chasing dance. So, by the time you reach your table in this long, narrow room with its cleverly positioned levels, you are convinced that nothing but good is in store. Indeed, you could be tempted to come for the serenity alone, but the Chinese food is among the best in town, especially the lemon chicken and beef and pine nuts. Children love to be here for the 7:30 PM feeding of the bright koi in the plant-rimmed pool. The hostess rings a gong and the fish rush to nibble food from her hand. Of course there's a fortune cookie to end the meal, and if you don't get just the one you like, you can buy a *box* of them on your way out. Information: *Noodlemakers,* 122 Powell St. (phone: 604-683-9196).

PINK PEARL: A longtime favorite among locals and visitors alike, this dim sum destination rivals most in this town — or, for that matter, any town. Come Sunday morning (early — they open at 9:30 AM, but the lines form at 9 AM) and bring your appetite. The *har gow,* the Chinese steamed shrimp dumpling, is the most succulent to be had this side of Taiwan. The place is renowned for its seafood, but don't let the carts of ribs with plum sauce, steamed crêpes with beef filling, and pork dumplings with wonton wrap go by untouched. The ambience complements the authenticity of the food: Look around and you'll see Chinese extended families seated around tables, chattering away, directing carts their way with a wave of their hands. Some of the dishes that the locals appear to be relishing may not be to your liking — this is, after all, the real thing — and some foods demand an acquired taste, but don't worry: If one cart's contents don't please you, the next one's will. Vegetarians will want to try the peanut-and chive-filled dumplings, or *chiu chow* — a crunchy, steamed vegetable combination. For those not coming for dim sum, there's a first-rate seafood dinner menu, with lobster, crab, prawns, and eel. Information: *Pink Pearl,* 1132 E. Hastings St. (phone: 604-253-4316).

SOOKE HARBOUR HOUSE: If you're going to make one dining foray outside the city make it this place (on Vancouver Island, 23 miles/35 km from downtown Victoria). Everything — from the setting (a snug candlelit room with a panorama of the wind-swept sea and huge rocks and the Olympic Mountain Range as a backdrop) to the menu, fresh from the sea — is perfection. Seafood here really is "the catch of the day"; some is even brought up from the deep by guests who dive with innkeeper-chef Sinclair Philip for such underwater exotica as sea cucumbers, singing scallops, spider crabs, and sea urchins. Meat from local farms is organically raised and Metchosin rabbit is a specialty. From the inn's garden come parsnips, leeks, brussels sprouts, spaghetti squash — whatever is in season — all cooked in a fashion to inspire the vegetarian in you. The menu, which varies from day to day, might include salmon with pickled blackberry butter, served with braised cabbage and purple potatoes; shrimp sautéed with salmon roe; or abalone with plum vinegar sauce. A before- or after-dinner walk, to watch the sea birds dodging whipped waves on the Whiffen Spit at the entrance to Sooke Harbour, is a fitting end to this true-blue West Coast experience. To get there, take Douglas Street (Hwy. 1) to Gorge Road (Hwy. 1A) to Colwood, BC; take the Sooke cutoff, and follow Sooke Road to the harbor. Information: *Sooke Harbour House,* Sooke, BC (phone: 604-642-3421).

WILLIAM TELL: Restaurateur Erwin Doebeli was a championship archer in Switzer-land and he's got the medals and awards — and the crossbows — to prove it. They're on display, together with a large tapestry that tells the story of that other Swiss archer named Tell and his apple-topped son. The first restaurant by this name opened in 1964, and fast became the city's favorite formal dining room. But unlike its dark, atmospheric predecessor, this version (opened 10 years ago) is bright, airy, high-ceilinged, with soft-peach walls, pale green carpeting, and servers dressed in burgundy and blue. Brick archways link four dining rooms in cozy intimacy. Ask to talk to the archer himself, a congenial greeter and crossbow presenter, before sampling your *café diablo,* a house specialty. Tableside is a firing range in itself, where Caesar salads are tossed and desserts flame and sizzle. Chef Pierre Dubrulle, whose cooking school in the city is legendary, has built a well-deserved reputation with his veal escallopes with morel sauce and one of the best chateaubriands in town. The wine list is a consistent medal winner at the *Vancouver Wine Festival.* Because the restaurant is on the theater route, you may want to have dinner early and return after the show for your sweets: pastries and cakes or ice creams and sorbets. The meringue glacé with dark chocolate sauce is a real winner. Information: *William Tell,* 765 Beatty St. (phone: 604-688-3504).

Vancouver Shopping Spree

Canada's tony tinsel-town is at its best along Robson Street, at *The Landing* in Gastown, or at *Sinclair Centre* on Hastings Street. Designer boutiques abound. Yet this is the place where the mall began in Canada (*Park Royal Shopping Centre,* ca. 1950) and in some ways it is still king. In the rain, legions of shoppers head to the dry indoor "streets" of Vancouver's 17 major shopping centers, some of which have more than 200 stores. Double that size, with department store giants *The Bay, Woodward's, Eaton's,* and *Brettons, Metrotown* in Burnaby is the largest in town. Below, the best buys for every whim and wallet.

MAIN STREET, Victoria: BC's capital has assiduously retained its "bit of Olde England" feel, particularly in the first few blocks of Government Street, where the best of woolens and bone china can still be found. Of special note along Government Street are several shops, among them, *Sydney Reynolds* (No. 801; phone: 604-383-3931), which has an impressive selection of fine china. But the throne of British supremacy has its challengers. Native art and crafts — totems, rattles, Cowichan sweaters, moccasins, Salish weavings — have a growing constituency at such stores as *James Bay Trading Co.* (No. 1102; phone: 604-388-5477); *Hill's Indian Crafts* (No. 910; phone: 604-385-9311); *Cowichan Trading Co.* (No. 1328; phone: 604-383-0321); and *Sasquatch Trading Co.* (No. 1233; phone: 604-386-9033). *The Quest* (No. 1023; phone: 604-382-1934) is one of the best around in quality Canadian crafts. And no trip to Victoria would be complete without a visit to *Roger's Chocolates* (No. 913; phone: 604-384-7021). They've been selling their renowned Victoria creams from this same location since 1916.

PUNJABI MARKET: Those wanting a taste of the East don't have to restrict themselves to Chinatown. Part of the mosaic that is Vancouver, this conglomeration of about 100 stores and services, which extends over a 3-block section of Main Street between 49th and 51st Avenues, is the best such market this side of the Punjab. The biggest lure for shoppers outside the Indo-Canadian community is the 25 fabric shops and 16 jewelry stores. Also appealing are textiles from Japan, South Korea, China, Pakistan, and the subcontinent, as well as saris and other garments — all exceptionally low priced because merchants buy directly from manufacturers. The jewelry shops showcase bangles, necklaces, and earrings of unique design, many in gold, and are a must-stop for those looking for something quirky and distinctive to add to their wardrobe.

ROBSON STREET: If you begin to feel as if you're in a sequel to *Pretty Woman* here, it's no wonder. This strip is often called the Rodeo Drive of the North. Indeed, no place in Canada seems so suffused with designer boutiques. At one time an Old World boulevard dubbed Robsonstrasse — the *Heidelberg House* restaurant (No. 1164; phone: 604-684-0817) remains true to the old spirit — today's Robson Street is all panache and style. Well-heeled high-steppers have caught on with shops in the mold of *Ferragamo* (No. 918; phone: 604-669-4495), the only Canadian location of this international shop for women's and men's shoes and leather accessories; *La Vie En Rose* (No. 1101; phone: 604-684-5600), which counts Liz Taylor and Lauren Bacall among its clients for fabulous lingerie, lace, and embroidery; and Canada's own *Alfred Sung* (No. 1143; phone: 604-687-2153), offering fashions and accessories for the elegant career woman.

SOUTH GRANVILLE: Those looking for an air of exclusive Old World luxury will do well south of the bridge, from 6th to 16th Avenues. Many of these high-end shops have a distinctly European flavor. Typical is *Atkinson's* (No. 3057; phone: 604-736-3378), perhaps the least intimidating (in spirit, if not in price) of the lot. Devoted to the "art of living well," owner John Atkinson's eclectic selection includes linen (Porthault, Pratesi), crystal (Baccarat, Lalique), china (Limoges), silver (Buccellati), teddy bears (Gund, Steiff), French perfume from Annick Goutal, and lizard, ostrich, and crocodile evening bags by Exotique. For the child in your life, from newborn to teen, there's *Bratz* (No. 2828; phone: 604-734-4344), with high-style European fashions, accessories, and shoes; there's also a hair salon devoted to the kiddy coiffed set. *Boboli* (No. 2776; phone: 604-736-3458) brings the latest in Italian designs for men and women each season and offers private, after-hours appointments; and *Bacci's* (No. 2788; phone: 604-732-7317) specializes in expensive European designer clothing and shoes for women. The *Mari Boutique* (No. 2439; phone: 604-732-8668) is the Asian entry on the strip, with men's and women's clothing and shoes from such Japanese designers as Issey Miyaki and Yohji Yamamoto. *Martha Sturdy Originals* (No. 3065; phone: 604-737-0037) is the home studio of the Canadian jewelry designer well known to readers of *Vogue*. Plastic, lucite, faux stones, and silver are combined in unusual earrings and bracelets. Look for her line of colored lucite candlesticks, too. A varied selection of menswear from European designers — Gianni Versace, Valentino, and Ferré — can be found at *Mondo Uomo* (No. 2709; phone: 604-734-6555). Special fittings are available by appointment. The Canadian designer who has worked to reverse the import trend is *Zonda Nellis* (No. 2203; phone: 604-736-5668). Her handwoven wool suits, dresses, coats, and shawls are exported to fine houses throughout North America.

YALETOWN: This old warehouse area on its ascent toward gentrification has drawn a following of bargain-hunting architects, designers, and TV and film producers. Located here is a small but thriving wholesale garment district, with upscale art galleries, restaurants, and coffee shops. Savvy shoppers head to the *Sample Room* (1000 Mainland St.; phone: 604-685-8485), which carries men's and ladies' fashions by well-known designers at half the retail price. Stock changes daily and many items are one of a kind, as is the venue itself: Under one roof is a good restaurant, a beauty salon, and a gift shop. *Shoes By Folio* (1005 Mainland St.; phone: 604-689-7110) is an attractive outlet for footwear that ranges from avant-garde to classic, all at a fraction of the normal cost. Art lovers will hit their stride at the studio of *Sergio Bustamante* (1130 Mainland St.; phone: 604-684-1340), featuring the acclaimed Mexican artist's vivid, androgynous, papier-mâché sculptures, and *Gabriel Gallery* (1033 Cambie St.; phone: 604-687-3384), which promotes new and established BC artists, sculptors, and potters.

Antiques Trail

Vancouverites delight in celebrating their past. For years, antiques shoppers confined themselves to Granville Street, between 6th and 16th Avenues, but in recent times, shops in other areas have begun doing well, too. Main Street, the site of many used furniture stores, has upgraded some of them to antiques status, and there are clusters of antiques shops in downtown tourist areas and throughout the city. The antiques focus has long been European, particularly British, but the Asian influence is waxing and there are several shops with wares from Pacific Rim countries. The following is an eclectic sampler of Vancouver's oldies but goodies.

BAKER'S DOZEN TWO AND BAKER'S DOZEN: Western Canadiana, the furniture of the hard-working Mennonites and Doukhoubors, shares display space with exquisitely handcrafted pond boats from Nova Scotia in the first of these jointly owned shops. A half block away, North American toy expert Heather Baker serves an international clientele. Her specialty? The original Dinky Toys. Information: *Baker's Dozen Two,* 3520 Main St. (phone: 604-879-3348); *Baker's Dozen,* 3467 Main St. (phone: 604-879-3348).

FRANKIE ROBINSON ORIENTAL GALLERY: This long, narrow shop, crowded with exotic items from tiny netsukes to huge chests, is a place of fact and fancy, the life's work of Frankie Robinson and Kelly MacKenzie, a mother/daughter team that has made 30 shopping trips to the Orient over the last 15 years. Japanese screens from the 17th, 18th, and 19th centuries with as many as nine panels, are hung on the walls or stand on a small platform under which smaller items are displayed. When sunshine hits the silver- and gold-leaf backgrounds of some of the wall-hung screens, the effect is nothing short of spectacular. The specialty here is chests: Japanese, of Keyaki wood, with its distinctive grain; Kiri (a lightly colored wood similar to pine), with ornate iron lockplates; and Chinese, of black wood and elm. Look for the newer items of fun folk art. Information: *Frankie Robinson Oriental Gallery,* 3055 Granville St. (phone: 604-734-6568).

GARDEN ANTIQUES: As the name suggests, the stock here is garden-based, with a healthy sprinkling of items from verandahs and conservatories. There are lots of old-fashioned gardening tools ("old" sometimes meaning from the 1940s and 1950s), along with turn-of-the-century wrought- and cast-iron gates and fence sections, Victorian wicker flower baskets, hand-tinted botanical prints, and croquet sets. Adirondack folding lawn chairs from the 1920s sit alongside old porch columns and newel posts. The biggest seller, especially to apartment-house gardeners, are old metal watering cans. Information: *Garden Antiques,* 3518 Main St. (phone: 604-876-2311).

UNO LANGMANN ANTIQUES AND ART: At the entrance to the city's posh South Granville shopping area, this spacious shop, with its wide, street-level windows and imposing grand stairway, is one of the most highly regarded purveyors of antiques. The gallery-like setting shows off the 18th- and 19th-century armoires and secretaries (predominantly British, but some continental) and other fine period furniture, along with paintings from the same era. Information: *Uno Langmann Antiques and Art,* 2117 Granville St., south end of Granville Street Bridge (phone: 604-736-8825).

VANCOUVER ANTIQUE CENTRE: Most of the dealer-operated shops in this cluster of 15 stores in the building that once housed the first Bank of British Columbia (1887) carry glass, china, and various bibelots. *Winchester's Antiques* (phone: 604-682-3573), through a brick archway on the first floor, also has an intriguing selection of Victorian scientific instruments and some early cameras. Thick-planked stairs lead to the second level of equally cluttered, grandma's attic–style shops. Information: *Vancouver Antique Centre,* 422 Richards St. (phone: 604-682-3573).

The *Antique Centre* building is shared by *Scandinavian Antiques* (it has its own entrance), a place that specializes in pine — armoires, blanket boxes, candle boxes, and bowls — from the late 1880s. Some pieces have original bright blue and green paint. Information: *Scandinavian,* 492 Hastings St. (phone: 604-685-7740).

FOR THE BODY

Downhill Skiing

Ask skiers if they had only a week to ski on this side of the ocean where would they choose to go and Whistler Resort (see also *Quintessential Vancouver*) finds its way to the top of most lists. Its two peaks, Whistler and Blackcomb, offer the longest runs in North America. Try, too, the city trio listed below. Because of the mild winters (by Canadian standards), cross-country skiing is not a popular pastime, but Whistler has track-set runs when conditions warrant.

CITY TRIO: Grouse, Cypress, and Seymour, the three Coast Range ski areas situated just a half hour's drive away from the city, offer urban skiing at its best: soaring verticals, easy accessibility, and spectacular views. Grouse Mountain, the best developed, has a 1,000-foot vertical and some satisfyingly steep expert skiing. There are also fine runs for beginners and intermediates; snowmaking, which ensures top conditions throughout the season, from mid-December to March; and long hours — from early every morning until 11 PM. Grouse Mountain also boasts the *Grouse Nest,* a fine dining spot, and *Jumpers,* a bistro, as well as a new *Theatre-in-the-Sky,* a year-round multimedia theater. More recently developed Cypress, 5 miles (8 km) from the Upper Levels Highway in West Vancouver, has 21 runs (the longest is 1,700 feet) and night skiing on its expert and intermediate runs. Mt. Seymour specializes in family skiing. It features one of the largest ski schools in the Pacific Northwest, the highest base elevation of the three areas, night skiing, and four double chair lifts. Seymour is about 10 miles (16 km) from the Upper Levels Highway in North Vancouver in an area known for its relative abundance of sunshine and wintertime warm spells. For those who like skiing hard-packed snow, Vancouver can provide some pleasant slope time. Information: *Grouse Mountain Resorts, Ltd.* (6400 Nancy Greene Way, North Vancouver, BC V7R 4N4; phone: 604-984-0661 or 604-986-6262 for snow conditions); *Cypress Bowl Recreations* (Box 91252, West Vancouver, BC V7V 3N9; phone: 604-926-5612 or 604-926-6007 for ski conditions); *Mt. Seymour Ski Country* (1700 Mt. Seymour Rd., North Vancouver, BC V7G 1L3; phone: 604-986-2261 or 604-986-3434 for snow report); and *Tourism Vancouver* (Pavilion Plaza, 4 Bentall Centre, 1055 Dunsmuir St., PO Box 49296, Vancouver, BC V7X 1L3; phone: 604-683-2000 for lodging and après-ski details).

WHISTLER RESORT: Nestled in the mountains 75 miles (120 km) north of Vancouver, along the spectacular Sea-to-Sky Highway, this resort has long been one of the giants of North American skiing. Yet, surprisingly, it was long known mainly to locals and day-trippers, and was until recently the sort of unspoiled western place frequented by youths investigating alternative lifestyles. This situation has changed — dramatically. Thanks to a multimillion-dollar development program, Whistler Village is now full of shops, restaurants, nightspots, hotels, galleries, and more. The skiing remains unparalleled. The resort's two ski mountains boast North

America's longest lift-served vertical drops — 5,280 feet at Blackcomb and 5,020 feet at Whistler Mountain. Side by side, this pair offers close to 2,000 acres of world class ski terrain, with over 180 trails up to 5 miles long served by more than 2 dozen lifts, and every type of skiing from forest-edged trails and paths through the glades to broad, groomed slopes and breathtaking alpine powder bowls. Whistler's snowfall often tops 450 inches a year. The resort frequently hosts the *World Cup* slalom and giant slalom competitions. Open year-round, with a special ski camp in summer. Information: *Whistler Mountain Ski Corporation* (PO Box 67, Whistler, BC V0N 1B0; phone: 604-932-3434 or 604-685-1007); *Canada Heli-Sports* (phone: 604-932-3512); *Whistler Heli-Skiing* (phone: 604-932-4105); and *Tyax Heli Skiing* (phone: 604-932-7007); *Whistler Cross-Country* (phone: 604-932-6436).

Golf

Though the rainy, mild climate here tests the time-honored adage, "It never rains on a golf course," it makes for some of the thickest fairways and lushest greens anywhere. A variety of public and semi-private courses are within a short drive of the downtown core. For the diehard, courses are open year-round, but are busiest from May through October. Expect busy phone lines during those months (especially when clear skies are forecast), but persevere to arrange tee times and enjoy some of the best golf in the country.

BURNABY MOUNTAIN: Aptly named, this 6,431-yard green monster doesn't give up any easy birdies, especially with the dozen water hazards that dot the green approaches; the hilly terrain affords some difficult lies. There are generous practice facilities, with two large putting greens, a chipping green, practice fairway for short irons, and a 40-mat driving range. To get here, take Lougheed Highway, via Kensington overpass, to Halifax Street. Information: *Burnaby Mountain,* 7600 Halifax St., Burnaby (phone: 604-421-7355).

FRASERVIEW: With about 90,000 rounds played here each year, this is the busiest golf course in Canada. Dave Barr, Canada's best-known golfer on the pro tour, notched his first birdies here. Although the well-treed, hilly course measures only 6,165 yards, it plays longer because of its uphill approaches. Each fairway and green on the 264 acres in South Vancouver is isolated from the others, so you are seldom aware of other golfers. All three of the par 5s are in the 450-yard range, while the four par 3s run from 155 to 201 yards. Take Marine Drive and turn north at Elliot Street or take 49th Avenue and turn south at Vivian Street. If you reach the corner of Boundary Road and 49th Avenue, which separates Vancouver from Burnaby, you've gone too far. Information: *Fraserview,* 7800 Vivian St. (phone: 604-327-3717).

GLENEAGLES: This 9-hole, par 35, 2,600-yard course is regarded by serious golfers as the best public course in Vancouver. Open year-round. Information: *Gleneagles,* 6190 Marine Dr., West Vancouver, BC V7W 2S3 (phone: 604-921-7353).

SEYMOUR: This private club (it opens 2 days a week — Mondays and Fridays — for visitors), across Burrard Inlet, has a mountainside, but playable, layout. At 6,288 yards, the course takes full advantage of the local vista. All greens and several of the fairways have traps and five of the generally wide fairways have small bodies of water. Unsheath your Big Bertha heavy-hitter for the par 5, 545-yard 6th that cuts across the south end of the course. To get there, take Mt. Seymour Parkway to the Seymour Mountain turnoff. Information: *Seymour,* 3723 Mt. Seymour Pkwy., North Vancouver, BC V7G 1C1 (phone: 604-929-2611).

UPLANDS GOLF CLUB: The wind always blows off the surrounding Pacific around here and probably provides the most difficult resident hazard. The 18-hole, 6,246-yard course was the site of the *Canadian Senior Championships* in 1972 and 1985. Information: *Uplands Golf Club,* 3300 Cadboro Bay Rd., Victoria, BC V8R 5K5 (phone: 604-592-7313; pro shop, 604-592-1818).

VANCOUVER UNIVERSITY GOLF CLUB: Situated on the university's Endowment Lands, this 18-hole, par 72, 6,584-yard course is open year-round. It has been upgraded, and is said to be considered one of the best public facilities in the entire country. Information: *Vancouver University Golf Club,* 5185 University Blvd., Vancouver, BC V6T 1X5 (phone: 604-224-1818).

Goin' Fishing: The Best Spots

 Few places are so closely associated with its catch of the day as Vancouver is with salmon. Shops across the country sell slivers of smoked Pacific Coast salmon, and you'll find it nearly impossible to resist the challenge of catching it fresh (and having it smoked on your own). Licenses are required for tidal, non-tidal, and freshwater fishing. No license is needed to go shellfishing in Howe Sound or around the Gulf Islands; however, there are some size limitations. Most marinas have up-to-date details on licenses and fishing seasons, or call the fisheries coordinator at 604-666-2268. For occasional red-tide warnings (unsafe conditions for catching shellfish), call 604-666-3169. Here are some of the best catches of the day — and that's no fish story.

SEWELL'S MARINA: The pros here have been taking fisherfolk into Howe Sound since 1931, so you can bet they'll track down the silver salmon if they're out there (and they usually are). Indeed, four out of five anglers who go out on a *Sewell* boat come back with either a chinook, coho, sockeye, or pink salmon. You can go out on your own (the pros there will give you tips on baiting and landing) in a 15- to 19-foot boat, or charter an 18-footer with a guide. Charter boats have fish finders, downriggers, and live-bait tanks. Howe Sound, home to the largest octopi in the world and 325 species of fish, is second only to the Red Sea in the variety of its underwater life. This deep fjord also has some of the most spectacular scenery this side of Scandinavia. Information: *Sewell Marina,* Horseshoe Bay, West Vancouver (phone: 604-921-3744).

WESTIN BAYSHORE YACHT CHARTERS: At the edge of Stanley Park, this marina provides skippered boats for a minimum 5-hour expedition. There's a guide, fishing gear, and license facility on board. You'll go where the salmon are biting: either at the mouth of the Fraser River or farther out in the Pacific. Chinook weigh about 10 pounds, although a 20-pounder is not unusual (catches are limited to two a day). The marina provides insulated boxes to keep your catch fresh for 24 hours until you can have it frozen. (Hotel kitchens usually provide this service.) A bonus here, in addition to the incredibly scenic surroundings, is that the marina is right downtown. Information: *Westin Bayshore Yacht Charters* at the *Westin Bayshore Hotel,* 1601 W. Georgia St. (phone: 604-691-6936).

FARTHER AFIELD: British Columbia's waters are an angler's Utopia. The sea is everywhere and lakes abound. The Okanagan in the BC interior boasts a multitude of trout lakes, with resorts and fishing camps to match. Anglers here are especially attracted to Kamloops trout, a good-tasting, good-fighting fish. In the same lakes are cutthroat, Dolly Varden, eastern brook, and lake trout, as well as salmon perch and bass. For information, contact the *Okanagan/Similkameen Tourist Association* (phone: 604-769-5959). The Cariboo-Chilcotin area, located due north of the city, has some of the world's most highly rated "fishing holes": landlocked sylvan lakes accessible only by float plane, and streams where trout are waiting in the shade of willows. The stocking of these waters is not wholly dependent on nature; fish hatcheries raise chinook salmon and rainbow trout to replenish the waters. For information call *Cariboo Tourism* (phone: 800-663-5885). Closer to home, Fraser Valley has a selection of good fishing lakes, including deep Chilliwack Lake, noted for its Dolly Varden and cutthroat trout. Contact the *Tourism Association of Southwestern BC* (phone: 604-876-3088). On Vancouver Island, Port Alberni bills itself as the Salmon Capital of the World. From the town on Highway 4, just south of Parksville, good fishing abounds in Barkley Sound, the protected waters of Alberni Inlet. The avid angler with more time can book the Charlotte Experience, a 4-day fishing adventure in the Queen Charlotte Islands through *Sewell Marina,* listed above.

Great Sailing

The vast, protected waters with their dozens of small islands, majestic mountain scenery, and wildlife viewings — whales, dolphins, eagles, deer — are why so many Vancouverites own sailboats. This is a great place to start a sailing career — in skippered boats available for novices, or, if time (and spirit) allows, a true wilderness adventure. The following is a sampling of the best sailing in this jewel of a port.

AR SEIZ AVEL SAILING: This company's 42-foot sloop, whose name means "Seven Winds" in the Breton dialect, takes advantage of the winds in its daily sails. Every morning at its downtown location at Coal Harbour the ship picks up its passengers (10 maximum) and heads out for an 8-hour tour. Cruises can vary depending on the wishes of the passengers, but usually include tours of the inner harbor, English Bay, and parts of Howe Sound. For lunch the ship anchors at either Bowen or Gambier Island. There is a boardsail on board, a few fishing rods, and even a dinghy for those who want to explore little coves along the shoreline. Upon its return at 6 PM, the ship stocks up in readiness for its sunset dinner cruise (for two or four people). For those with a little more time, 2- and 3-day trips can be arranged to the Gulf Islands and up the Sunshine Coast. Passengers on these trips must plan their own activities and do their own cooking. Information: *Ar Seiz Avel Sailing,* 101-1184 Denman St., Box 304, Vancouver, BC V6G 2M9 (phone: 604-682-8695).

COOPER BOATING CENTER: With a large fleet of 20- to 45-foot Catalina, Hunter, C and C, and locally built Maple Leaf craft, this Granville Island location is a popular spot for ancient mariners and novices alike. Visitors can hire a 20-footer with skipper for a 3-hour tour of local waters for CN$30, and bare boats can be rented for full or half days by those who have an international certificate or proof of boating experience. (Boaters are given an orientation during which skills are evaluated.) Would-be sailors often make a special trip here to take the 5-day Cruise and Learn Vacation course (about CN$700, including food, on-board lodging, and instruction); it sails to the Gulf Islands, Vancouver Island, Gibson's Landing, and waters in-between. Graduates receive certification and a log book that can be used as proof to rent a boat at any marina worldwide. There is also a summer sailing camp for children 13 and up. This day camp includes lessons, lunches, and 5 full days of sailing for CN$300. Course reservations should be made in advance; boats can often be rented with little notice. Information:

Cooper Boating Center, 1620 Duranleau St., Granville Island, Vancouver, BC V6H 3S4 (phone: 604-687-4110).

DUEN SAILING ADVENTURES: Not for the cocktail-hour cruiser, the wilderness trip offered by this firm aboard its Norwegian heritage vessel *Duen* is for serious sailors. Few attractions are as difficult to reserve — or as memorable — as an 8-day voyage aboard the 72-foot ship that makes its way to the Queen Charlottes, the emerald islands of the Pacific. As part of the expedition, the six to eight passengers paddle lightweight inflatable craft into the islands' rain forest to see the ancient middens (small hills) and totem poles of the Haida and the abundance of wildlife. Built in 1939 in a fashion that hadn't changed much from Viking days, the *Duen* (Dove) plied the waters of Norway for 30 years as a fishing craft before being converted to an oceangoing vessel. It has heavy beam construction, wooden-nailed planking, and 2,400 square feet of traditional rigged sail. Passengers can help sail the boat if they wish, but it's not a requirement. Reserve as far in advance as possible. Information: *Duen Sailing Adventures,* 876 Westview Cres., North Vancouver, BC V7N 3Y2 (phone: 604-987-7635).

Cycling

 What you'll soon discover about Vancouver is the grand scale of the place: There's so much to see, over so vast and scenic an area, that it makes perfect sense to do some of your exploring on two wheels (an extremely popular pastime among locals). There are miles of bike paths on which you can pedal about town, admiring the ever-changing majestic views of the North Shore mountains, the floatplanes and tugs of Burrard Inlet, the white caps of English Bay and the Pacific Ocean. Bear in mind that it's easy to get swept up in the grandeur of the place, so in the busy spots along the seawall that surrounds Stanley Park or along the Seaside Bikeway between the park and Pacific Spirit Regional Park be on your guard: You're sharing the route with joggers, walkers, meandering souls, and the inevitable speeding bike coming up from behind. Rent good wheels at *Spokes: Bike Rentals and Espresso Bar* (Denman at Georgia Sts.; phone: 604-688-5141) or *Stanley Park Bike Rentals* (near the park entrance; 676 Chilco St.; phone: 604-681-5581). Both carry mountain bikes with wide gear selections, free maps, and offer guided tours of the park, False Creek, and Granville Island. Visitors are welcome to join local cyclists on the regularly scheduled rides of the *Bicycling Association of BC* (phone: 604-731-7433). Following are popular routes for cyclists.

BRITISH COLUMBIA PARKWAY: An area of parks, gardens, and playgrounds beneath the *Skytrain,* it boasts a 10-mile bicycle path, the 7-11 Bicycle Trail, from False Creek to New Westminster. Theme parks along the route (you might want to plan a picnic here) include a rhododendron garden, a Japanese garden, and the "Dutch Mile," plus a jogging track. Take the *Skytrain* from Main Street Station to the Broadway Station and begin here. Where the route crosses streets, the intersections are marked by cylindrical striped poles, interlocking paving stones, and signs. It is well marked with information and safety signs and is the site of numerous bikeathons.

SEASIDE BIKEWAY: This 9.5-mile path between Stanley Park and Pacific Spirit Regional Park at the University of British Columbia is a long ride that might be taken in smaller segments to allow time to enjoy the parks and beaches along the way. The trail is very well signed, with large board maps at locations such as Jericho Park. It runs alongside the water wherever possible. You can make it as long, or as short, as stamina permits.

STANLEY PARK SEAWALL: A yellow dividing line separates cyclists from strollers and runners, but always watch for strays who cross the line. The round trip is almost 6 miles and features some of the city's most spectacular scenery. Early morning is the best time to ride here, especially on summer weekends. Signs near the entrance to Stanley Park will point you toward Second Beach, a good place to start the ride. You'll pass Ferguson Point, Prospect Point, Brockton Point, and Lost Lagoon before returning to Second Beach.

FOR THE MIND

Memorable Museums

 It's not surprising in a city whose heritage properties are just over a century old that its museums focus as much on the future as the past. Some of the freshest and most innovative museums are here. Set aside a good part of the day and join in on the fun with the spirited staff and volunteers who shape entertaining and educational experiences at Canada's westernmost metropolis.

BURNABY VILLAGE MUSEUM: Cross the wooden footbridge that spans the narrow ravine here and you'll step right into a time warp. Listen for the ringing clang of hot metal being pounded into horseshoes against the village smithy's anvil, or some honky-tonk music spitting from the player piano at the sheet-music store, or even a bit of "Oh, Promise Me" if there's a wedding at the tall-steepled chapel. In summer there's oom-pah-pah or a barbershop quartet at the bandstand, or a high-stepping, Yukon-style, vaudeville show at the theater. Guides in period costume tell historically accurate tales about the buildings and about real (and mythical) villagers, while others go about their everyday chores, as if oblivious to curious onlookers. Children are encouraged to get involved, and are sometimes shown how to roll hoops or use a washboard, or sit in a classroom straight out of their grandparents' memory. A microcosm of 1890–1925 life, the museum includes replicas, buildings moved here from other Burnaby locations, and one building native to the place, the Elworth kitchen (1922), which displays cooking implements of the 1920s. The chapel is a reconstruction, but its pews come from a 1905 church. Over at the newspaper office, a linotype operator, complete with green eyeshade, is working on real print jobs. An absolute must-visit is the Chinese herbalist shop, with its dozens of little wooden drawers stocked with exotic herbs, weeds, and medicinal wonders. It came intact from Victoria, where it was in operation from 1900 to 1971. There's also an *ofuro,* a Japanese version of a hot tub, a welcome tradition for tired Asian woodsmen a century ago, and *Old Curly,* the oldest surviving steam locomotive in BC. The ice cream parlor, with its paper doilies and mob-capped waitresses, serves pretty good old-fashioned food at reasonable prices, including ham and split-pea soup, thick-cut sandwiches, and deep-dish fruit pies à la mode. There are picnic tables, and the Elworth lawn is a great place to spread out a lunch. The museum can be reached by going east on Canada Way Highway to Sperling Avenue. Open daily April through May, 11 AM to 4:30 PM; June to *Labour Day,* 10 AM to 5 PM; September and *Thanksgiving* weekend (October 9–11), 11 AM to 4:30 PM; and for part of December for *Heritage Christmas,* 1:30 to 9:30 PM. Admission charge. Information: *Burnaby Village Museum,* 6501 Deer Lake Ave., Burnaby (phone: 604-293-6501).

CANADIAN CRAFT MUSEUM: On few other occasions has such good come from bad, or so the story goes. A few years ago, the usual sound and fury from historic preservation groups greeted developers' plans to demolish the Georgia Medical-Dental Centre and put up a high-rise. Well, the demolition went ahead, but you won't hear a peep from any of the original protestors today. As part of his building plan for the green-roofed Cathedral Place (see *Special Places* in THE CITY), architect Paul Merrick created this museum, with a separate Hornby Street entrance and a stone-arched cloister courtyard that fronts it and separates it from the complex. (The developer had the facility built as part of a city-sponsored program that waived urban density regulations for the construction of an arts center.) The interior was designed so that the exhibits, not the architectural flourishes, attract the eye. Since opening in 1988, it has become a showcase for Canadian and international crafts both contemporary and historical, with a focus on postwar items. Founded in 1980 as the *Cartwright Gallery* on Granville Island, it is now the only museum in Canada devoted to crafts in all five media: metal, clay, wood, glass, and fiber. Exhibitions run the gamut — from functional and decorative Canadian crafts, to Finnish sculpted glass and textiles, to ancient Asian snuff bottles, to dolls from the renowned *Yokohama Doll Museum* in Japan. Interspersed with these exhibits are smaller, timely displays: BC birdhouses, or entries from a Best Vancouver Sweater Contest. There are four to eight major exhibitions each year. The smaller displays are in the mezzanine space. A gift shop offers local and international crafts. Open Mondays through Saturdays from 9:30 AM to 5:30 PM, Sundays and holidays from 12 to 5 PM. There is an admission charge, which is waived on first Thursdays of each month. Information: *Canadian Craft Museum,* 936 Hornby St. (phone: 604-687-8266).

MUSEUM OF ANTHROPOLOGY: Located on the campus of the University of British Columbia, this musem has a major collection of Indian artifacts, focusing on the northwest and coastal tribes, as well as natives of the Americas, the Pacific Islands, Asia, and Africa. An intriguing aspect of this museum is that it's arranged like a library. The entire collection is displayed in the public galleries, and information about each item is available in a computerized catalogue system. Curious laymen and serious researchers alike can search through the catalogue, read an entry about an interesting artifact, and then find that artifact in one of the glass cases or drawers. Conversely, visitors can browse through the collection, then turn to the catalogue for additional information. Among the collection are woodcarvings, 150-year-old house posts, bentwood boxes, and a variety of dishes and bowls. A unique group of totem poles is displayed in the North Hall. This is the place to see the best of Indian culture, for it is the repository of much that was lost to European settlement. *Museum of Anthropology,* 6393 NW Marine Dr., University of British Columbia (phone: 604-822-5087).

SCIENCE WORLD: When the 12-day tour of "carol ships" along the waterfront serenades the city with *Christmas* music (see *Special Events* in THE CITY), no single site is as fantastic as this dome, dazzlingly bathed in thousands of lights like a castle in Oz. In daylight it looks like a giant golf ball teed up before a water hazard. Yet this spectacular legacy of *Expo '86* is no figment of the imagination; the science and technology museum is one of the most popular institutions in the city. The emphasis here is on interactive learning. Mesmerized children learn how to blow a square bubble inside a round bubble, or how to make their hair stand on end. There are demonstrations of lightning bolts and laser beams at the *Science Theatre;* and an authetic, giant-size, walk-and-climb-through beaver lodge at the entrance to the immensely popular Search Gallery. Here everyone from toddlers to young adults will want to stand inside the trunk of a western cedar, play in the costume corner, where there are uniforms of all types, and watch the drones and worker bees buzz about the queen bee in a glass-encased hive. On the second level, the colorful Canada Promenade features an area of scientific demonstrations; from there, visitors move on to the main gallery, with its more than 50 hands-on exhibits. The dome itself provides the spherical surface for *Omnimax Theatre,* the world's largest, where films about such topics as Antarctica, earthquakes and volcanos, and mountain gorillas are shown. The center has been a colossal hit since its first show, a temporary exhibition of dinosaurs, drew close to 400,000 visitors during a 4-month run. Traveling exhibitions from other science museums — the *Reuben H. Fleet* in San Diego and the *Smithsonian,* among others — are regularly mounted. There's a large cafeteria and a well-stocked gift shop. Open July to *Labour Day,* 10 AM to 6 PM, Saturdays until 9 PM; the rest of the year, 10 AM to 5 PM, Saturdays until 9 PM; *Christmas* hours vary. Admission charge. Information: *Science World,* 1455 Quebec St. (phone: 604-687-8414; for tape-recorded, 24-hour message, call 604-687-7832).

VANCOUVER MUSEUM: Located in a futuristic-looking building that has alternately been described as an old Haida hat, a spaceship at takeoff, and Taj Mahal by the Creek, this place is the granddaddy of them all. In 1894, the original incarnation was called the *Vancouver Art, Historical and Scientific Association Exhibit Hall* (claiming a stuffed white swan as part of its collection); since then it has become one of the leading civic institutions in the world, housing more than 300,000 artifacts. It was given a new lease on life when it moved to the museum and planetarium complex built in Vanier Park by architect Gerald Hamilton in 1967, Canada's centennial year. A more beautiful setting, with its background of water and mountains, is hard to imagine. The most fascinating permanent exhibit is the interpretative displays of life during the city's first years; featured are a street setting and reconstructed rooms, complete with furniture and household items, even wallpaper, from local homes. Selections from the Asian art collection, started over 90 years ago, are beautiful reminders of the city's ties to the Pacific Rim. In cabinets with "Please Open" drawers are combs, buckles, fans, footwear, and other personal items of early immigrants from China, Japan, Burma, Thailand, Tibet, India, Indonesia, and Nepal. Noteworthy long-term exhibitions, such as "Panache," devoted to the history of women's dress, and "Making a Living," about the changing face of jobs and work habits, have toured worldwide. On guard by a pool by the entrance is a gleaming stainless-steel crab sculpture by George Norris, its tentacles waving welcome. The museum gift shop is noted for its Indian and Inuit art and local crafts. The *Vanier Room* restaurant (phone: 604-738-6336), with its idyllic view, is open Tuesdays through Sundays from 8 AM to 5 PM; Sunday brunch is a specialty. Located below the *H.R. MacMillan Planetarium,* the museum is wheelchair-accessible and open Tuesdays through Sundays, and holidays, 10 AM to 5 PM. Admission charge. Information: *Vancouver Museum,* 1100 Chestnut St. (phone: 604-736-4431 or 604-736-7736 for taped information).

Glorious Gardens

 For those whose idea of a garden is daffodils in spring and roses in summer, public gardens here are an awakening. If hockey is *the* game, gardening is *the* pastime; scarcely a backyard or balcony is without one. Year-round, gardens are a riot of color, a symphony of smells. Close to 50,000 flowering plum, crabapple, and cherry trees blossom each spring, lining streets and parkways, blanketing sidewalks with pink petals. Then magnolias, dogwoods, and rhododendrons have their turn and, in autumn, it's maples, sumacs, and beeches. And towering green firs always provide contrast. The following public gardens are Vancouver's most colorful spots.

BUTCHART GARDENS, Victoria: Shortly after the turn of the century, Jenny Butchart chafed at the site of a worked-out limestone quarry, an ugly scar on her 130-acre estate, and managed to convince her cement-maker husband that what was needed there was a little garden. And Jenny, how your garden did grow! At 50 acres now, it is one of the most famous of its kind in the world. This place gives new meaning to the term eclectic: There's a formal Italian garden; a Japanese garden; an elegant-looking fountain; a pool with floating water lilies; English-style perennial borders; sweeping lawns; and an English rose garden. The centerpiece remains the sunken garden on that old quarry site. Although multitudes of blossoms bloom throughout the year, it is in winter that you really can see the layout of the gardens that Jenny built. Yet the place is no sleepy hollow. In summer, the gates don't close until after dark; there are fireworks display on Saturdays during July and August. From June 15 to September 15, thousands of colored lights are tucked among the flowers to transform the garden into one of the world's most fantastic nature shows. During the *Christmas* season, it is open again in the evening, with featured areas of the garden glowing with lights and festive touches. Enjoy afternoon tea, lunch, or dinner at the old Butchart home, or snack at the *Blue Poppy,* a flower-filled greenhouse. The gift shop has freshly packaged seeds from the gardens, preserves and jellies. Open daily at 9 AM. Call for closing hours. Admission charge. Butchart Gardens is 13 miles (21 km) north of Victoria. Take Blanshard Street north (it becomes Highway 17/Patricia Bay Highway) for about 10 miles. Turn left at the Keating X Road/Butchart Gardens exit. Continue straight on Keating, and follow the signs to the Butchart Gardens' entrance. Information: *Butchart Gardens* (phone: 604-652-4422).

DR. SUN YAT SEN CLASSICAL CHINESE GARDEN: Your first impression of this very special corner of Chinatown is of a strange familiarity, as if you are looking at the design of an antique Asian dish or painting come to life. Not the old blue willow pattern that everyone knows; something more exotic. And that impression lingers as you make your way through this, the only full-size classical Chinese garden outside that country. Unlike the other gardens in town, this one is best viewed with a guide. On your own, you might miss too many nuances: The whys and wherefores of this uniquely formal garden are precise and intense; everything has a reason. An indoor garden of the type one would find at a scholar's home during the Ming Dynasty (1368–1644), it seems more like an original than a replica — probably because the 52 artisans who created it came from Suzhou, Jiangsu Province, and used only the traditional tools and methods of the period. They brought with them the rare, eerie T'aihu rocks, and the tiles and woods for the carved pavilions. From almost every angle there is a vista, a combination of light and textures, as you view the jade-green water, the grotesque rocks, the tangled plantings, the latticework. The garden was named for Dr. Sun Yat Sen, the first President of the Republic of China, who visited Vancouver many times to raise funds for the 1911 revolution, which brought about the downfall of the Manchu rule and earned him the title Father of the Country. Through the garden's moon window, the public park bearing his name is visible. Tour guides are available at the entrance. Call for opening hours. Admission charge. Information: *Dr. Sun Yat Sen Classical Chinese Garden,* 578 Carrall St. (phone: 604-662-3207).

NITOBE MEMORIAL GARDEN: An authentic example of a Japanese garden, with its idealized conception of nature, here is a blend of waterfalls, trees, and shrubs. Designed by Kannosuke Mori, who supervised the placement of each plant and rock, it was officially opened in 1960 on the campus of the University of British Columbia as a memorial to Dr. Inazo Nitobe, a Japanese educator, scholar, and diplomat who died while visiting BC in 1933. The still pond in this serene oasis, which is almost stark in its design, was created to reflect the colors of the changing seasons. Laid out in the traditional circular fashion, which symbolizes the cycle of life, the garden has a tranquillity that encourages quiet contemplation. Japanese lanterns, an informal stroll garden, and a tea garden with a ceremonial tea house add to this serenity. Open daily. Call for hours. Admission charge can be combined with entrance to the nearby UBC Botanical Gardens (see below). Information: *Nitobe Memorial Gardens,* UBC campus, NW Marine Dr. (phone: 604-822-4208; 604-822-6038 year-round).

PARK AND TILFORD GARDENS: This charming oasis is pure Vancouver: In the shadow of a shopping center, towering trees and beautiful flowers grow. Shoppers seeking Zen-like relaxation to go with their browsing flock here to the eight theme gardens on just 2½ acres of land in North Vancouver — a living testament to the city's innovative land-use policies. Once a noted display garden, it was redeveloped and enhanced after the shopping center of the same name was completed. The circular herb garden, near the greenhouse, is especially aromatic with its variety of mint, thyme, bee's balm, and lavender; the Rock Pool area, with outsize boulders arranged atop each other, has a tropical look, enhanced by clumps of ornamental grasses. Magnolia trees — some 50 feet tall — cast their spell, as does the English-style rose garden of clematis and climbing roses. The native garden is where BC plants and trees — plus those from Alaska to northern California — come into their own in this simulated coastal rain forest atmosphere of Douglas fir, hemlock, birch trees, sword ferns, and trilliums. A timber bridge crosses a bog with such natural surprises as skunk cabbage. Not far away — and in complete contrast — is the Colonnade, with 60 hanging baskets and an air of early Rome. But one of the garden's unique attractions is the white garden. A tradition in British gardens, it is rarely seen outside the British Isles. With white flowers and plants that have silver or grey leaves, it is designed to allow a viewer to study plant form, size, and texture. Nearby, the Asian Garden is created for contemplation, with bonsai-pruned Japanese maples, ornamental bonsai pines, all sizes of bamboo, and a tea house. Rest here beside the pond with aquatic plants and an Oriental-style bridge; goldfish swim here, to the delight of the herons who occasionally drop in for a free lunch. Surrounding the rose garden, herb garden, and white garden is a post-and-beam patio strung with hanging baskets. From its benches are some of the garden's prettiest vistas. Open daily from 9:30 AM to dusk and in December, when visitors come from all over the city to enjoy the light-strung gardens and *Christmas* music, until 9 PM. No admission charge. The gardens are located in North Vancouver about a mile west of Second Narrows Bridge, behind the *Park and Tilford Shopping Centre.* Information: *Park and Tilford Gardens,* Main St. and Brooksbank Ave. (phone: 604-984-8200).

QUEEN ELIZABETH PARK: Much of this 121-acre park, located at the center of the city, is devoted to gardens. Originally known as Little Mountain, this onetime quarry provided crushed rock for Vancouver's first road. Named not for the current Queen of England but her mother, the Queen Mum, the gardens began to take shape in the mid-1950s when the larger of the two quarries was transformed with a 50-foot waterfall, which drops into a series of landscaped pools on the floor of a quarry garden. The picturesque viewpoint bridge was installed then, too. On Saturdays the garden fills with wedding parties posing for pictures, and every morning hundreds of people practice tai chi and other exercise workouts. On weekends overexuberant children tend to turn the elevated pools and fountains at the reservoir area into make-believe wading pools. The Bloedel Floral Conservatory, in its ultramodern dome, is considered the park's crowning glory. In a controlled environment, it houses plants and flowers from three climate zones: desert, tropical, and rain forest, along with a population of parrots, free-flying tropical birds, and brilliant koi. On the surrounding plaza is a Henry Moore sculpture, *Knife Edge-Two Pieces,* and from this site are some of the most spectacular views of downtown and the mountains beyond. Because this is the highest elevation in the city, the views, enhanced by well-positioned telescopes, are magnificent. Throughout the park, the lifelike statues by Seward Johnson always rate a double take. The garden is also home to the famous Gregg Collection of rhododendrons. There is a well-signed parking lot at the reservoir level. Open daily; April through September weekdays 9 AM to 8 PM, weekends 10 AM to 9 PM; October through March 10 AM to 5 PM. Admission charge to the Bloedel Conservatory. Information: *Queen Elizabeth Park,* 33rd Ave. at Cambie St. (phone: 604-872-5513).

UBC BOTANICAL GARDEN: Considered by some to be the city's best-kept secret, this place is no mystery to Vancouver's horticultural volunteers. The oldest university botanical garden in Canada (1916), there is a 2-year waiting list to get into the *FOG* (*Friends of the Gardens*), whose members perform tasks not handled by the pros. These tenderhearted folk mind the well-stocked gift shop with its gardening paraphernalia, books, seeds, and, on occasion, rare plants. Stretching over 75 acres, the display gardens are an aromatic mélange of old and new. Just beyond the entrance is the David C. Lam Asian Garden and Forest, a rich variety of magnolias, rhododendrons, rare trees, and vines that is especially lovely in spring, when brilliant blossoms sharply contrast with dark forest trees and ferns. The E.H. Lohbrunner Alpine Garden with its mountain plantings, including edelweiss, wild orchids, blue gentians, and BC's native alpine trilliums, is a scenic spot, as is the native garden, an aromatic woodland and meadow trail, peat bog, brook, and pond. From the province's desert area there are sagebrush and cacti. Appropriately bordered by a hedge of yew, whose anti-cancer properties are just being realized, is the Physick, a 16th-century medicinal garden. It features plants — laid out in formal display around a sundial — that have been used to cure ailments since ancient times. Plantings from the famous Chelsea Physick Garden in England formed the nucleus of this one. A stroll through an arbor of climbing plants and vines leads to the kitchen garden with its vines, berry bushes, and fruit trees, many grown in the traditional espaliered style. The gardens are open daily. Call for hours. Admission charge can be combined to include entrance to the Nitobe Memorial Garden (above). Information: *UBC Botanical Garden,* 6804 SW Marine Dr. (phone: 604-822-4208; 604-822-3928 year-round).

VAN DUSEN BOTANICAL GARDENS: Those traveling with children will not want to miss the Children's Gardens here, with topiary and hedges that form an Elizabethan maze. Take a breather while your small ones wend their way through these luxuriant corridors where plants, flowers, and shrubs from every part of the world have taken root, 400 feet above sea level. Within a short stroll are BC red cedars, cedars of Lebanon, and blue cedars native to Algeria and Morocco. Quaint rustic wooden bridges lead from one ecological niche to another and link such beautiful areas as the Meadow Garden and the Rhododendron Walk. There are several massive stone sculptures, too, the legacy of a stone symposium that attracted sculptors from France, Austria, Yugoslavia, Poland, Italy, and North America. The Walk in the Forest exhibit, built by the local MacMillan Bloedel forest products company, guides people along a forest walk that illustrates the life cycle of BC's trees. In December the entire garden complex is transformed into a *Christmas* wonderland, with thousands of lights, holiday displays, and music. Once the site of the 55-acre *Shaughnessy* golf course, it is located only a few blocks away from Queen Elizabeth Park. The gardens are open daily. Admission charge. Information: *Van Dusen Botanical Gardens,* 37th Ave. at Cambie St. (phone: 604-266-7194).

A Shutterbug's Vancouver

 If you can get it to hold still long enough, Vancouver is an exceptionally photogenic city. There is architectural variety: Old is juxtaposed with new, ornate with ordinary, and a skyline bristling with the temples of modern commerce against a backdrop of forested hills. Rhododendrons embroider a park footpath, ivy inches up a red-brick building, and a summer sunset sparks the water ablaze. There's human variety as well: Newcomers exchange the latest gossip in rapid-fire Asian dialects and shop at the down-to-earth *Punjabi Market,* and sports fans sit cheek by jowl dressed in their team's full colors. The thriving city, the shimmering sea, the parks, the people, and traces of rich history make Vancouver a fertile stomping ground for shutterbugs. Even a beginner can achieve remarkable results with a surprisingly basic set of lenses and filters. Equipment is, in fact, only as valuable as the imagination that puts it into use. (For further information on equipment, see *Cameras and Equipment* in GETTING READY TO GO.)

Don't be afraid to experiment. Use what knowledge you have to explore new possibilities. At the same time, don't limit yourself by preconceived ideas of what's hackneyed or corny. Because the Marine Building has been photographed hundreds of times before doesn't make it any less worthy of your attention.

In Vancouver, as elsewhere, spontaneity is one of the keys to good photography. Whether it's a sudden shaft of light bursting through the clouds and hitting English Bay just so, or a man practising tai chi at Little Mountain as dawn creeps over the city, don't hesitate to shoot if the moment is right. If photography is indeed capturing a moment and making it timeless, success lies in judging just when a moment worth capturing occurs.

A good picture reveals an eye for detail, whether it's a matter of lighting, of positioning your subject, or of taking time to frame a picture carefully. The better your grasp of the importance of details, the better your results will be photographically.

Patience is often necessary. Don't shoot a view of the sails of Canada Place if a cloud suddenly dulls their look. A rusted old Volkswagen in the center of your Gastown scene? Reframe your image to eliminate the obvious distraction. People walking toward a scene that would benefit from their presence? Wait until they're in position before you shoot. After the fact, many of the flaws will be self-evident. The trick is to be aware of the ideal and have the patience to allow it to happen. If you are part of a group, you may well have to trail behind a bit in order to shoot properly. Not only is group activity distracting, but bunches of people hovering nearby tend to stifle spontaneity and overwhelm potential subjects.

The camera provides an opportunity, not only to capture Vancouver's varied and subtle beauty, but to interpret it. What it takes is a sensitivity to the surroundings, a knowledge of the capabilities of your equipment, and a willingness to see things in new ways.

LANDSCAPES, SEASCAPES, AND CITYSCAPES: Gastown's Steam Clock and flatiron buildings are most often visiting photographers' favorite subjects. But the city's gardens and waterways provide numerous photo possibilities as well. In addition to the Marine Building, the gate to Chinatown, and its pagoda accents, be sure to look for natural beauty: flowering plum and cherry trees that line the streets in springtime, the well-manicured plots of flowers in Van Dusen Botanical Gardens, and the sailboats that skim along English Bay are just a few examples.

Color and form are the obvious ingredients here, and how you frame your pictures can be as important as getting the proper exposure. Study the shapes, angles, and colors that make up the scene and create a composition that uses them to best advantage.

Lighting is a vital component in landscapes and seascapes. Take advantage of the richer colors of early morning and late afternoon whenever possible. The overhead light of midday is often harsh and without the shadowing that can add to the drama of a scene. This is when a polarizer is used to best effect. Most polarizers come with a mark on the rotating ring. If you can aim at your subject and point that marker at the sun, the sun's rays are likely to be right for the polarizer to work for you. If not, stick to your skylight filter, underexposing slightly if the scene is particularly bright. Most light meters respond to an overall light balance, with the result that bright areas may appear burned out.

Although a standard 50mm to 55mm lens may work well in some landscape situations, most will benefit from a 20mm to 28mm wide-angle. The round globe of *Science World,* with city skyscrapers looming in the background, allows for the type of panorama that fits beautifully into a wide-angle format, allowing not only the overview, but the opportunity to include people or other points of interest in the foreground. A flower, for instance, may be used to set off a view of Queen Elizabeth Park; or people can provide a sense of perspective in a shot of Granville Island.

To isolate specific elements of any scene, use your telephoto lens. Perhaps there's a particular carving in a historic church that would make a lovely shot, or it might be the interplay of light and shadow on a cobblestone Gastown street. The successful use of a telephoto means developing your eye for detail.

PEOPLE: As with taking pictures of people anywhere, there are going to be times in Vancouver when a camera is an intrusion. Your approach is the key: Consider your own reaction under similar circumstances, and you have an idea as to what would make others comfortable enough to be willing subjects. People are often sensitive to having a camera suddenly pointed at them, and a polite request, while getting you a share of refusals, will also provide a chance to shoot some wonderful portraits that capture the spirit of the city as surely as the scenery does. For candids, an excellent lens is a zoom telephoto in the 70mm to 210mm range; it allows you to remain unobtrusive while the telephoto lens draws the subject closer. And for portraits, a telephoto can be used effectively as close as 2 or 3 feet.

For authenticity and variety, select a place likely to produce interesting subjects. Granville Island is an obvious spot for visitors, but for local color visit Chinatown or Stanley Park, where people gather in all their diversity, or walk around Vanier Park, where everyone seems to flock to enjoy a sunny day. Aim for shots that tell what's different about Vancouver. In portraiture, there are several factors to keep in mind. Morning or afternoon light will add richness to skin tones, emphasizing tans. To avoid the harsh facial shadows cast by direct sunlight, shoot in the shade or in an area where the light is diffused.

SUNSETS: The sky above the waters of English Bay is a rosy, magical sight in the evening, while gold glints off North Shore mountains, coloring skimming sailboats pink. When shooting sunsets, keep in mind that the brightness will distort meter readings. When composing a shot directly into the sun, frame the picture in the viewfinder so that only half of the sun is included. Read the meter, set, and shoot. Whenever there is this kind of unusual lighting, shoot a few frames in half-step increments, both over and under the meter reading. Bracketing, as this is called, can provide a range of images, the best of which may well be other than the one shot at the meter's recommended setting.

Use any lens for sunsets. A wide-angle is good when the sky is filled with color-streaked clouds, when the sun is partially hidden, or when you're close to an object that silhouettes dramatically against the sky.

Telephotos also produce wonderful silhouettes, either with the sun as a backdrop or against the palette of a brilliant sunset sky. Bracket again here. For the best silhouettes, wait 10 to 15 minutes after sunset. Unless using a very fast film, a tripod is recommended.

Red and orange filters are often used to accentuate a sunset's picture potential. Orange will help turn even a gray sky into something approaching a photogenic finale to the day, and can provide particularly beautiful shots linking the sky with the sun reflected on the ocean. If the sunset is already bold in hue, the orange will overwhelm the natural colors. A red filter will produce dramatic, highly unrealistic results.

NIGHT: If you think that picture possibilities end at sunset, you're presuming that night photography is the exclusive domain of the professional. If you've got a tripod, all you'll need is a cable release to attach to your camera to assure a steady exposure (which is often timed in minutes rather than fractions of a second).

The best time for night photography is during the 12-day "carol ships" tour at *Christmastime,* when lights adorn countless waterfront vessels and *Science World* transforms into a shimmering golden ball. For situations such as evening concerts at Kits Beach or nighttime harbor cruises, a strobe does the trick, but beware: Flash units are often used improperly. You can't take a view of the skyline with a flash. It may reach out as far as 30 feet, but that's it. On the other hand, a flash used too close to a subject may result in overexposure, resulting in a "blown out" effect. With most cameras, strobes will work with a maximum shutter speed of 1/125 or 1/150 of a second. If you set the exposure properly and shoot within range, you should come up with pretty sharp results.

CLOSE-UPS: Whether of people or of objects such as totem poles, close-ups can add another dimension to your photography. There are a number of shooting options, one of which is to use a 70mm or a 210mm lens at its closest focusable distance. Unless you're working in bright sunlight, a tripod will be worthwhile. If you are very near your subject and there is a good deal of reflective light, it may pay to underexpose a bit in relation to the meter reading.

If you do not have a telephoto lens, you can still shoot close-ups using a set of magnification filters. Filter packs of one-, two-, and three-time magnification are available, converting your lens into a close-up lens. Even better is a special macro lens designed for close-up photography.

The following are some of Vancouver's truly great pictorial perspectives.

A SHORT PHOTOGRAPHIC TOUR

DAWN ATOP LITTLE MOUNTAIN: The golden morning light of a Vancouver sunrise viewed from Queen Elizabeth Park at 33rd and Cambie Streets offers the early-bird photographer an opportunity to capture the freshest image of the downtown skyline. Not only will you have the tranquillity of a morning in the park, but also the clearest skies of the day. The best shots will be taken from the plaza in front of the Bloedel Conservatory. From this point the city's most prominent landmarks will be outlined against the backdrop of the spectacular North Shore mountains. (The sun rises over your right shoulder.) Use the Harbour Centre Tower, with its flying saucer–shape revolving top, to create the right-hand boundary of the photograph, the snow-capped twin peaks of The Lions to create the left, and rhododendron bushes for the foreground. A walk around the quiet park will offer many other perspectives of the awakening city.

GRANVILLE ISLAND: This onetime sandbar is now a rich mosaic of photo subjects. There is no single approach here: Just take camera in hand and shoot whatever strikes your fancy. The mix of shoppers, buskers, strollers, and structures, combined with the bustling waterfront setting, will ensure that every photograph contains something of interest. An intimate look at the city's maritime heritage can be captured from the pier adjacent to *Bridges* restaurant. Look west and, using the fishing and pleasure boats as foreground, photograph the comings and goings of the vessels in the harbor. Then wander down to dockside for action shots of the perky little Granville Island water taxis.

GASTOWN STEAM CLOCK: Probably Vancouver's most photographed landmark, this ingeniously designed curiosity has a personality of its own (see *Walk 2: Gastown* in DIRECTIONS). It is difficult to get a photograph that captures this, so take a little extra time to ensure a pleasing result. Stand by the south side of Water Street at the corner of Cambie Street, and position yourself so that the clock is in the center of the open space created by adjacent buildings. Use the mosaic brick of the street as a foreground, and the sky and mountains as a backdrop. Fill the viewfinder with the flags suspended from the brick building on the left and wait for the plume of steam the clock emits every 15 minutes to capture a quintessential Vancouver moment.

DOMINION BUILDING AND THE CENOTAPH: At the corner of Cambie and Hastings Streets, the picturesque red-and-gold Dominion Building and the adjacent Victory Square make a great subject. Move up the hill toward the center of the park. From this elevated perspective, using the cenotaph to block off the Toronto Dominion Bank sign from the foreground, fill the rest of the viewfinder with the building. From here you'll best capture the beautiful curving roofline, the arched windows, and the massive stone pillars out in front.

MARINE BUILDING: This holdover from the Roaring Twenties can be photographed from many locations. One of the more interesting shots can be taken by focusing in the opposite direction on the Daon Building (on the northeast corner of Hastings and Burrard Sts.). The full image of the wedding-cake-shape Art Deco building shimmers on this reflective surface and makes a compelling contrast of old and new. This shot is most successful on a sunny day at high noon.

STANLEY PARK SEAWALL: Seascape and cityscape views from many perspectives along this seawall make for spectacular shots. One that will capture the essence of Vancouver is from a point between the *Vancouver Rowing Club* and the entrance to the Naval Reserve at Deadman's Island. That protected bay is a picturesque haven for countless small boats. Frame it so that you have the forested point and five sails of Canada Place on the left, the bay and the docks in the foreground, and the cityscape behind.

THE HOLLOW TREE, STANLEY PARK: For generations, this giant cedar stump has been *the* must shot. But many have come away disappointed because they did not shoot it with a fill-in flash. If you don't have a flash, place your subjects far enough in front of the tree to ensure adequate lighting. There are lots of enormous, gnarled roots radiating from the trunk, worn smooth by weather and climbing children. (Please note: Visitors are no longer allowed to climb into the trunk.) Take time and use these to advantage to create both serious and humorous pictures.

ENGLISH BAY: This lovely open stretch offers a panorama of sea, the land of Point Grey, and a 180°, south-facing view of downtown Vancouver. Photos can be taken from any location along this beach; the scene is constantly changing: freighters at anchor, fishing trollers, and, on breezy days, the firefly-like sails of windsurfers scooting across the water. The best shots include the beach in the foreground and should be taken from the elevated perspective of the sidewalk above a grassy knoll. An interesting Inuit sculpture, located at the east end of the beach, serves nicely as foreground in west-facing photos.

TOTEM POLES, MUSEUM OF ANTHROPOLOGY: No Vancouver photo story would be complete without a shot of totem poles. Located behind the museum, with a spectacular forest backdrop, are weathered Haida totem poles, a longhouse, and mortuary chamber. You'll have to move around and take several photos, from different angles, to include everything. For a good overall shot, stand, facing the longhouse, in the open area to the right. From atop a grassy mound, use the tall raven-topped memorial pole as your left border, the short and stouter eagle-topped pole as your right border, and the mortuary chamber and longhouse as the center. The evergreens in the background will nicely fill out the frame. The image will be best revealed in early evening light.

CHINESE GATE, CHINATOWN: Located at the entrance to the Chinese Cultural Centre and Dr. Sun Yat Sen Park on Pender Street near Carrall Street, this grandiose structure is a delight of whimsy and fancy that is best shot during the day or, with the right equipment, at night, when lights enhance its many textures and bold colors. For the night shot you'll need a tripod and a camera with a slow shutter speed. Stand across the street and select an angle that most pleases your eye, but avoid shooting straight-on because this tends to make the gate appear one-dimensional.

DIRECTIONS

Introduction

In spite of a first-impression British demeanor, most Vancouverites are actually the laid-back, West Coast, let-the-good-times-roll type. They can be serious — dealmakers take their cellular phones to the ballpark or the beaches — or lighthearted — "Look! Isn't that a bit of blue sky over there?" goes the excited refrain. "No, just another shade of gray."

Which doesn't mean that Vancouver can't move up-tempo when it wants to. Just watch the bicycle couriers darting and weaving through traffic with their precious cargo. Actually, one look at the car-clogged downtown streets and crammed parking lots will attest to the city's other side.

Visitors should remain true to cool, Canadian West Coast–style, setting out on these walks via the whisper-quiet *Skytrain,* the spotless, steady-as-she-goes *SeaBus,* or one of the clean mass-transit buses. Indeed, outside of the occasionally outraged suburban-bound motorists and the daring couriers, Vancouver is thoroughly civilized at its shake-a-leg pace.

For a modern city, downtown Vancouver is comfortably condensed. Neglected until the 1970s, when a newfound sense of heritage put a halt to rampant demolition, the downtown core is today a mix of renovated, derelict, and reconstructed buildings. (At times, it can be hard to know which is which.) The Art Deco Marine Building, a one-of-a-kind structure tinted in sea green and touched by gold, typifies those that dodged the wrecking ball, and Cathedral Place, with its *Canadian Craft Museum,* the scintillating new breed of glass towers. The historic routes outlined here pass by remnants of the city's heritage; with a bit of imagination, you should be able to visualize Vancouver as it once was — from its Gastown roots through its early growth. You'll see the roles that rail and steamships played; learn the city's pioneer beginnings in such places as the *Burnaby Village Museum;* and discover its native communities in the galleries of Indian art and culture and in the *Museum of Anthropology,* which boasts the world's finest collection of Northwest Indian art.

The sun needn't shine in order to enjoy this harborfront city. Bring along a brolly (just in case), and take the time to explore the streets, parks, and gardens of this clean, friendly, and thoroughly modern city that winks at the past. But, a word of warning: Don't take the spirit of good citizenship for granted. Lock your rental car and keep valuables in the hotel safe. After all, this is a major port city with all the potential dangers of any metropolis. So stay alert.

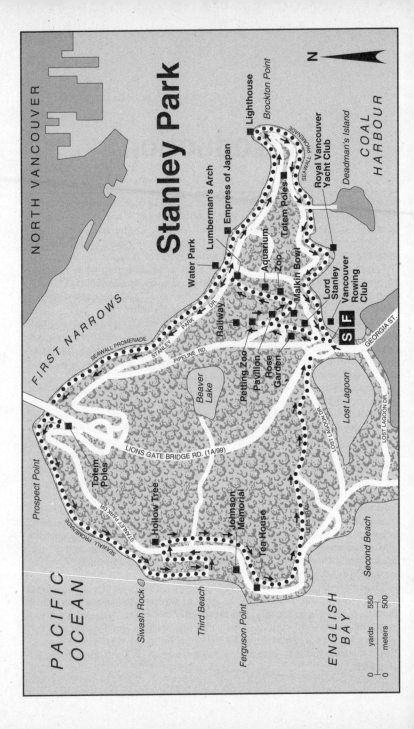

Walk 1: Stanley Park

This lush, sprawling, 1,000-acre woodland had its beginnings in a smoke-filled room. In its first official act, the city council in 1886 petitioned the federal government to create a park — not in the spirit of shaping a romantic oasis for its citizenry, but rather to attract the citizenry in the first place. This sound business reasoning came at a time when most of Vancouver was forest. To developers, hungry to build up the western end of the city, the park was to be a promotional amenity, a carrot to lure the investment that would quickly make this a major city. The rest, as they say, is history.

Located at the end of a peninsula that almost closes Burrard Inlet at First Narrows, Stanley Park is surrounded on three sides by the sea and has majestic views of the North Shore mountains, the peaks of Vancouver Island, the city skyline, and freighters and ocean liners heading to and from port. And while gleaming office towers have risen only a stroll away, the building ban in Stanley Park has remained firm, leaving its towering natural wonders, the Douglas firs — some reaching heights of 150 feet — untouched. (Although it was extensively logged before the turn of the century to provide mast and spar timbers for the British Navy, the park is now 500 acres of forest, covered with hemlock, western red cedar, and Douglas fir.) It's a place to stroll where only the trailmaker and other strollers have been — or head to the gardens, lakes, lagoons, tennis courts, and bowling greens that have been developed over the years. The *Vancouver Aquarium,* one of the world's best, is here, as are restaurants, coffee shops, snack bars, and a small zoo. There are 27 miles (43 km) of trails and an encircling 5-mile (8 km) seawall promenade. For generations now, Vancouverites have been coming here to cycle, jog, swim, play tennis and cricket, picnic, sip tea, and generally take it easy.

As in any great park, you can't do it all in a day — or a week. (At 1,000 acres, Stanley Park is 160 acres larger than New York City's Central Park.) The Stanley Park walk is best split into three 2-hour parts, each of which provides a good introduction to this magnificent wooded peninsula. Those with time and energy might want to combine these segments for a fuller experience. Each 2-hour walk allows plenty of time to take pictures, admire the scenery, or have a snack (or two). Get here on *BC Transit* (phone: 604-261-5100) or take a taxi from downtown — in summer and on balmy weekends, parking here is horrendous, so if you drive plan to arrive early and park close to the entrance, where this walk begins.

The first known occupants of the coastal lands here were Musqueam Indians of the Coast Salish group, who paddled out to meet Spanish explorer José Narváez in 1791. A peaceful people, they lived in harmony with the neighboring tribes, the Tsleilwaututh and Capilano, weaving elegant baskets and carving mortuary boxes; they found shelter from the rain in the smokey haven of 1,500-foot longhouses they built from the plentiful cedar. The Squamish Indians, another Coast Salish group — among the first workers in the first sawmills — were living in the traditional way on the Burrard Inlet peninsula when the area was surveyed in the 1850s. Their way of life was disrupted when the British Navy seized the strategic point of land in the early 1860s and erected the First Narrows Military Reserve. Built because of fears of US expansionism, specifically to ward off any possible backdoor attack by US forces based on the San Juan Islands, the reserve gave way in 1888 to the park plan submitted by real-estate developer Alexander Ross. Named after the governor general of the day, Lord Stanley (1841–1908), the park was officially opened the following year.

As you enter from Georgia Street, Lost Lagoon is on the left and Coal Harbour on the right. Poet-actress Pauline Johnson (1862–1913) so named the lagoon because its waters seemed lost at low tide. A daughter of a Mohawk chief and an Englishwoman, she was a well-known stage performer at the turn of the century. For years before her death, Johnson paddled her canoe here; today the waters at the southern edge of the park are the year-round home to swans, mallards, and Canada geese — unfortunately, canoeing is now discouraged. To the right, the body of water adjacent to the towers of modern Vancouver was named after a seam of coal that was discovered in the city's West End. This coal was used to fuel pioneer industries, notably the brick factory of "the three greenhorns" (see THE CITY) and spurred early interest in the site.

From the bus loop, at the foot of Georgia Street, follow the pedestrian walkway beneath the underpass. On the right is the *Vancouver Rowing Club.* Its "Victorian eclectic" clubhouse was built in 1911 in the spirit of a 19th-century Cambridge boathouse, complete with reading room and hardwood floors. It's as old as the city: The first club, the *Vancouver Boating Club,* held its charter meeting in 1886; it merged with the *Burrard Inlet Rowing Club* to become the *Vancouver Rowing Club* 13 years later. A familiar sight south of here, in the relatively calm waters of Coal Harbour and False Creek, are the skimming sculls keeping that tradition fresh. Even today, many athletes take rowing very seriously: Teams from the Vancouver club have been national champions, and many Canadian Olympians have first learned their skills here. Indeed, a rowing squad from this club won the 1964 *Olympic* gold for Canada.

On the left, stop for a moment at another legacy of Vancouver's British heritage, the city's first public monument: a memorial to Queen Victoria. Today about half of Vancouver's population is of non-British descent, but that change has been relatively recent (40 years ago, about 75% of Vancouverites claimed UK ancestry). And "Victoria the Good," the monarch at the time of Canada's Confederation in 1867, has a special place in English Canadian history: Canada led the nations of the Commonwealth in proclaiming a legal holiday to celebrate the queen's birthday (the Monday before May 24). The monument, one of many to her majesty that went up across Canada in the years following her death, was designed by James Blomfield, a craftsman from a family of stained glass artists; some of his work is on display at the *Vancouver Museum.*

Up an incline to the right of this monument is a statue to a figure prominent in the literary history of the British Isles: poet Robert Burns. If you've ever visited the poet's birthplace, near Ayr, Scotland, this statue of the bard gazing over Coal Harbour might look familiar; the 1884 original is near the Ayr railway station. Burns's fans will recognize the bronze bas-relief signs around the granite plinth that illustrate scenes from his poems.

A few yards north of Burns's statue, his arms open in welcome, stands Lord Stanley, better known to some for his cup than his park. Stanley's name is on the lips of most Canadians throughout April and May during the National Hockey League playoffs as the man who donated the *Stanley Cup,* the birdbath-size trophy that signifies supremacy in hockey; he also dedicated the park "to the use and enjoyment of all colors, creeds, and customs for all time." As part of the park's opening ceremonies, Lord Stanley, who was Governor General of Canada from 1888 to 1893, was promised a statue to immortalize those words — but it was a long time in coming: The city didn't raise the money for the statue until the 1950s, and on the day the bronze arrived from London, officials began wrangling anew on its placement. It finally was unveiled in March 1960.

Walk past the statue; behind it and past a playground is the Rose Garden, which is at its peak in early June. The first rose bushes, donated by the *Kiwanis Club* in 1920, were planted near the Shakespeare Memorial Garden, which had been created 4 years earlier to commemorate the 300th anniversary of the bard's death (most of the plants and trees in the Shakespeare Garden were chosen because they were mentioned in his works). In the Rose Garden, stop and smell the flowers; there were 5,000 rose bushes at last count. Then walk to the south wall of the park maintenance compound and look for a brick monument with a stone bas-relief of Shakespeare's head, commissioned and built for Vancouver's *Jubilee* in 1936. As you stroll through the garden, look for plaques honoring people and events connected with Vancouver theater.

After perusing the plaques, look for an enormous cedar nurse tree on a grassy triangular patch, bounded by the Rose Garden, Pipeline Road, and the sidewalk to Lost Lagoon. Here is a memorial dogwood planted in honor of the beloved Canadian actor John Drainie, a Vancouver native who became immensely popular for his work in radio dramas in the 1940s and on early television shows. His *Stories with John Drainie* on CBC Radio — original short stories by Canadian writers that Drainie read 5 days a week on the national radio network — helped launch many authors' careers and was a critical success during its 6-year run in the 1960s. Nearby, too, is a pair of expansive silver oak trees. One, dedicated to Shakespearean Tragedy, was planted by touring actress Eva Moore in 1921; the other, saluting Comedy, honors Sir John Martin, the British thespian. Linger here on a park bench for a few minutes, and friendly squirrels will approach looking for handouts.

Now head over to the chalet-style Pavilion adjacent to the Rose Garden for a coffee break. The onetime parks board office is now home to a refreshment stand, a restaurant, and a banquet hall. And if checkers is your game, don't miss the action a short distance northwest of here. The regulars who play on a larger-than-life checkerboard — using a shuffleboard cue stick to slide the oversize red and black checkers — take kindly to newcomers. Then fall into the current of young folks heading north to the children's petting zoo, where small fry flock to frolic with baby farm goats, sheep, rabbits, and chickens (small admission charge). Across from the zoo is a popular attraction for the Casey Jones crew: For an admission fee, a miniature railway takes adults and children through a forested area, over streams, and by simulated Indian villages and a mock miner's hut. The train, with its scaled-down open carriages, runs in summer and during the *Christmas* season.

Backtrack to the Pavilion and note the impressive stone-and-bronze statue of US President Warren Harding. His visit to Vancouver in 1923 marked the first time that a US president had ever come calling in Canada. But he wasn't here on official government business. His was a social call as a Kiwanian, in response to a request to speak to the *Vancouver Kiwanis Club;* the speech he gave was one of his last (he died a month later).

The fence you see here surrounds *Malkin Bowl;* a place to visit on a summer evening, this is the home of *Theatre Under the Stars.* Since its inception in 1940, this company has featured performances by local talent (including a young Robert Goulet), presented here at twilight during the summer months. Now walk east along a forested path toward the Vancouver City Zoo (no admission charge). Listen to the raucous chorus of birdlife, the chatter, caw, and trill of Canada geese, ducks, sea gulls, and crows who call the area home. Closer to the zoo, the birdcalls mingle with the music of buskers, a saxophone player, violinist, or guitarist. Here, too, you'll see a balloon man, face painter, or puppeteer ready to amuse the young (and young at heart). Allow some time to watch the seals, playful river otters, and high-swinging monkeys.

Beside the stream that separates the zoo from the aquarium is the cylindrical Japanese Monument. Erected in 1920 in memory of Japanese Canadians who perished in the First World War, it has an impressive backdrop of Japanese cherry trees, especially splendid in spring, when they are in blossom. Two plaques on the base of the monuments list the names of those who died in World War II and the Korean conflict.

At the *Vancouver Aquarium* (admission charge; phone: 604-682-1118), one of the finest in Canada, enjoy the underwater play of five beluga whales, natives of Hudson Bay, and other creatures of the north in the Arctic Sea display. You might want to return to see the killer-whale shows here and watch the public feedings of the playful seals and sea otters, and ever-popular sharks. If time is short this time around, this place is worth a return visit.

From the Japanese memorial follow a path toward the waterfront; in a few minutes you'll reach Lumberman's Arch, a triangular portal made from old, massive logs — a tribute to BC loggers and the province's number one industry. The first arch on this spot — built in 1912 for a visit of the Duke of Connaught and his wife — was one of a dozen lumber arches erected along their parade route through Vancouver; the current arch was erected in 1952. There are picnic tables and a concession stand for snacks. On this site was a Squamish Indian village known as Whoi Whoi (the Masks), which figures in Pauline Johnson's book, *Legends of Vancouver,* a compilation of her newspaper columns, published in 1913. You can end your walk here, or continue by walking beneath the overpass. When you reach the seawall you will see the Variety Club Water Park, a playground for the physically challenged; those who want a seaside walk, with some diversions, can continue to the right, while those craving a longer hike — along the seawall to Third Beach and through a forest glade to Lost Lagoon — will turn left.

For the seawall tour (back toward the entrance), turn right as you face the water at the Variety Club Water Park. Be sure to walk on the pedestrian side of the yellow line, away from cyclists. The first point of interest along the seawall is the *Empress of Japan* figurehead. Recast from the original in 1960, this fiberglass replica was on one of three liners owned by the *Canadian Pacific Railway* that sailed the Pacific from 1891 to 1922 (the others were the *Empress of India* and the *Empress of China*), bringing Oriental goods — silks, ivory, tea — and Asian immigrants to the West. As she came into port, the *Empress* passed near the point where the figurehead now stands.

A bit farther along the seawall, the sculpture perched on a rock offshore is no mermaid, but *The Girl in a Wetsuit,* by Vancouver artist Elek Imredy; he created this statue of a skin diver as a symbol of the modern spirit of exploration. Keep going along the path toward Brockton Point, the easternmost point of the park, stopping to take pictures of the sailboats and marine traffic on Burrard Inlet, the downtown skyline, and the mountains of the Coast Range looming in the distance.

Before reaching the lighthouse at Brockton Point, leave the seawall promenade, turning right to Stanley Park Drive, the paved road that circumnavigates the park, and walk toward the group of totem poles. Four of the poles, which honor Northwest Coast Indian culture, were presented to the city in 1912; the others were purchased in 1936 and 1963. The Kwakiutl tribe is represented by the Wakius pole, the Tsa-wee-noh house post, and the Nhe-is-bik pole. The Tinglit group is represented by the Si-sa kau-las pole, and the Haida Indians, who live in the Queen Charlotte Islands, are represented by a Skedan Mortuary pole. The colorfully decorated poles of ravens, bears, and wolves are kept looking that way with regular touch-ups from the historically correct park staff. A few yards west, between the seawall and the road, is a large boulder with a plaque honoring Captain Edward Stamp, the founder of Hastings Mill. It was on this site that the pioneering Vancouver businessman set up his first lumbering operation. He soon moved his headquarters to the foot of what is now Dunlevy Street; 2 years later, in 1867, "Gassy" Jack Deighton, the irrepressible publican, set up his *Globe* saloon at the edge of the mill site — and the seeds of Gastown were sown.

Return to the promenade, turn right, and walk to the Brockton Point Lighthouse, where the views of busy Burrard Inlet, with floatplanes landing and taking off, and of the majestic North Shore mountains, are at their best. Walk around the point; just ahead is a small, cage-like structure that houses the Nine O'Clock Gun, a naval-type, muzzle-loader gun that was set up in 1898 by the Federal Department of Fisheries to warn fishermen of the nightly fishing curfew. Since then Vancouverites — just plain folk and celebrities such as actors Raymond Burr and Michael J. Fox — have set their watches to the city's traditional time signal, which is fired every night at 9 o'clock sharp. Continue along to an outsize boulder near where Johnny Baker, the last British holdout on the peninsula, lived until homesteading was declared illegal. At the turn of the century, the Salvation Army used the clearing, and it earned the nickname Hallelujah Point. To the left is the entrance to Deadman Island, home of the Naval Reserve HMCS *Discovery;* the island is connected to Stanley Park by a causeway. For centuries it was an Indian burial ground; during the smallpox epidemic of 1888 it was turned into a quarantine area. Next along is the exclusive *Royal Vancouver Yacht Club* (which has another site west of here along English Bay). There is a visitors' center kiosk (open during summer months) at the zoo level parking lot near the yacht club. Also here is *AAA Horse Drawn Carriage, Ltd.* (phone: 604-681-5115), offering narrated tram tours of the park (May through September, 11 AM to 4 PM). Just beyond the yacht club marina is the *Vancouver Rowing Club.* Now cross Stanley Park Drive to the Queen Victoria monument; retrace your steps to the bus loop or, if you drove, return to your car.

For those choosing the longer route, turn left (facing the water) at the Variety Club Water Park. (Again, be careful not to stray over the yellow line that separates cyclists from pedestrians.) At low tide you'll find sunbathers and picnickers sitting on huge driftwood logs below the wall, or beachcombers picking through shells and elaborate flotsam. Steep stone steps are carved into the wall at intervals to provide access to the shoreline for those who feel the need to get even closer to the salty spray. On one side are endless expanses of water and views of the North Shore of Vancouver; on the other are ferns clinging to rock face, old trees green with velvety moss, and fir trees climbing as high as the eye can see. There are cutoffs into forest paths, with signs that warn against cycling on environmentally sensitive trails. Here, too, directly ahead as you walk along, is the impressive-looking Lions Gate Bridge, which Canadian trivia buffs know was built by a foreign brewer: the Guinness Brewing Company of Ireland built the mile-long suspension bridge in 1938 to provide access to the family's residential land, British Properties, across the inlet in West Vancouver. The bridge takes its name from the two hovering Lions Mountain peaks. Since 1986 it has been illuminated at night.

Keep your head up, watching for cyclists and sprinters along the straightaway, and stop a while when you come to Prospect Point, the northernmost point of the park, just west of the bridge. (Across the strait at First Narrows to the west of the bridge is West Vancouver, where residents claim the highest per capita income in the country.) It was here at Prospect Point that the SS *Beaver,* the first steamship to ply the north Pacific coast, ran aground on the rocks in 1888. In its glory days with the Hudson's Bay Company, from 1835 to 1874, the brig-rigged paddle wheeler took supplies from the south to northwest outposts and returned with furs to southern markets. A few of the ship's relics are on display at the *Maritime Museum* (south of here at Vanier Park at the entrance to False Creek; see *Museums* in THE CITY).

Walk uphill at Prospect Point to Stanley Park Drive. The totem pole here was carved by the great Squamish leader, Chief Joseph Capilano, the keeper of the legends transcribed in Pauline Johnson's *Legends of Vancouver.* This pole commemorates the meeting of Captain George Vancouver and members of the Squamish tribe in 1792. As members of the Musqueam tribe did the year before when Spanish explorer José Narváez arrived, the Squamish paddled their canoes to the ship in the waters off the wooded peninsula.

Stop here for a breather or a snack at the *Prospect Point* restaurant and café (phone: 604-669-2737). There's a take-out area for hot dogs, ice cream, and other snacks, and a gift shop. The picnic grounds nearby often are the site of a longstanding North American tradition: a family reunion. The Canadian variety is a very organized affair; planned for months in advance, it brings family members together from across the country. On sunny days many reunions will be going on at the same time. Watch for the traditional races — three-legged, egg and spoon, and wheelbarrow. At one time, this site — where, on these occasions, grandfathers and grandmothers are kings and queens for the day — was a water reservoir; when the city's water plant was modernized, it was transformed into picnic grounds.

Now return to the seawall and continue walking a very short distance to Siwash Rock. According to Johnson's *Legends of Vancouver,* Skalsh, a young Squamish brave, was transformed into this rock as a reward for his unselfishness, his spirit to emanate for all time from this imposing spot near shore. From here the view of English Bay, a line of anchored freighters, and Point Grey jutting into the sea is simply spectacular. On the tall cliffs that border the seawall, just beyond Siwash Rock, look for the plaque honoring master stone mason James Cunningham, who worked on the seawall for 32 years; unfortunately, Cunningham would never see the 5-mile (8 km) promenade finished. Begun in 1913 to stop erosion, the seawall wasn't completed until 1983.

As you pick a place to sit among the park benches that line the walk, read the little plaques of dedication: Many are birthday or retirement gifts to seniors, or memorials to honor departed friends, colleagues, or loved ones. The view from here of English Bay and, on a clear day, Vancouver Island, is the most unobstructed of the walk. Farther along the seawall is the best family beach action at Third Beach, the next stop along the promenade. At the beach, take the easy uphill path to a concession stand located at Stanley Park Drive. Carry your coffee and salmon burger back to the beach, or eat it right here at a stone picnic table.

From here, cross the parking lot to Stanley Park Drive and turn left. Walk along the sidewalk for about a quarter of a mile; on the right is the Hollow Tree, which plays an integral part in the city's lore. The tree is actually the tall stump of an 1,100-year-old red cedar. After the First World War, a photographer was allowed to set up his camera and take shots of people visiting the tree. Thousands of photos still exist, showing people, some in their Sunday best, posing in horse-drawn carriages or even in early automobiles. Though reinforced by iron rods, the stump has become too fragile for such carryings-on, but the stump itself still makes for a memorable photograph.

Return to the sidewalk and turn left. Continue along this road (do not turn off to the concession stand) for about another quarter of a mile. As you reach the crossroad, you will be facing the water; on the right is a small clearing. Cross over to view the Pauline Johnson monument, erected in 1922. A poet who devoted herself to immortalizing the Indian people, she is the only person officially interred in Stanley Park. Credited with bringing the rhythmic and picturesque side of Indian life to the Western World, Johnson dressed in buckskins and used her Indian name, Tekahionwake, during her stage career, which included successful tours of New York City and London. The hush in this cathedral-like area, created by the intertwining of arched tree branches and the decades-thick carpet of pine needles, is true to the spirit of the place.

From here go back across the road and follow the path around the *Ferguson Point Teahouse* (phone: 604-669-3281), once a World War II officers' mess. In 1937 the point was turned into a defense station, complete with gun batteries, and when war was declared by the Canadian government 2 years later, it was put into active use (although the guns were never fired in combat). At the end of the war, only the mess remained; today it a pleasant place for some first-rate fare and fine tea (what else?). Across its driveway is a grassy promontory with benches and a view across English Bay of Point Grey, home to the University of British Columbia, one of Canada's leading institutions of higher learning (also see *Walk 5: Point Grey*).

Return to the sidewalk and watch for a sign on the other side of Stanley Park Drive that marks Lees Trail. Cross over to the marker and follow this trail through the forest. Here you will truly experience the woodland park's flora and fauna: centuries-old trees, mossy logs, ferns, salal, huckleberry, and, punctuating the stillness, chittering black squirrels, rabbits, raccoons, and the music of songbirds. The flat, well-kept trail is shaded by cathedral-like arbors. Stop at the intersection that leads to Second Beach, a favorite swimming hole for Vancouverites since 1900. The beach itself is near a miniature-golf course, tennis courts, and a swimming pool; go there if you'd prefer, but for more sights and sounds of a Pacific Coast forest, continue until you arrive again at Stanley Park Drive at Lost Lagoon, a freshwater spot for a variety of birds. Locals keep the birds, squirrels, and raccoons well fed, sometimes to the consternation of park officials, and depending on the time of your visit, you will see a variety of migratory birds, as well as the year-round residents: swans, mallards, and Canada geese.

The fountain here, sometimes illuminated, was erected as part of the 50th-anniversary celebrations held during Vancouver's *Jubilee.* You are now an easy stroll from the park entrance and should be able to see the outstretched arms of Lord Stanley, where the first walking tour of this beautiful seaside city began.

Walk 2: Gastown

The birthplace of Vancouver is said to be at Maple Tree Square, which isn't a square and doesn't have a maple tree. But it was, and it did, in 1886 when the first election notice for the City of Vancouver was nailed to the sturdy trunk of a maple tree. This area had for 20 years been dubbed Gastown in honor of its loquacious first settler, the publican "Gassy" Jack Deighton, the most colorful character in Vancouver history. The tree may be gone, but in the middle of the square is a statue of Gassy Jack, standing atop a barrel, welcoming visitors in the same spirit as when he served his first shots of whiskey back in 1867. Maple Tree Square is at the intersection of Water, Carrall, Powell, and Alexander Streets and is a good place to begin a walk of this historic area. The walk that follows should take about 3 hours. Tours in the summer months (conducted by guides in period costume) can also be arranged through *Gastown Historic Tours*. For dates and hours, call the *Gastown Business Improvement Society* (phone: 604-683-5650).

By the time that election notice was posted, Gastown had grown considerably from the forest it was when Englishman Jack Deighton arrived by canoe with his Indian wife, her mother, her cousin, and all their belongings — the most important being a barrel of whiskey. Legend has it the wily entrepreneur rolled that barrel into Maple Tree Square, near the vicinity of the Hastings sawmill, and offered workers booze in return for help in building his saloon. If there were a record for such things, Deighton's *Globe* would be in the running as the fastest-built saloon ever. (Until then, thirsty workers had to trudge 12 miles/19 km away to New Westminster for a drink.) Within 24 hours, the saloon doors were flung open, marking the settlement that would grow to become downtown Vancouver.

In 1870, Gastown's leading citizen built the *Deighton* hotel, complete with a saloon, billiards room, and a verandah that enjoyed the shade of the big maple tree. In these boom-and-bust days, Gassy Jack was booming; but 5 years later he became ill and died. Meanwhile, the settlement's fortunes grew. The big push came in 1884 when the *Canadian Pacific Railway* announced its plans for a port and terminus development; soon Gastown was awash not just in rumors that the line would extend to this site, but with saloons and hostelries ready to handle the influx of settlers and with food warehouses and retail stores designed to serve the thriving logging industry.

After that first election notice was posted, campaigning began in earnest for the votes of the 2,500 residents, and in true Old West style, it went ahead without a voters' list: Bogus ballots were cast along with legitimate ones; losers denounced winners as crooks and finaglers (but fell short of carrying out death threats); and in May 1886, the first city council of ten aldermen and a mayor took office.

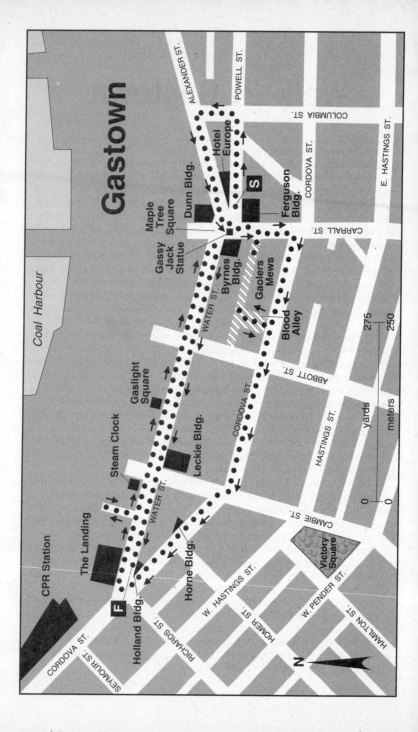

But a month later disaster struck. On Sunday, June 13, fires, ordered by the new council to clear the land, raged out of control; although there were only about 20 human casualties, most of the city's 800 buildings, many in various stages of development, were razed. When the smoke cleared it was back to Maple Tree Square again: Mayor Malcolm McLean had a sign that read "City Hall" tacked to the tree and the council met there under a tent. Despite the loss of life and property, the councillors reasoned that since the clearing work was done, building could begin; on that day bylaws were passed that limited construction in Gastown to structures of stone, brick, or iron. Today these century-old buildings stand as testament to this early pronouncement, and although the maple tree is long gone, it's said that its roots lie buried deep beneath the statue of Gassy Jack.

Directly across from Deighton's statue is one of Vancouver's most interesting edifices: a flatiron building known as the *Europe* hotel (now a subsidized housing facility). The original building on that site, the *Tivoli Saloon,* where a 5¢ beer bought a free lunch, was the first of four hotels to occupy this land. That early wooden structure was destroyed by the Great Fire, but two later buildings, both built by Angelo Colari, an Italian stonecutter, one in 1890 and another in 1895, were later incorporated into the pride of his complex, the *Europe* hotel, which was completed in 1908. This imposing building — the first reinforced concrete structure in the city and the first fireproof hotel in western Canada — added a touch of class to distinguish Vancouver as more than a rowdy logging town. The *Europe*'s autobus service between the hotel and the steamship docks at Columbus Street made it especially popular among sophisticated travelers.

From the statue, notice the hotel's corniced roofline and the pillared point that was once the lobby (now closed off for safety reasons). Stroll over and peer inside the window at the lobby with its exquisite tiling, beveled glass, marble-and-brass stairway, and cast-iron walls. Also look at the glass blocks set in the pavement around the point of the building; they were there to provide light to the basement. The street level of the building houses retail shops; on the Powell Street side is the entrance to a poster shop, once the hotel's dining room. Go inside and browse the pop art as you walk on the original tile flooring.

From here walk east along Powell Street toward Columbia Street. There are several interesting antiques shops along this block. The large building that takes up the rest of this triangular site once housed the *City* hotel. The *Al Forno* restaurant (103 Columbia St.; phone: 604-684-2838), one of the best pizza places in town, occupies the hotel's former billiards room. Internationally known rocker Bryan Adams owns the 3-story red-brick warehouse at the southeast corner of Powell and Columbia Streets and is converting it into a recording studio. Note the small, weathered brick building at the north end of Columbia Street. In Vancouver's early days, this was where people awaited news of loved ones in times of peace and war: the telegraph office.

Turn left onto Alexander Street. Redevelopment has converted the former warehouse row on the north side into condominiums; offices for a food wholesaler were once located on this block as well. The 3-story Dunn Building (at the corner of Water Street) was erected 95 years ago on the site of a boat shed that was used as a first-aid shelter for victims of the Great Fire. Built by former Alderman Thomas Dunn, it was opened with great fanfare, including a grand ball; the next day it began business as a ship chandlery and hardware store that prospered by outfitting men heading north to seek their fortunes during the Klondike Gold Rush of 1897 and 1898. Behind this building is a refurbished dining car that brought some of the first transcontinental passengers to Vancouver; it is now home to *Le Railcar* restaurant (106 Carrall St.; phone: 604-669-5422).

Walk back to the Gassy Jack statue. On the southwest corner of Water and Carrall Streets on the site of the former *Deighton* hotel stands the Byrnes Building, now home to several small boutiques and an ice cream shop. One of the city's first brick structures, it was erected by a Victoria real-estate speculator in 1886, shortly after the fire. The *Alhambra* hotel, which was once located here, was a precursor of the city's modern-day luxury hotels: Every room had a stove or fireplace, hot running water, and fabulous views. Look up at the ornate window pediments, the pilasters on the top floor, and the fancy cornices. If you stand back far enough, you can see the chimneys on the roof, one for each fireplace.

Now walk across Carrall Street. On the southeast corner of Powell Street is the second Ferguson Building. Before the fire, a wood-frame structure built for railway tunnel contractor A.G. Ferguson was the city's first office building; it housed the *CPR* land office and a dry goods and grocery store. The building was destroyed in the fire and Ferguson built this replacement. From the edge of the square you can see its stilted arch windows and the bracketed cornice that tops the structure. Farther south on Carrall Street is the building that claims the city record as having the longest continuous hotel on one site. In 1888, this Italian Renaissance Revival–style building (now the *Spinning Wheel* hotel) was the first brick hotel in Vancouver, although its design was much like its wooden predecessor, the *Tremont* hotel, noted for its metropolitan-style bar. During the gold rush, it operated as the *Klondyke* hotel.

Cross Carrall Street to an alley that leads into a little brick annex known as Gaolers Mews. The site of the city's first lockup, it has a realistic replica of the tiny, barred jail on the right. In 1871, Burrard Inlet residents began to feel some concern for keeping law and order in the growing settlement and asked the newly proclaimed provincial government in Victoria for help. The request stirred little interest at the time (Granville was no more than an unruly logging outpost), but finally Jonathan Miller, a local merchant, was appointed chief constable, and a cottage for his use and a jail were built near what is now the Water Street entrance to the Mews. Here, between two saloons, stood the little jail, with two cells that had no locks. Indeed, for that first election (just prior to the Great Fire), the dining room in Miller's cottage served as the only polling station. Today, looking upon this up-to-date mews (built in 1972), home to designers, architects, boutiques, and delis, it's hard to imagine such humble beginnings.

Now backtrack to Carrall Street and continue south toward Cordova Street. The building on the right (which has kept its name but now houses artists' studios) was the site of the *Bodega* saloon. It, too, started out as a wooden structure, was destroyed in the fire, and was rebuilt in 1887. City Hall movers and shakers hatched more than a few early decisions over a pint or two here. The building with the stone façade adjoining the *Bodega* once housed the *Boulder* saloon (1889); a notorious watering hole in Klondike days, it has housed banks and hotels through the years and is now the *Meatmarket* restaurant (1 W. Cordova; phone: 604-685-1122). Its plain rectangular windows, set into an unornamented masonry wall, were unusual in this area. The third floor of the building was erected about 1909; it blends so well that to the naked eye it is hard to detect that it was a late addition.

In post-fire Vancouver, the corner at Carrall and Cordova Streets became one of the city's main intersections; from here for 2 blocks west to Cambie Street, Cordova was the main shopping district, until business and society shifted to *CPR*-promoted Hastings Street (see *Walk 3: Historic Hastings*). Now turn the corner on to Cordova Street. Before the fire, this street on the outer limits of Gastown was no more than thick forest and pungent swamp, but in the late 1880s buildings started going up, and streets of 3-foot-wide wood planks were laid over the muddy ground. In 1890 it was traveled by Vancouver's first streetcar, and 7 years later it was the busiest street in town, filled with gold-seekers stopping for supplies en route to the Klondike.

The site of the present *Army and Navy* discount store (on the south side of Cordova St.) was once considered the finest commercial building in the city. The Italian Renaissance–style structure was built in 1889 by Alderman Dunn and Constable Miller. Go to the north side of the street for the best view of the terraced building, which is reminiscent of Georgian England. Its upper stories were once home to the city's first library — known at the time as a subscription reading room — the former *Knights of Pythias* service group, and to the city's first synagogue. The *Vancouver Electric Railway and Light Company,* proprietors of the popular new streetcar of 1890, were here, too. During the gold rush, A.H. Lonsdale purchased the building and renamed it for himself; in the mid-1970s the *Army and Navy* store restored its façade.

Continue walking on the north side of the street; three doors past the *Meatmarket,* turn right through a passageway. On this site once was the funeral parlor of Frank Hart, the city's first undertaker, best known for donating coffins and burial services for victims of the Great Fire. In 1907, the *Stanley* hotel was erected on his old premises, and in 1971 this brick passageway was constructed leading to the shops of Gaolers Mews and Blood Alley (the nickname for Trounce Alley) Square. Turn right, and as you walk through this area note the brick façades, greenery, and back doors of downtown businesses. Legend has it that in old-time Vancouver, fistfights in this alley were commonplace (thus the nickname); there were many saloons at street level, and brothels on the upper floors, where, from time to time, bodies would be thrown from open windows to the street below. This area was also the site of more civilized concerns: horse stables, a blacksmith shop, a Chinese laundry, and a bathhouse boasting fresh- or saltwater baths.

Return to Cordova Street. In recent years, this onetime retail district, which had grown shabby and rundown, has undergone a revival, with several shops and galleries moving in. From here look over to the building on the southwest corner of Cordova and Abbott Streets to a point high atop its roof. The huge red neon "W" marks *Woodward's* department store (101 W. Hastings; entrance off Cordova; phone: 604-684-5231). The "W" was first placed atop an Eiffel Tower–style structure on the roof as a promotional gimmick in the 1920s, and it quickly became a familiar, well-loved landmark. The first store was built in 1891 at what is now Main and Georgia Streets by Charles Woodward; the chain now has stores throughout western Canada. For his second store, Woodward bought swampland at Hastings and Abbott Streets; the city installed drains, and a 4-story department store was erected in 1902. An addition that spread along the rest of the block down Hastings Street to Cordova Street was completed in the 1920s. Once the flagship of the ever-growing chain, this store is today a warehouse outlet for factory-direct specialty shops.

Cross Abbott Street and continue to the corner of Cambie Street. The modernistic CP Telecommunications Building, built in 1968, will give you an idea of what Gastown might have become if preservationists had not resisted change. Erected as the first stage of a Gastown redevelopment scheme, the building instead stirred interest in the preservation of the area's heritage properties. Indeed, critics helped call a halt to further plans for modernization and the redevelopment project was scrapped. And instead of bulldozing the area and building high-rises and office towers, plans for the restoration and renovation of this down-at-the-heels area began in earnest.

Cross Cambie Street; on the corner where Cordova Street angles toward the waterfront is another flatiron building, the former Masonic Temple. Masons were very active in frontier inlet communities (Gassy Jack was a Mason; he is buried in the Masonic Cemetery at New Westminster), and the 1888 building was an important meeting place of the day. The small storefronts, with their arched windows, recessed doors, and cast-iron pillars, make this an especially popular turn-of-the-century backdrop for filmmakers. Today a mix of trendy shops, ranging from the very upscale *Peter Fox* shoe store (303 W. Cordova St.; phone: 604-662-3040) to several antiques and collectibles outlets, do business here.

Follow along the north side of Cordova Street to just about where Richards Street ends and stop before one of the most elegant-looking structures in Gastown, the Victorian Italianate building, with its carved wood pilasters and Juliet balcony, which once sported a dome on its top. Known as the Horne Building, it was built by James Horne, a well-heeled Winnipeg real-estate magnate who moved to Granville in 1885 and soon was the largest holder of real estate in the city. As a politician, Horne served as chairman of the parks board and helped finance the Stanley Park Zoo. Next door is the flatiron-style Holland Building, another structure built to take advantage of a triangular lot. The San Francisco–style bay windows along its Cordova Street side were designed to increase light on the two upper levels. (Because of the post-fire bylaws, the windows were not allowed to project more than 3 feet over the street.) The street-level entrances and windows are framed by cast-iron pillars.

If hunger strikes about now, you'll find plenty of eating places from which to choose by crossing Water Street and entering *The Landing* retail complex on the north corner. Originally the warehouse for the Kelly Douglas food wholesaling business — which opened in 1896 and prospered during the gold rush — this place houses some of Vancouver's most upscale boutiques as well as several food outlets, and some of the best views of the industrial waterfront, the largest Pacific port in all the Americas. From the floor-to-ceiling windows opposite the entrance (at the newsstand), and from windows in *Pastel's* cafeteria (375 Water St.; phone: 604-684-0176) to your right, you'll see rows of rail cars on sidetracks, a busy truck route and, beyond, the harbor with freighters waiting to load and unload cargo. Every year, the *CP Rail* terminal moves between 60 to 70 million metric tons of coal, grain, sulfur, potash, lumber, and other commodities. Beyond the wharves, look for the tugboats and sailboats, the floatplanes and helicopters. You may want to end your tour here over a cup of coffee and a snack, enjoying the view. (Maple Tree Square is only a short stroll east of here.)

For a tour along what once were the working wharves of old Vancouver go back out on Water Street and walk east. The next building was once a warehouse of W.H. Malkin, a grocery wholesaler who in time would have three properties on Water Street. Many of these warehouses were built on pilings, because the inlet lapped right up to the edges of the street during high tide. Next along the route is the Greenshields Building, erected in 1909 for a wholesale dry-goods merchant. Stand back and look up at the thin vertical openings above the arched windows and at the carved faces that represent Vancouver's early ethnic mix. Then sidetrack down the lane here toward the railway tracks. At the foot of the lane look down the roadway at the backs of these warehouse buildings and see how close they were built to the tracks. Imagine, too, the waters from the inlet flowing beneath them when they were still on pilings.

Now return to the street and walk east. The next building, Hudson House, a brick structure with stone trim, was built in 1897 as a warehouse for the Hudson's Bay Company and now has been renovated as office and retail space. For several years it was considered the tallest building in the city. Look up to the twin pointed parapets atop the façade. Next door, W.T. Dalton, the architect who built this warehouse, was influenced by the US architect Henry Hobson Richardson, whose round-arched variation on the Romanesque theme spread north from Seattle at the turn of the century and is seen on several Gastown buildings.

At the corner join the cluster of people, stake out a good spot, and wait. The first steam-powered clock in the world, the Gastown Steam Clock, is probably the most photographed object in the city. People gather here and wait, because every 15 minutes the Westminster chimes play and, on the hour, the steam whistle sounds. The mechanically minded usually pay a visit to the clock's builder Ray Saunders, who runs the nearby *Gastown Steam Clock Company* (123 Cambie St.; phone: 604-669-3525), with its interesting collection of old timepieces.

Cambie Street itself was one of the first streets cleared in Granville (Gastown) and was the first skid road for logs that were sent sliding down the sloping road into the inlet. On Water Street, a half block east of Cambie Street, at the site where Malkin built his first warehouse, is Gaslight Square, to the left. Continue east along Water Street to the northwest corner of Abbott and Water Streets; a structure built in 1905 for the Canadian Fairbanks Company, a machinery and outfitters' wholesaler, it has been nicely renovated and now houses the *Vancouver Rug Company*. Around 1873, this site was the center of early Vancouver's religious life. On the corner was the Methodist parsonage of missionary-pastor Reverend James Turner, who vowed to bring God to the Indians and to serve the fledgling Methodist congregation of Scottish loggers and wharf workers; 3 years later the Methodist church itself was built here.

Cross Abbott Street; continue on Water Street to the *Old Spaghetti Factory* restaurant (No. 53; phone: 604-684-1288), one of the first Gastown renovations. Built in 1907 and added to in 1911, its wood posts with their cast-iron accents and timber beams are visible from the ground floor. Continue walking east; on the northwest corner of Water and Carrall Streets is the *Packing House,* a center of offices and shops in the renovated Swift meat-packing building. In 1871, George Black built the first abattoir and butcher's shop here, right across Water Street from Gassy Jack's place. It projected out over the water on pilings, and cattle were slaughtered on the back platform. (Undoubtedly, it was not a pretty sight for patrons of the *Sunny Side* hotel, an impressive property with a 600-foot-long wharf, which went up next door in 1873.) Thirteen years later, during the Great Fire, a *CPR* land agent dashed over to the *Sunny Side* with the office cash and stashed it in the hotel safe. Luck was on the agent's side that day, because when the burned building collapsed, the safe fell into the water and its contents were later retrieved, soggy but intact. All other safes and their contents in Vancouver that day were destroyed.

Cross Water Street, past Gassy Jack's statue, and pick up an ice cream cone at *Miriam's* (2 Water St.; phone: 604-685-9985) to enjoy as you continue your walk. This time you will be going west, walking on the south side of Water Street. As you go, try to imagine that in early days the shoreline ran right up as far as this sidewalk and that on the next block, between Abbott and Cambie Streets, the shore was just slightly north of the street. In its early days, Gastown was roughly bordered by Carrall, Abbott, Water, and Cordova Streets.

On Water Street, in historic buildings that now house shops and offices, was the site where Gassy Jack's neighbor, Ebenezer Brown, ran a saloon (at No. 28). The *Granville* (1874) was the first in a row of no-nonsense hostelries and restaurants, a popular breakfast stop for loggers, who started with oysters and ended, several courses later, with pie. After the fire it was rebuilt in Victorian Italianate style, and if you stand back and look at the upper floors, you will see that the window arches are of different shapes and colors. The *Terminus* hotel (1886), which was located next door, featured San Francisco bay windows. Its name honored the fact that Vancouver was chosen as the endpoint of the national railway. Billy Blair, the hotel's owner, also operated Blair Hall behind the hotel; a popular spot for social gatherings, dances, and meetings, it was here in 1885 that Father Fay celebrated the first mass in Gastown, 4 years before becoming parish priest of the first Holy Rosary Church (now a cathedral) at Richards and Dunsmuir Streets (see *Special Places* in THE CITY).

The building that houses the *Town Pump* restaurant (66 Water St.; phone: 604-683-6695) is on a site with a long and fabled history. A widow, Mrs. Sullivan, managed the first restaurant on this spot after her husband, a saw-mill cook, died. A staunch Methodist, the widow provided space in her kitchen for the first services of Reverend James Turner, whose parsonage was later built across the street. Later, with her son Arthur, a popular musician, she parlayed her hospitality talents into managing the *Gold House,* one of the most prestigious hotels of the day.

Next door to Mrs. Sullivan's, at the corner of Water and Abbott Streets, was the *Hole in the Wall* saloon (now the *Lamplighter;* 210 Abbott St.; phone: 604-681-6666), which opened in 1868, just a year after Gassy Jack set up his establishment. Its proprietor was Joseph Simmons, whose Indian wife, Sylvia, gave birth to Gastown's first baby. Today's owners poke fun at the past by having named their pub after John Clough, the town's lamplighter and a regular of the saloon, who was often here "getting lit" instead of lighting lamps.

Cross Abbott Street and continue west along Water Street to the parking complex. A major hotel and a saloon were among the buildings torn down to make room for this structure. The 3-story *Carter* hotel and saloon was one of the settlement's largest buildings. Next door was the *Stag and Pheasant* saloon, the first establishment to yield to pressure from the Women's Christian Temperance Union and put up a lighted beacon in front of its door. The WCTV's idea was to let people know that this was a notorious place; instead the lamp merely served as a streetlight — and free advertising (especially after the owners came up with the idea of painting their logo on its frosted glass).

Continue west along Water Street; at the next corner (there's an entrance on Cambie Street) is the Leckie Building, Gastown's most recent multimillion-dollar restoration. Erected in 1908 as a warehouse and factory, it housed the Leckie Shoe Company, a well-known firm in Canada. A major supplier of boots for the Canadian Army in both World Wars, its "cork" boots were popular with loggers; school boys all wanted to wear the thick-soled ankle boots with cleats called "Leckies." The factory closed in 1950 and the building housed many small businesses until its renovation last year. Sandblasting restored the brickwork to its original hue, and other exterior features, such as the neo-classical windows, have been refurbished. Go inside to see such heritage features as Douglas fir beams and posts and exposed brickwork.

Across Cambie Street, on the corner, is the site of the only building to survive the Great Fire — now a refurbished complex of shops and offices, with the *Water Street Café* (300 Water St.; phone: 604-689-2832) on the ground floor. The *Regina* hotel was being constructed on this site when the flames reached it; construction workers formed a bucket brigade on the roof and lined the walls with wet blankets — and saved the building. But in 1906, it was torn down and replaced by the iron-and-steel-framed *Edward* hotel.

The cast-iron columns and decorated steel beams can still be seen in the restaurant. Farther along this block is another Romanesque–style building, erected in 1899, the work of Seattle architect Henry Hobson Richardson. The stonework seems deliberately chiseled to give it an unpolished look. Next door is *Le Magasin* (No. 332), a collection of small shops and eateries. Have a look at the faces on the building's frieze: They represent the movers and shakers of the 1960s and 1970s who prompted the Gastown revitalization.

Across the street is *The Landing* retail development and the end of the Gastown walk. And to the west, at the edge of Gastown, is the beautifully restored *CPR* Terminal (see *Walk 4: Canada Place*).

Walk 3: Historic Hastings

From the moment you catch sight of the Marine Building — with its impressive wedding-cake tower, it was the city's first skyscraper — you'll get the picture of what this walk is all about. The Marine Building is the touch of class of which the early founders of Vancouver's prestigious Hastings district would be proud. Gastown could have its Blood Alley; Hastings would have Blueblood Alley.

The walk through historic Hastings that starts and ends here at the foot of the Marine Building, on the corner of Burrard and Hastings Streets, should take about 3 hours. Parts of this section of town are in the midst of renovation and are a bit shabby, so it is best to tour during business hours. Ironically, Hastings was the choice of barons and businessmen in Vancouver's early days, but Gastown has been the district of choice in this era of gentrification. Happily, renovations are now restoring much of Hastings Street's past glory.

Proclaimed by the railway barons after the Great Fire as a place of distinction, a sanctuary removed from the rogues and ruffians of Gastown, Hastings Street soon became *the* place to build in the new city of Vancouver. Shortly after the fire, the *Canadian Pacific Railway* paved Hastings Street (once the trail to the Hastings sawmill) and Pender Street, 1 block farther south, and moved its land office from Gastown to the corner of Hastings and Richards Streets. It actively promoted that section of Hastings Street (nicknamed Blueblood Alley) west of Granville Street as an exclusive residential neighborhood, and *CPR* executives set the pace by erecting stately mansions and forming such private domains as the *Vancouver Club* and the *Terminal Club* in its enclave. The Bank of British Columbia's decision to move to West Hastings Street 3 years after the fire influenced other banks and businesses to do the same; within a decade Hastings Street had become the city's financial district.

Although the Marine Building, built in 1929, postdates these developments, its grandeur is certainly in their spirit. Stand back to the edge of the sidewalk to get the full impact of the design of this structure, which, according to Gregory Edwards, author of the book *Hidden Cities,* is one of the world's great masterpieces of Art Deco style. Its builders, the Vancouver architectural firm of McCarter and Nairne, included a 40-foot arch in bas-relief terra cotta that illustrates the story of sail on one side and of steam on the other. The magnificent entrance is topped by friezes of stylized bronze Canada geese flying in formation against the rays of the setting sun; here, too, intricate brass castings of lobsters, crabs, and starfish mingle in a forest of seaweed, prompt-

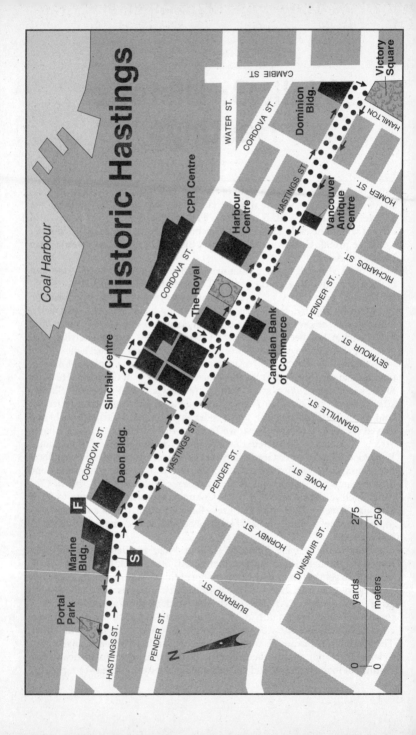

Historic Hastings

Coal Harbour

CPR Centre

Harbour Centre

The Royal

Sinclair Centre

Canadian Bank of Commerce

Daon Bldg.

Marine Bldg.

Portal Park

Dominion Bldg.

Vancouver Antique Centre

Victory Square

WATER ST.

CORDOVA ST.

CORDOVA ST.

CORDOVA ST.

CORDOVA ST.

HASTINGS ST.

HASTINGS ST.

HASTINGS ST.

HASTINGS ST.

PENDER ST.

PENDER ST.

PENDER ST.

PENDER ST.

CAMBIE ST.

HAMILTON

HOMER ST.

RICHARDS ST.

SEYMOUR ST.

GRANVILLE ST.

HOWE ST.

HORNBY ST.

BURRARD ST.

DUNSMUIR ST.

F

S

N

yards   0   275
meters   0   250

ing McCarter and Nairne to say that the building represented "some giant crag rising from the sea, clinging with sea flora and fauna, tinted in sea green and touched by gold." Take the time to examine the work to discover etchings representing all kinds of small marine life.

The Marine Building escaped the wrecker's ball in the 1970s and is now protected as a heritage building by City Hall — the one property in town that locals would man the barricades to defend. But it wasn't always this way. For years, the wedding-cake tower was referred to as Vancouver's Folly, and for close to a decade after it opened with great fanfare in 1931 it stood almost empty, a victim of the Depression. For a short time in 1933 it was the property of the Guinness family of Ireland, who bought the building for $900,000; an elevator was added to connect the 18th floor to a lavish penthouse suite with majestic views of Burrard Inlet, the North Shore mountains, and the sea beyond. The suite was built for the managing director, but when the director's wife found she had an aversion to heights, they moved out.

Enter the lobby. Unfortunately, only the exterior of the building is designated historic, so some changes have been made here, but the huge stained glass window remains. (Not surprisingly, John Gread, one of the designers, moved on to Hollywood to become a set designer.) On the east wall, showing the kitschy opulence of the era, is a clock whose "numbers" are denizens of the deep, and the floor is inlaid with the 12 signs of the zodiac. The elevators are still magnificent; in their heyday they were the fastest in town, gliding at a speed of 750 feet a minute when the average was 150. Take special note of the cast bronze doors with their design of sea flora. Above them, lobby lights are set in small plaster ships, and beyond the bronze doors, the elevator walls are inlaid with 12 kinds of hardwood. A small alcove features photographs and clippings that illustrate the building's history from groundbreaking to opening.

Walk through the lobby to an adjacent area where, on the mezzanine level in the former Grain Exchange, you'll find the *Imperial* (355 Burrard St.; phone: 604-688-8191), one of the city's best Chinese seafood restaurants. Take a peek at the splendid, finely detailed, carved-jade Chinese junk housed in a glass case at the top of a short flight of marble stairs. Now might be a good time to reserve a table for some of the best dim sum in town; you'll probably be hungry at the conclusion of this walk, which ends here. There is an eclectic gift shop — *Tangram Design* (phone: 604-669-6789) — on the main level, and two coffee shops.

Leave by the Burrard Street entrance of the Marine Building, turn right, then go around the corner on to the West Hastings side of the building; just above eye-level is a terra cotta strip that portrays transportation forms of the past: biplanes, dreadnoughts, steamships, and zeppelins. The drawings were made here, but US craftsmen with the Seattle firm of Glading and McBain did the carvings.

Continue walking west along Hastings Street for about a half block, past the Guinness Tower, to a little urban gem: Portal Park. This city oasis, built atop the entrance to an old *CPR* tunnel, has four portals, small arched columns set with stained glass, and a large glass dome above a relief map showing Vancouver's relationship to other Pacific Rim cities. A plaque calls this point "Vancouver's Gateway to the Pacific"; we call it a great place to relax and enjoy the view. The 1,000-square-foot triangular park has flower-filled cement planters, squares of grass, and curved stone benches that overlook the busy harbor.

Now go back to the corner of Burrard and Hastings Streets and cross Burrard, keeping in mind (always, if you know what's good for you) that in Canada "Don't Walk" signals are to be taken literally. This is the heart of the city, so be aware, too, of cycling couriers who wheel and weave through traffic on their appointed rounds. Get your bearings on the northeast corner from the large mosaic of a compass (embedded in the sidewalk) registering true north before crossing the small plaza to the 19-story Daon Building on Hastings Street. Built in 1980, it's an outstanding example of modern West Coast architecture; the distinctive golden hue of its glass façade is created by the addition of real gold to the glass. If you happen to time your visit around noon and it's a sunny day, the building will pick up a remarkably clear reflection of the Marine Building that emphasizes the contrast in their designs. Go into the lobby for a close look at the tapestry hanging here. This Vancouver cityscape, designed by local resident Joanne Staniskis, was used as a backdrop for Queen Elizabeth's state dinner, held at the *Westin Bayshore* in 1983.

Continue walking east along Hastings Street and you'll begin to appreciate the essence of Blueblood Alley. At No. 915 stands a proud — some might say pompous — survivor: the *Vancouver Club,* a private men's organization. Others like it may have changed their ways, but not this old warhorse. Built in the Georgian Revival–style, the club has been the exclusive preserve of Vancouver's male high society since it opened back in 1889. A few hundred yards away stands another exclusive men's club, the *Terminal Club,* in the stone-arched modern brick building at the foot of Hornby Street, on the site of the original. Glance through street-level windows (or stop in and shop) at *Chong's* (No. 409; 683-6012), an Oriental home furnishings store that offers a wide assortment of traditional Chinese vases.

Continue east to the corner at Howe Street, and near the building's free-standing office directory, note a huge chunk of granite on the sidewalk. Part of the first masonry wall erected in Vancouver, it surrounded the residence of H. B. Abbott, the first superintendent of the western division of the *CPR* and an early resident of Blueblood Alley.

Cross Howe Street for a look at one of Canada's most interesting and unique restorations. Taking up a full city block, *Sinclair Centre,* an amalgamation of four historic buildings united by a glass atrium, is a mini–walking tour of its own. Beginning at Hastings and Howe Streets, from west to east on Hastings, the first segment was once the R. V. Winch Building. Built in 1908 with a steel frame and reinforced-concrete floors for the former cowboy and railroad worker (Winch later made a fortune in salmon canning and real estate), it was the first commercial building west of Granville Street. For the best look at the exterior of *Sinclair Centre*'s second building, walk downhill on Howe Street, past the west entrance, to what was once a brick warehouse of the Department of Canada Customs. Built in 1913, its location across Cordova Street from the *CPR* station and docks made it handy for processing federal customs forms; it was converted to office space in 1958. Turn right onto Cordova Street and go east, past another entrance to the center, to the third structure, the Federal Building. Built in 1937 as an expansion of the post office, it is one of the city's few remaining examples of Art Deco design.

Turn onto Granville Street and climb the hill. From here you'll see the most attractive of the quartet, which was, from 1910 to 1958, Vancouver's main post office, an Edwardian baroque structure, complete with a clock tower. Papers of the day called it "a palatial monument of chiseled stone," and that stone, both outside and inside, has been carefully restored. Ten years ago *Sinclair Centre* was dedicated to the late Honorable James Sinclair of Vancouver, a longtime member of Parliament and federal fisheries minister, who is perhaps better known as the father of a bride — in 1971 his daughter Margaret married Pierre Trudeau, then the Prime Minister of Canada. Turn onto Hastings Street and enter *Sinclair Centre* through the main doors. Here is an alcove of archival pictures and informative plaques and beyond is the bright, airy, exclusive mall and atrium. Some of the city's chicest shops are located here, among them *Leone's* (No. 757; phone: 604-683-1133), featuring designer fashions by such well-known names as Gianni Versace and Giorgio Armani, and *Plaza Escada* (No. 757; phone: 604-688-8558), carrying European designer wear for men and women. On both levels, have a close look at how the granite and limestone façades have been turned into interior walls. The elegant friezes and hand-carved newels uncovered during the refurbishing of the now-restored *Sinclair Centre* add a touch of elegance. Go down the wide stone steps, with their ornate green, wrought-iron trim, to the food court, an area encircled by a variety of small shops. This is a good place to stop for a snack; at certain hours a piano player adds music to the air; at *Christmastime,* costumed carolers entertain shoppers and office workers.

Take the Hastings Street exit. As you cross Granville Street note the tall arched windows along the side of the corner structure, one of the most magnificent bank buildings in the city: the Royal. Do some moneychanging here and then take a short stroll around (browsers are not discouraged). Enter through the huge, arched doorway that leads to the Romanesque main banking hall. The outsize mirror at the far end that reflects the tall columned arches replaced a window that once overlooked the mountains (were it not for the building of an adjacent parking garage, that view would be here today). If you get the feeling you're in an Italian palazzo, it's not surprising. The high ceiling was designed and built by Italian artisans; brass chandeliers in the center area weigh 2,000 pounds each, while those on the sides are a hefty 1,200 pounds. When improvements were carried out in the 1980s, it was impossible to create a single template to help with the repainting of the ceiling because each piece of the original artwork was done freehand. The walls of both the main and lower banking halls are of variegated Indiana limestone; the floors are of travertine marble from Italy, as are the counters on the main floor. Go down the marble staircase to the lower banking hall to see the Belgian black-and-gold marble counters. The bank's original ornate brass doors are on display, one at the foot of each section of the staircase. Construction began in 1929 and the bank opened in 1931 as the main Vancouver branch of the Royal Bank of Canada — which it was until 20 years ago, when regional headquarters moved to Georgia and Burrard Streets.

At the corner of Seymour and Hastings Street is the Price Waterhouse complex of modern curved lines, including a circular space with blue benches and lots of greenery beneath a high glass dome. There's a muffin shop alongside this space, so you can get coffee and relax for a bit.

Cross Seymour Street to *Harbour Centre,* one of the city's best vantage points. Originally the site of the Molson Bank, and then of *Spencer's* department store — which became *Eaton's* in 1948 — its current life began in the mid-1970s when *Eaton's* moved its flagship store to Georgia and Granville Streets. The building underwent extensive renovations and attracted shops and galleries, a 400-seat international food fair on the lower level, and even the downtown campus of Simon Fraser University. But it's perhaps best known for *The Lookout!,* its observation deck perched like a flying saucer on top of the block-long complex. Take one of the two glass elevators to the 553-foot level for this view (admission charge) or, if you'd rather, try the revolving restaurant, *The Top of Vancouver* (No. 555; phone: 604-669-2220), 1 floor above, that completes a 360° turn every 90 minutes. The panoramic view is from the highest point in town. Also at the top, a 12-minute multi-image presentation, "Once In A World, Vancouver," tells the story of the city, and plaques will help you identify the sites: Gastown and Chinatown, and on a clear day, Washington State's Mt. Baker. From here you will see that the Marine Building (toward the west) is just as impressive from this height, as is the Dominion Building (on the east side; you'll see it up close a little later). Helicopters and floatplanes, which have proliferated in the port area along with the Vancouver-to-Alaska cruise business, soar into view all day long.

Back down to earth, cross Richards Street. A vintage 1930's neon sign will alert you to *Millar and Coe* (No. 419; phone: 604-685-3322), one of the city's most noted china shops. Since 1912, the shop has carried name china and crystal at discount prices.

Continue until you cross Homer Street and walk another block to the ornate heritage building at Cambie Street. The Dominion Building (on the corner) has been cleaned and refurbished and looks much as it must have when it was considered the jewel in the crown of the Hastings Street financial district. In 1889, the lot sold for $1,500 and in 1906, when the Dominion Trust Company wanted to erect this 13-story skyscraper, it paid $15,000 to build it, then promoted it as the tallest office building in the British Empire and the most modern in Canada. The original main floor mezzanine and high ceilings have been altered, but much of the building's ornate marble tile and woodwork is still in place. The financial collapse of the Dominion Trust in 1914 sent shock waves along Hastings Street and spelled the end, for some years, of frenzied real-estate speculation. However, the building, with its rose-colored marble pillars flanking the entranceway, continues to be known as the Dominion and remains one of Vancouver's legendary landmarks, a favorite backdrop for Hollywood filmmakers and television producers. With no interior well for daylight, all the offices face outside, a standard design feature of turn-of-the-century architecture.

Cross Hastings Street to the almost triangular Victory Square, where Vancouverites commemorate the war dead on *Remembrance Day* (November 11). This was Court House Square from 1888 until 1906, when the law courts moved to Georgia Street (to a building that now houses the *Vancouver Art Gallery*). Decades ago, the *Province* newspaper raised funds to renovate this once desolate square and it was turned into a pleasant city park complete with flowers, trees, and benches, and, on the south side of the square, a cast-aluminum sculpture by city artist Gerhard Class.

Exit the square at Hastings and Hamilton Streets; on the building on the southwest corner note a plaque on the wall that commemorates the spot "in the silent solitude of primeval forest" where Lachlan Hamilton began surveying the city's streets in 1885; he named the first one for himself. Continue back west on Hastings Street to Homer Street and on the corner look for the city's first temple-style bank building. Built in 1903, it was the local head office of the Royal Bank of Canada until 1931, when headquarters moved to the splendid building you walked through earlier. Now closed, its fate is being decided — as are others in this area — by developers and heritage committees.

Continue west to Richards Street, the next corner, and home of the *Vancouver Antique Centre* (422 Richards St.; phone: 604-682-3573), a 3-story building that was erected in 1889 as the Bank of British Columbia. This place has had many lives through the years and the only relics of its previous existence are the wide-plank stairs and a few brick arches; today it houses 15 shops crammed with collectibles. For a one-of-a-kind browse of Victorian scientific instruments and early cameras try *Winchester Antiques* (same phone as above).

Cross Richards Street. The Standard Building, an award-winning renovated edifice, is the site where the *CPR* established its land sale offices and began the vigorous promotion of Hastings Street. When the present 15-story building, with its neo-classical façade, was completed in 1915 it was one of the tallest structures in Vancouver. The lobby is a prime example of florid, overdecorated Edwardian exuberance; a display of vintage photographs illustrates the building's construction. Original plans called for it to be crowned with Gothic cresting similar to that of the Woolworth Building in New York City, but the onset of the 1913 Depression squelched that idea. The rebuilt main floor extends the lobby into an adjacent Venetian-style cappuccino bar, a good stop for a pick-me-up. Today the building houses a mix of office and retail space. At street level, the *Pen Shop* (No. 512; phone: 604-681-1612) claims the largest pen selection in the Canadian west; a quick look around seems to confirm its claim.

Next door is the Innes Thomas Building, built in 1889 for F. C. Innes and Company, one of the city's first established realtors. This charming little office building, with its Romanesque arches, was designed by Charles Osborne Wickenden, the architect of Christ Church Cathedral (see *Special Places* in

THE CITY); its neighbor, the now vacant Toronto Dominion Bank building, is also worth a peek. The site of the first Bank of British Columbia, which spurred the buildup of the Hastings financial district, the current structure is of second Renaissance style and was finished in 1920.

Walk west to the corner, cross Seymour Street, and halfway up the block is the Canadian Bank of Commerce. Built between 1906 and 1908, it was designed to inspire confidence by resembling an ancient Roman temple. Now cross Granville Street again and continue toward Howe Street; halfway up the block is the *Jolly Taxpayer Pub* (No. 828; phone: 604-681-3574), complete with darts, Guinness stout, and inexpensive British pub-style lunches. If your heart isn't set on dim sum at the *Imperial,* this is a convivial place to end the walk.

For those heading on, a few doors farther west is the BC and Yukon Chamber of Mines office, with its wide sampling of regional ores just inside the door. Next door is the cute-as-a-button, red-brick Ceperly Rounsefell Building, erected in 1921 by Sharp and Thompson, the architects who designed the slightly grander *Vancouver Club* across the street. The Georgian Revival–style building housed the offices of a pair of real-estate developers. One partner, Alexander Ross, first came up with plans to create Stanley Park; the other partner, Henry Trace Ceperley, is remembered for his donation of a children's play area at the park, and other philanthropies. Dwarfing this lovely 2-story structure is the Credit Foncier next door, considered to be one of the most distinctive buildings in Vancouver. It was built in 1914 for a Montreal-based mortgage company in Roman palazzo–style, complete with 36 Corinthian columns; the building is currently undergoing heritage renovation.

Cross Hornby Street and walk west to Burrard Street. Here are superb views of the Marine Building's ornate façade from the small plaza beside the Canadian Imperial Bank of Commerce Tower. To make your way back to this Art Deco landmark, cross Hastings Street, then Burrard Street. Go to the mezzanine level of the building and enjoy your dim sum treats at the *Imperial,* with its tall-windowed view of the harbor, or top off your walk with a cappuccino and croissant at the street level *L'Express* (phone: 604-662-7041).

Walk 4: Canada Place

To discover why so many well-to-do Asian immigrants are choosing this place as home, stand for a moment at this modern wharf development along Burrard Inlet. To the right is Vancouver harbor, the largest Pacific port in all the Americas; to the left, the straits of the Pacific Ocean and, farther south, the mighty Fraser River. The Chinese are drawn to Vancouver because it is a "Good Luck" city, says Joseph Ip, a leading businessman in the city.

From Canada Place, the trade and convention center whose series of scalloped roofs are meant to evoke the five sails of a clipper ship, the future of Vancouver is best realized. Even during the recession of 1991 and early 1992, this "good luck" waterfront has attracted investment interest: The omnipresent *Canadian Pacific Railway* intends to develop its 82-acre Coal Harbour railyard east of Stanley Park into residential units and more than 2 million square feet of commercial space; and Hong Kong billionaire Li Ka Shing and his associates plan to turn the former *Expo '86* site, along the north shore of False Creek, into 12.2 million square feet of residential and commercial space. In no small measure Canada Place has helped chart that course; like the *Sydney Opera House* in Australia, it has been a potent symbol of change. From here begins a waterfront promenade from which the future complements the past like few other walks of its kind. This walk, including a trip aboard the *SeaBus,* will take about 2½ leisurely hours.

The earliest inhabitants of this area, the Coast Salish Indians, relied on the bounty of the sea for their livelihood, building their homes and places of worship along the junction of these two bodies of water. Their early maps show directions using waterways only; they felt no need to penetrate the heavily forested land beyond. And when the British settlers came, they realized the commercial value of the sea: Long before the railway was built in the late 1880s, thousands of board feet of Douglas Fir cut at Hastings sawmill went to European markets aboard the immensely profitable ships of the empire.

Begin the walk a bit to the east of the landmark sails at Canada Place Way at the foot of Howe Street. Before climbing the steps to the promenade, stop at the information kiosk for a brochure. Not far from here, on May 2, 1986, the Prince and Princess of Wales, Charles and Diana, cut the ribbons when the complex opened as the Canadian Pavilion of *Expo '86.* To the left of this booth is a digital clock with times of major cities around the world. Press a button to see what time it is back home, and then climb the stairs to the promenade "deck" overlooking the harbor. If you are facing the water, the white teflon sails will be on the same level to the left. Quite likely there will be a cruise ship, bound to or from Alaska, in a slip to the right.

Just like a cruise ship, Canada Place has several encircling decks. The

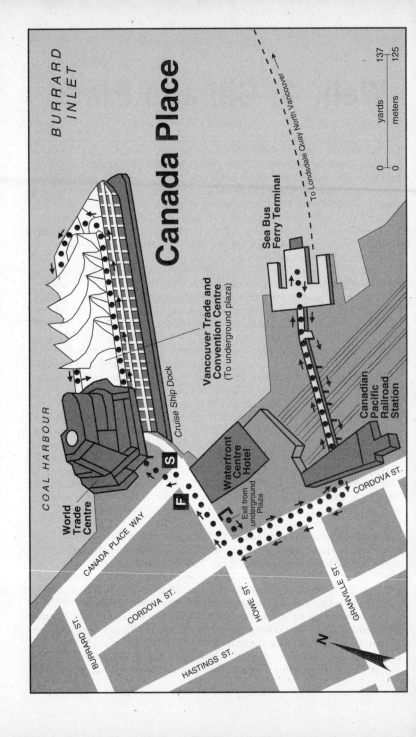

Canada Place

BURRARD INLET

COAL HARBOUR

World Trade Centre

Cruise Ship Dock

Vancouver Trade and Convention Centre
(To underground plaza)

Sea Bus Ferry Terminal

To Londsdale Quay North Vancouver

Waterfront Centre Hotel

Exit from underground Plaza

Canadian Pacific Railroad Station

CANADA PLACE WAY

CORDOVA ST.

CORDOVA ST.

BURRARD ST.

HOWE ST.

HASTINGS ST.

GRANVILLE ST.

S

F

N

yards   0   137
meters 0   125

promenade deck itself is well marked with historical and viewpoint information, and each is represented by a plaque designed to look like a page out of the city's past. Here you're standing on the site of historic Pier B-C, which, when it opened on July 4, 1927, was the most modern and efficient terminal for *Canadian Pacific Railway*'s rapidly growing trade route with the Orient. (And those straits of commerce have not waned; this is far and away Canada's busiest deep-sea harbor.)

Yet it was the *"Empresses,"* the grand old ladies of Vancouver's economic history, that set the stage for that success. Three decades before the opening of Pier B-C, the *Empress of India,* the *Empress of China,* and the *Empress of Japan,* members of the *Canadian Pacific Railway*'s merchant fleet, began trading with their Oriental partners from the port of Vancouver. Onetime members of the Cunard line, the *Empress* liners filled their holds with the finest of teas, spices, and silks from the Orient; they also carried the Royal Mail of Great Britain (the railway won the trans-Pacific contract in the 1890s). The ships sailed across the Pacific and docked here, where *CPR*'s "Tea" and "Silk" trains stood at the ready. With such precious cargo, these trains were given top priority as they whistled their way on the 4-day transcontinental run to Montreal. From there, silks were re-routed by ship to London and by rail to New York. The *Empress of India,* which was the first one to arrive in Vancouver on April 28, 1891, had on board 131 salon passengers, 355 Chinese immigrants in steerage, and cargoes of tea, silk, opium, rice — and the Royal Mail. The British were elated with the first *Empress* sailing: Mail delivery using the Yokohama-Vancouver-Montreal-London route took 26 days; the previous route through the Suez Canal took 45 days.

Walk along the promenade toward the water. To the right, beyond the cruise ship dock, the *SeaBus* catamarans glide in and out of the docks of the old red-brick, stone-trimmed *Canadian Pacific Railway* station, now the terminal for this streamlined commuter ferry. Beyond the station, note the green dome of the Sun Tower on the skyline. When completed in 1912 for the now-defunct *World* newspaper, this was the tallest building in the British Empire — and the place where Sarah Ann MacLagen became the first woman editor/publisher in Canada. As you walk along you'll hear the Westminster chimes of the Gastown Steam Clock announcing the time on the quarter-hour.

On a clear day from this spot along the promenade you can see on the distant horizon Washington State's Mt. Baker or, as native legend calls it, the Great White Watcher (because of its snow-capped summit). Lummi Indians referred to it as Shot at the Point, because of its history of volcanic activity. The last recorded eruption was in 1843, but steam and volcanic gasses regularly escape.

As you continue north along the promenade a bright red building will come into view on the waterfront: The oldest existing tenant here is CanFisco, the Canadian Fishing Company. Benefiting from its proximity to the railway for quick transportation to world markets, this fish-processing plant began as a halibut processor for the then-parent New England Fish Company. Today that connection still works to bring canned BC salmon to market, a 76-year tradition. Indeed, BC salmon processing has been a major industry in the province since the first cannery was built on the Fraser River in 1870. Note the fishing boats in the waters of Burrard Inlet here. A flurry of sea gulls will pinpoint the seiners and trollers with their catches of salmon, sole, and shellfish. Early vessels used in BC were constructed in the style of Atlantic schooners, but the traditional West Coast design, which moved the wheelhouse forward, allowing more fishing gear on board, is what you'll see on the water today.

Look across the inlet to North Vancouver, where the Second Narrows Bridge (the bridge over the Second Narrows) has been taking traffic from downtown since the first one was built in 1925. At the North Shore shipyards at the foot of the bridge an important moment in military history was played out when submarines were secretly built for the Imperial Russian Navy to help the Allied cause of World War I. Today, shipyards along the inlet are kept busy with less clandestine projects, including the refitting of *BC Ferries.* Continue walking to the north end of the promenade, and go down a set of steps and then up another to the circular observation deck, where two metal lions appear to be jumping through a hoop of lights. These feline fellows point out the location of Vancouver's famed Lions mountain peaks. From here you can see it all: the harbor, railway, Stanley Park, floatplanes and helicopters, tugboats and dredges, even a grebe, or gull, or duck, or wayward sea lion. And above it all, those legendary lions. The peaks have had other names, but this one, which refers to their resemblance to the crouching lions of British heraldry, has long reigned.

Leave the observation deck. The steep stairs down on the left lead to a brick courtyard with tiered benches that are perfect for sunning if the day is right. The *Prow* restaurant (phone: 604-684-1339), with its expensive fare and great views, is in a niche to the left. If you prefer an easier route, follow the curve of the observation deck to the left, go down 6 steps, veer to the right and follow this walkway. You're now 1 deck below the sails. Continue past the glass elevators on the right to a ramp that leads up to the *CN IMAX Theatre* (phone: 604-682-4629), or go down to the next level. With film presentations on its giant, 5-story-high screen, the *CN IMAX* theater is well worth a stop — you might want to pick up a program or tickets and come back later. Some of the original titles are still the best: Watch for *North of Superior,* Graeme Ferguson's film of majestic Northern Ontario scenery; or *Volcano,* a film by Christopher Chapman. Proceed down the winding ramp to the bottom. A few feet from the base, on the left, is a door to an inner staircase that leads to the cruise-ship level and to the *Gourmet Express* food fair, where you can have an inexpensive snack with a million-dollar view. For a change of pace, try some traditional BC native fare, some salmon or a buffalo burger on bannock bread from the *First Nations* food stall. Nonie Hall serves up fresh barbecued sockeye, caught by her father on the Fraser River, and Rena Henry, of the Cowichan Band, bakes the best crusty bannock you'll find in these parts. The West Coast bannock is pan-fried, much like the fried bread made by Native Americans throughout the US and Canada.

On this level are shops and the entrance to the cruise ship arrival and departure terminals. Like Seattle to the south, Vancouver is a terminus for cruise operators who run sightseeing and nature trips along the coasts of north British Columbia and Alaska. (In 1991, 400,000 passengers made the trip in 22 ships from 12 lines.) Go back up the stairs and continue walking along the deck. All along this lengthy promenade are white metal benches and flower-filled planters, making it a pleasant place to watch the harbor traffic. In summer, you will probably see a cruise ship berthed on the right. Directly ahead, the blue-glass towers of *Waterfront Centre* reflect the clouds of the mountains, while the regal Marine Building peeks out from behind its sleek, modern neighbors.

Walk toward the "stern" of Canada Place, and, with the sails on your left, you will see a portion of Stanley Park across Coal Harbour to the right. At Lumberman's Arch was the village of Whoi Whoi (the Masks), home of the Squamish Band of the Coast Salish Indians (see *Walk 1: Stanley Park*). The grassy area visible from here is Hallelujah Point, the place where the Salvation Army prayed, sang, and picnicked at the turn of the century, and to the left of the point, outlined by blue-topped boathouses, is Deadman's Island, home to the Naval Reserve HMCS *Discovery*. For centuries, it was an Indian burial ground; during the smallpox epidemic of 1888 the island was turned into a quarantine area.

Continue to the end of the promenade and enter the Vancouver Trade and Convention Centre through the glass doors on the left. Look up to the second story of this atrium, above the ballroom doors, and you will see a waterfall. In the lobby there are some fine examples of West Coast Indian totem poles of animals and legendary figures. The pole on the right, carved by the Kwaki-utl tribe, stands 45 feet high and for 50 years was in Stanley Park; the remaining ones were carved by the 'Ksan, who lived on the Skeena River. All of the poles are more than 80 years old. Walk toward the street-side doors; to their right is an escalator leading to the underground walkway that con-nects the convention center with the *Waterfront Centre* hotel. On this lower level are shops and a food court in a nautical theme. (Even the servers at *McDonald's* wear sailor-type uniforms.) An outside seating area is enhanced by another waterfall.

Cross through this underground plaza to the street exit, where you'll emerge at the corner of Cordova and Howe Streets; go east on Cordova to the historic *CPR* station. Enter the renovated terminal through the heavy wooden doors, pick up a cappuccino from *Starbuck's* (phone: 604-682-0721), find a bench, and sit beneath the vaulted dome and listen to classical music being played by the tuxedoed piano player. Lovely. A glance at the upper reaches of this neo-classical building reveals a series of 16 paintings depicting the scenes a traveler would encounter on the train ride across Canada. The station — now funneling commuters, not chamomile — was restored in the 1970s and is a pocket of extreme civility for surburbanites who seldom take time to enjoy the soft colors, potted plants, tile floors, and Ionic columns of a more graceful age. Built from 1912 to 1914, this is the third *CPR* station on this site. The first, a wood-frame building, was erected in 1887 to welcome the inaugural transcontinental train to the new city of Vancouver.

Walk to the *SeaBus* through the wide central arch, following a lengthy passageway that leads to the docks. There is a row of ticket-vending machines at the entrance. Ferries leave and return at 15-minute intervals 7 days a week (first runs are later in the day on Sundays and holidays) and return late into the night. The one-way fare is good for 90 minutes and can be used for return within that period. The trip takes less than a half hour. Once on board, try to find a seat at the front so that you have a good view of the inlet in action. On the port side, look for the commuter floatplanes that fly passengers to points all along the coast and to Vancouver Island. A heli-jet pad, to star-board, is the terminal for regular flights to Victoria. You will see seiners, pleasure boats, tugboats, perhaps a cruise ship, and always a line of freighters in the harbor, waiting to load or unload at a harbor terminal. From here ships load grain and lumber, and unload cars, appliances, and other consumer goods from Japan. The perspective from the water is entirely different from the one you get from land, but always there are the surrounding mountains to frame it, just so. If you want, you can stay on board for a couple of rides and really experience this very inexpensive "harbor cruise."

At the ferry terminal on the North Shore is the *Lonsdale Quay,* a market-place with produce stands, upscale shops and boutiques, and dining spots. If you stop to explore, you can return to the ferry along the brick overpass, following the signs. On your return, exit the *CPR* terminal and walk west to Howe Street, then north 1 block to Canada Place Way.

Walk 5: Point Grey

Walks in other parts of the city are rich in pioneer history, in ethnic diversity, in bustling urban energy, but for the spirit of the place come here, to the cliffs of Point Grey. Seen from the air, the coastal land that makes up modern-day Vancouver resembles a great elk, with Stanley Park, Canada Place, Gastown, even historic Hastings making up the antlers. Point Grey, the site of the University of British Columbia (UBC) and its *Museum of Anthropology,* are the mouth of the beast.

Long before there was a university here, long before there was a Vancouver, the waters off this point of land, jutting 200 feet above the Strait of Georgia, were making history. It was off these cliffs, in June 1792, that the last Spanish exploration of the inlet took place. (Spain had a long history in these waters. In 1592 Greek navigator Apostolos Valerianos, who sailed for Spain under the assumed name of Juan de Fuca, named the saltwater arm of the Pacific Ocean separating the southern part of Vancouver Island from mainland US. In 1795 the Spaniards ceased their expeditions, thus ceding the land to the British.) That month in 1792 Captain George Vancouver was doing his surveys for the British when, quite by chance, his vessel, the *Discovery,* came upon the Spanish ships *Sutil* and *Mexicana,* captained respectively by Dionisio Alcala Galiano and Cayetano Valdes. They exchanged information and all continued the exploration together. Sixteen years later, Scottish fur trader Simon Fraser (of the North West Company), traveling upon the river that now bears his name, paddled close to these cliffs, having completed his historic trek. Fraser was the first explorer to blaze an overland route to the Pacific.

The best place to begin a tour of the University of British Columbia — arguably one of the most beautifully sited universities in the world — and a bit of Pacific Spirit Regional Park, is at the main bus terminal — known as "The Loop" — at University Boulevard. There is bus service to this point from all areas of the city (call *BC Transit;* phone: 604-261-5100); if you're driving from downtown, go south on Burrard Street and cross the Burrard Street Bridge (keeping to the left lane and following the street's curve). At 12th Avenue, turn right, and drive west (12th will become 10th and then becomes University Boulevard). Turn right at Westbrook Mall and continue for a short distance to Student Union Boulevard. Turn left and follow the sign to North Parkade (admission charge).

Roughly the same size as Stanley Park, the UBC campus and its environs is an inviting place for walking. This stroll will take about 2 hours, longer if you visit the museum and gardens. Wear sturdy (comfortable) shoes.

Just 4 years ago these cliffs and the forest adjacent to UBC were dedicated as part of Pacific Spirit Regional Park, so nature and wilderness trails and

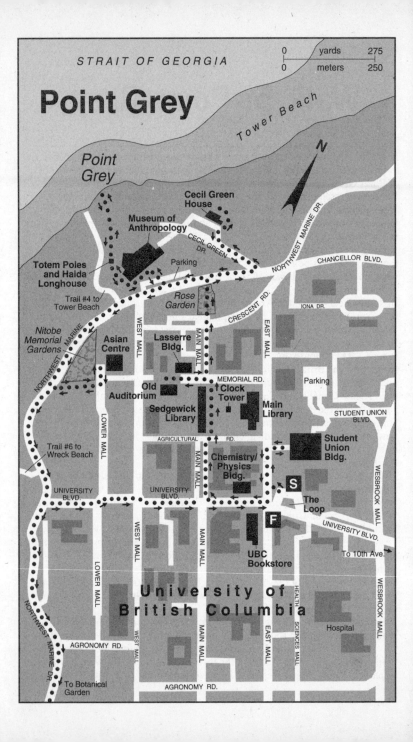

facilities here are still being developed. But the cliffs themselves — with their windswept brush, trees, and grasses — offer spectacular views of the cobalt-blue waters of the Strait of Georgia. At the foot of the cliffs are cobble and sand beaches.

Follow the signs to the Student Union Building and pick up a free map from the information desk. From here in summer you can join a student-guided campus tour. The 90-minute tours leave twice a day Mondays through Fridays at 10 AM and 1 PM, from May to August. Tours starting at 3 PM and on weekends can also be arranged (UBC Dept. of Community Relations; phone: 604-822-3131). Pick up some lunch (go West Coast with a vegetarian sandwich — avocado, tomato, bean sprouts, and cream cheese on whole-grain bread — and natural fruit juice at the sandwich bar of the *Gallery Lounge,* along with a cookie or chocolate bun at *Blue Chip Cookies*) to enjoy as a picnic on your walk.

Walk toward the Loop. In front of the Student Union Building on the right as you exit is a 12-foot faux-marble statue of the Goddess of Democracy, a replica of the torch-bearing goddess that was destroyed June 4, 1989, during the Tiananmen Square student uprising in Beijing. The replica was erected 2 years after the incident by three groups: the *Chinese Students and Scholars Association;* the *Vancouver Society in Support of the Democracy Movement;* and the *UBC Alma Mater Society.*

At University Boulevard (the Loop) turn right. You may want to cross the street for a browse at the *UBC Bookstore* (6200 University Blvd.; phone: 604-822-2665), the largest academic bookstore in the country, which has a good selection of university souvenirs, from sweaters to spoons.

Follow University Boulevard to Main Mall. The university's oldest building (on the right) is the Chemistry/Physics Building, begun in 1913. Turn right on Main Mall with its grassy median to the Great Trek Cairn, the first official structure of UBC.

Advanced learning in the province had begun in 1908 at Fairview Campus, today the site of Vancouver General Hospital. The school was an affiliate of Montreal's McGill University, one of Canada's oldest seats of higher learning; it didn't take long for the Vancouver branch to become overpopulated, and by 1913 there was a growing movement for a BC university. Land was acquired on historic Point Grey, clearing began, and construction was just getting underway when building plans were shelved at the onset of World War I. Students, ever more insistent on independence from McGill, fought for the establishment of the University of British Columbia — with or without new buildings; and in 1915, the university, the province's first, was born. But after another 7 years of inaction, with no telling when building on the Point Grey site would begin, BC's first "Student Power" demonstration swung into action. A precursor of successful student-run actions in the 1960s and 1970s that influenced provincial politics here, the class of '22–'23 took matters into its own hands: They arranged a public awareness week, sent a 60,000-name petition to the legislature, and marched on Point Grey by the hundreds; this show of support for the new university would go down in Vancouver history as the Great Trek. The march — on October 28, 1922 —

concluded with the installation of the cairn, the first official structure on the promised academic land.

Not long after that, work resumed on the Chemical/Physics Building, and construction of other university buildings began in earnest. Since those days, two plaques have been added to the cairn: one for the time capsule commemorating the Great Trek, prepared by alumni and sealed in 1972 by the march's chairman, Dr. A. B. Richards. The other is a 1967 tribute to Canada's 100th birthday, a Centennial Time Capsule, added by the *UBC Science Undergrad Society.*

Continue walking toward the courtyard and note those rather strange-looking orbs poking up from the ground. Fir trees and mountains in the distance reflect off the surface of these architectural curiosities, which act as light collectors for the cavernous, below-ground, modern Sedgewick Library. (It was situated underground to preserve the trees and the view above.) Year-round, trees along this route are rich in bird life, with starlings, towhees, chickadees, and rosy finches in the maples.

To the right is the gray granite Main Library, the second-oldest building on campus. Look closely above the entrance and note a pair of gargoyles (one a monkey and the other a bearded old man), which were carved and installed at the time of the famous Scopes trial in the 1920s. The library itself, which has the largest collection of books in the province, was finished in 1925 and is one of 21 libraries on campus. In front of the library to the left is the Ladner Clock Tower, with its 150,000 chimes. Atop this landmark UBC's engineering students have (on more than one occasion) hoisted a Volkswagen as part of their zany orientation rituals.

The best view of the library is from a bench near the fountain (not far from the Ladner Clock Tower). It is in this core area of campus that Frank Buck, UBC's professor of landscape architecture from 1920 to 1932, designed these grounds of grassy hills, shrubs, and trees. One of his more notable achievements was the planting of the giant sequoia, a towering evergreen native to the mountainous regions of Southern California; this is an especially magnificent sight when lit for *Christmas.* The tree that stands at the northwest corner in front of the Main Library came from a Fraser Valley cutting. It's believed gold seekers from California coming to Canada in the mid-1800s planted the first giant sequoias in the Fraser Valley.

Return to the Main Mall, keeping an eye on the flagpole ahead, a helpful aid to navigation on this walk. Sidetrack down Memorial Road to view the 2-story, Gerhard Class sculpture, the *Tuning Fork,* in the courtyard between the Lasserre Building and the Old Auditorium where Faculty of Music students practice. With "Wet Coast" weather in mind, Class created his sculpture using corten steel, a metal that rusts easily. The vermillion-colored water that continually drains from the sculpture adds to its character.

Follow beneath the covered walkway, with its columns that are illuminated at night. At the end of this path, almost mesmerizing with its steadfast gaze, is the marble *Asiatic Head* by Otto Fischer-Credo, a work donated to UBC in 1958. Turn the corner; on the left is a bust of Dr. Norman MacKenzie, one of the longest-standing presidents of the university (1944–1962); the

Centre of Fine Arts bears his name. To the right, with a background of foliage, is the sculpture *Three Forms,* by the multitalented actor, Robert Clothier, who became internationally known to television audiences in the role of Relic, a disreputable character on "The Beachcombers," a TV series that depicted life in and around BC coastal settlements. Clothier's sculpture won the University Purchase Prize in UBC's first Outdoor Sculpture Show in 1956. Nearby is *Reclining Figure,* a small red stone sculpture created by artist Jan Zach.

Now go toward that helpful flagpole and on a railing, just behind it, is a cast bronze plaque that identifies the North Shore mountain peaks that you can see in the distance.

Walk down the small flight of stone steps to the little Rose Garden, a richly perfumed area of 300 different types of roses, more than enough to provide a fitting background for the wedding photographers who are often at work here. Also at work are gray squirrels, who frolic among the bushes in fearless abandon, clamoring for handouts. Continue along the path, with its fragrant border of daphnes, toward the water and Northwest Marine Drive. Cross the roadway and on the sidewalk turn right. Walk for a short distance and turn into the lane marked Cecil Green Park Drive.

Here you will find one of the earliest buildings on Point Grey. This mansion was known as Kanakla (House on the Cliff) when it was built in 1912 for lawyer Edward P. Davis, who watched the university grow up around him. In 1967, Canada's centennial year, it was purchased by industrialist and founder of Texas Instruments Cecil Green and his wife Ida and donated to the university as a social hall. The house is not open to visitors, but the porte cochere at the entrance is accented with trailing wisteria and on the right is a 2-story coach house where you'll see large rings that were used for tying up horses.

Circle the house going toward the water, and, from the large verandah, peek in the front windows at the parquet floor, the crystal chandeliers, and the grand piano, which is said to have been played by the great Polish concert pianist Ignace Jan Paderewski. The verandah steps are the best spot on the point to take time out for that picnic lunch as you admire the breathtaking views of the mountains and the Georgia Strait.

Backtrack to Northwest Marine Drive and follow the signs to the UBC *Museum of Anthropology* (phone: 604-822-5087). Vancouver architect Arthur Erickson (whose work includes the Canadian Embassy in Washington and the San Diego Convention Center) designed this award-winning structure, incorporating the theme of totems, mountains, and ocean. Have a close look at the large cedar entry columns and doors which illustrate the Skawah legend; they were carved by 'Ksan craftsmen at the restored Gitskan village near Hazelton, in northwestern BC. The doors were a gift to the university from the graduating class of 1974 (with financial assistance from the *National Museum of Man* in Ottawa). You will probably want to return for a relaxed visit to this museum. Closed Mondays; admission charge (see *Memorable Museums* in DIVERSIONS).

Circle to the back of the museum. Here in a natural setting, not far from the cliff's edge, with the mountains in the distance, are six authentic Haida totem poles. Standing stark and weathered by the elements, the totems create a mystical aura: Shin-high wild grasses wave in the constant breeze, bald eagles soar above. Two of the poles here were carved by the late Mungo Martin, a revered Haida craftsman who was the creative spiritual link for a new generation of carvers to their almost forgotten past. The best-known is artist Bill Reid, a man of Haida heritage whose monumental bronze sculpture, *Spirit of the Haida Gwaii* (Islands of the People), has been admired by thousands in the courtyard of Canada's much-praised embassy in Washington, DC. Look closely at Martin's memorial poles to Chief Kwekwelis and Chief Kalilix. Other totems here include the traditional Hok-hok (a bird-monster), the Ancestral Chief with Frog, Bear with Salmon, Killer Whale, and the Beaver with Human Face on Tail. Sunsets from this vantage point in the western skies over the Pacific Ocean are phenomenal.

To the left of a grassy area (when you are facing the water) sits a Haida longhouse and mortuary chamber. Reconstructed in 1958 by Reid (whose work you will also see inside the museum), the buildings are representative of Haida villages around Skidegate and Masset on the lush Queen Charlotte Islands and of the southern part of the Alaska panhandle. Before the decimation of the Haida population — due to the introduction of smallpox by white settlers in the late 19th century — each family dwelling held an average of 25 to 40 members. The houses here are currently used for museum receptions, workshops, and theatrical performances.

Walk across the grass to the chain-link fence erected at the edge of the cliff. Down below is Tower Beach; a favorite of students, it is less crowded and a bit easier to reach than other beaches along the point. The concrete blocks visible at water level are remains of military buildings constructed during World War II to help warn the city of expected attacks from the Pacific. The shore is also rich in marine life, including harbor seals, Stellar's sea lions, blue herons, bald eagles, and sea gulls. (To reach Tower Beach, return to the sidewalk at Northwest Marine Drive, turn right, go past the museum's parking lot, and follow signs that lead to Trail No. 4, the path to the beach.)

Return to Northwest Marine Drive; with the water on the right, follow the signs that lead toward Nitobe Memorial Gardens. At Trail No. 6 a very steep path leads down the cliff to Wreck Beach, which most Canadians will cite as evidence of Vancouver's wacky image. This 6-mile (10-km) strand is Vancouver's only "clothing optional" beach. Popular with nudists since the 1920s, it is the site of special events on *BC Day* weekend (the first weekend in August), including sand-castle contests, body painting, and family barbecues, when 10,000 free-spirited participants join in. From the roadside the landscape of thick rhododendron bushes and towering Douglas firs conspires against voyeurs. Indeed, only the very agile should descend the steep trail to the beach.

Return to Northwest Marine Drive and follow the signs to Nitobe Memorial Garden, on the left. Designed by Kannosuke Mori in the late 1950s and opened in 1960, the garden is dedicated to the memory of Dr. Inazo Nitobe, a Japanese educator, scholar, and diplomat who died while visiting Victoria in 1933; admission charge (also see *Glorious Gardens* in DIVERSIONS).

Backtrack on Northwest Marine Drive to the other side of the Nitobe Gardens on Lower Mall; cross the Mall, and in a woodsy setting you will find the not-to-be-missed *Asian Centre* (1871 West Mall; phone: 604-822-2746; open Mondays through Fridays 9 AM to 5 PM). Designed to resemble a Japanese farmhouse, the building was the Sanyo Pavilion at *Expo '70* in Osaka, Japan. To the right, resembling a giant wishing well, is the Pacific Bell Tower with its pagoda-style roof, from a design that dates back 800 years. A gift in 1983 of the Japanese government, the bell is one of two in North America (the other is in San Diego) designed by Masahiko Katori, a celebrated Japanese artist who also created the Hiroshima Peace Bell. The characters etched on the bell translate to "Clear Thoughts Lead to a Tranquil Mind."

The landscaping here is the handiwork of Kannosuke Mori, the man responsible for the Nitobe Memorial Garden. If the center is open, cross the walkway between the two green still ponds and enter the building. From the entranceway look behind you at the reflecting pools with their mirror images of bushes, fir trees, and the Bell Tower. At one time the ponds were stocked with goldfish, but bald eagles and blue herons considered them a special treat, so they were replaced by the less vulnerable (but no less colorful) carp. Look up at the center's white ceiling beams, whose installation was a challenge for the builders. The structure had been dismantled, and each piece numbered, when it was sent from Japan. But the beams were left outside while the rest of the building was being erected and all the numbers washed off in the rain, leaving construction workers with a giant-size puzzle. The building houses one of North America's largest collections of Asian books and manuscripts, the oldest dating back to AD 986, as well as a noted collection of Japanese woodblocks and copper-engraved maps. Visitors are welcome to tour the rooms where these artifacts are on display.

Return to Northwest Marine Drive and continue walking to the left. In a brief time, the peace may be shattered by the sound of blaring stereos perched on the windowsills of coed housing as Northwest Marine Drive curves along the waterfront. There are washrooms and pay telephones at Beach Trail No. 6, as well as bicycle racks and a car park. Bus No. 47 (call *BC Transit;* phone: 604-261-5100) stops here. Avid and weekend gardeners alike will want to continue to the UBC Botanical Garden (it's about a 25-minute walk); established in 1916, it is the oldest university botanical garden in Canada (see *Glorious Gardens* in DIVERSIONS). Admission charge.

If you are not going on to the garden, turn left at University Boulevard, then walk along the boulevard for a block or so to the *Ponderosa Café* (2071 West Mall; phone: 604-822-2372) for a cinnamon bun (a UBC specialty) and coffee. It was on this site in 1916 that "Botany" John Davidson, the first botanist hired by the provincial government, started the original botanical garden. Brought in 4 years earlier to do a botanical survey of British Columbia flora, he started a herbarium of pressed specimens that now numbers 500,000. In 1913 he started his garden in Colony Farm in Essondale and 3 years later transferred almost 30,000 herbs, shrubs, and trees to a 7½-acre site on the university grounds as a living classroom. The garden was dug up in the 1950s and the herbarium and sundial were moved to the present site of the UBC Botanical Garden. After a rest here you'll be ready to continue back to the bus loop where the walk began, or to the parkade.

Walk 6: Historic Steveston

With its bountiful gardens and splendid sea vistas, Vancouver offers solitude and calm as do few other modern cities. But even here the visitor may feel the need to get away from the city, and when that spirit strikes, head for historic Steveston. This quaint, picture-postcard-pretty fishing village, about a 45-minute drive south of downtown, is also the largest commercial fishing harbor in Canada. To experience it to the fullest, it's best to start out from downtown in mid-morning, tour the village, have a fish lunch (or the more traditional fish 'n' chips or bowl of chowder from a dockside takeout), and take an inexpensive 30-minute harbor tour to get a close look at the wildlife (bald eagles and red tail hawks) and marine life (sea lions) aboard a flat-bottom boat (see below). Then go for a walk along the dikes. In all — depending on how long you'd like to linger — this walk should take about 2½ hours.

The most relaxing way to get here is by city bus from downtown Vancouver. (Although the village has developed separately from Vancouver, it is a part of the district of Richmond, which in turn is a part of the Greater Vancouver Regional District.) In the morning you'll be going against rush-hour traffic. *BC Transit* (phone: 604-261-5100) buses run several times each hour from the Hastings and Howe Streets area. If you drive, take Highway 99 south and exit onto Steveston Highway. (In summer and autumn, stop at some of the roadside fruit-and-vegetable stands along the way, and pick through the fresh peaches, plums, berries, tomatoes, and squash; this part of Vancouver has the best farm land.) Go about 5 miles (8 km) and turn left onto No. 1 Road, going about a kilometer to the traffic lights at Moncton Street. This takes you to the 3-block heritage area that is the heart of the place. Although this entire area is not an officially designated historic site, new construction must be approved by a design panel of local residents, and building codes are in effect.

The historic section of the village is along Moncton, Chatham, and Bay-view Streets, from No. 1 Road to Third Avenue. Intermingled with points of historic interest on this walk is a lively variety of shops featuring local crafts, art, antiques, souvenirs, and several catch-of-the-day seafood restaurants. Just 4 blocks farther west, along picturesque streets with several 1-story, false-fronted shops (reminiscent of a western movie set), is Garry Point Park; rimmed by a dike, it affords views of the North Shore mountains and, to the south, the American Gulf Islands. A block south of this historic little enclave is one of the only remaining stretches of waterfront in North America where

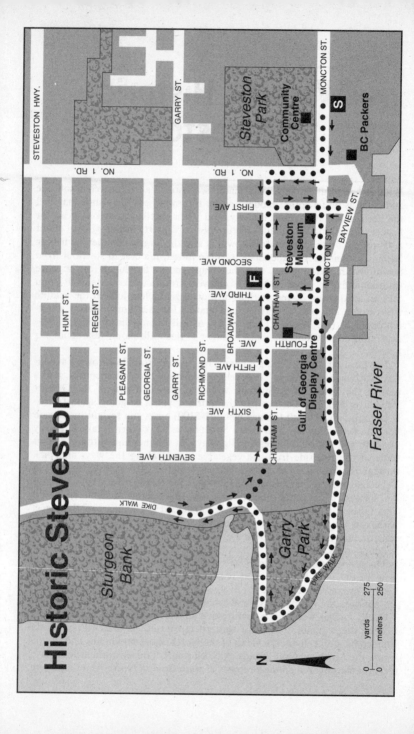

Historic Steveston

STEVESTON HWY.

NO. 1 RD.

GARRY ST.

Steveston Park

Community Centre

S

BC Packers

HUNT ST.

REGENT ST.

PLEASANT ST.

GEORGIA ST.

GARRY ST.

RICHMOND ST.

FIRST AVE.

SECOND AVE.

F

THIRD AVE.

BROADWAY

FOURTH AVE.

FIFTH AVE.

SIXTH AVE.

SEVENTH AVE.

CHATHAM ST.

Steveston Museum

MONCTON ST.

BAYVIEW ST.

Gulf of Georgia Display Centre

DIKE WALK

Sturgeon Bank

Garry Park

DIKE WALK

Fraser River

N

yards 0   275
meters 0   250

the L-shape canneries and wharves designed for three-masted sailing vessels still stand.

Start this walking tour at the village park and adjacent community center (No. 1 Rd. and Moncton St.), which is close to both a bus stop and a parking lot. If you come here on July 1, you're in for a major treat. That's when the park, and the whole area, celebrates the *Salmon Festival.* An annual event since 1944, this has become the largest 1-day community festival in Canada. Up to 1,700 pounds of salmon (and 3,000 plates of chow mein) are served, and some of the best anglers in BC converge for the King of the Fraser fishing competition. The railway tracks here were once part of the *Sockeye Limited,* the name given to the Steveston tram that operated between the village and downtown Vancouver from 1906 to 1959. Part of the inter-urban line that replaced stagecoaches, it was the rapid transit of its day; its loss is still lamented by car-pooling commuters.

Look toward the water; just a bit south on No. 1 Road you'll see the largest legacy of the early salmon canning industry. The blue-and-white building is the headquarters of BC Packers, heir to the Imperial Cannery, which opened for business on the waterfront in 1893. Today this packing company processes 40 million pounds of seafood each year.

Walk 1 block north on No. 1 Road to Chatham Street. Near this site in 1895, the Japanese Fishermen's Benevolent Fund founded the first area hospital. Now the Telephone Exchange Building, where for 40 years (until 1954) operators for BC Tel put through calls for villagers, this was the fishing community's third telephone link. The first (and, at the time, only) line from Vancouver was installed in 1891 at the general store on Second Avenue by the New Westminster and Burrard Inlet Telephone Company. Youngsters made a habit of hanging around here so that they could deliver messages to villagers, at 10¢ apiece. In 1904 the BC Telephone Company took over. This wood-frame building was awarded landmark status 2 years ago. Adjacent is the Bill Rigby senior complex for retired fishermen, a property owned by the *United Fishermen and Allied Workers Union.*

Walk west on Chatham Street. At the northeast corner of Second Avenue is the *Steveston Bicycle Shop,* housed in a former United Church building (1894), a gray stucco structure complete with steeple and pink, green, and blue trim. Built for the Methodist congregation at a cost of $700, the church had an adjacent house for the minister and for missionaries who flocked here during the summer salmon run, when the population swelled with rowdy itinerants who were considered prime candidates for soul-saving. Directly north of the building is the church that replaced the original on this site in 1977.

Walk back (east) to First Avenue and go south 1 block to Moncton Street for a look at the *Steveston Museum* (no admission charge; 3811 Moncton St.; phone: 604-271-6868; open Mondays through Saturdays 9:30 AM to 1 PM and 1:30 to 5 PM) housed in an original (1905), cream-colored, pre-fab bank building. This branch of the Northern Crown Bank (which was absorbed by the Royal Bank of Canada in 1918) is the only remaining building of what was once Northern's 350 western Canada branches. It was built in 4-foot sections by the BC Mills and Trading Company in New Westminster, shipped down the Fraser River, and assembled on this site. In addition to being the village museum, the building today houses a post office. Its entrance is draped with fishing nets and on the first floor the bank manager's office is just as it was in 1905, complete with business machines of the day. (In 1918, it escaped a devastating fire that destroyed most of the town south of Moncton Street.) On the second floor is a turn-of-the-century dining room and bedroom with furnishings arranged in the style of the day. Also here are Japanese and Chinese memorabilia, including fan-tan stones, a ginger jar, and a portrait of laborers dressed in their Sunday best. Early Asian workers toiled under contract at farms and at work sites building dikes and irrigation ditches. Look for old photos of the *Steveston* hotel with tent camps of the "Sockeye Fusiliers" (more about them later). Behind the museum is a pleasant little park, complete with benches; it's a restful place for a moment's repose.

When Vancouver was in its infancy, Steveston was a bustling Saturday night boomtown, where in excess of 10,000 people would come to promenade the boardwalks above its muddy streets. Fishing fleets, with their land-hungry crews lusting for excitement, joined hundreds more men who toiled at the village's dozen canneries. Hotels, saloons, and houses of prostitution all did a brisk business.

Ironically, this little fishing village owes its beginnings to a farmer. Manoah Steves, the first white settler to bring his family — his wife and six children — to Lulu Island (now Richmond) arrived in 1877; he bought 300 acres of good farm land. Other farmers soon followed his lead, and today Richmond's dairy industry is an important part of the BC farm economy. Not far away, at the mouth of the Fraser River, the first cannery, the Phoenix, was built in 1882; others quickly sprang up. In 1889, deciding to compete with the newly declared city of Vancouver, Manoah's son, William took it upon himself to lay out the town site of Steves (which later was changed to Steveston), where the canneries were being built.

That same year the first Japanese fishermen arrived from the village of Wakayama, beginning a link between the two fishing villages that has remained intact — except during World War II, when Canadians of Japanese ancestry and Japanese immigrants were interned in holding camps away from their BC coastal villages. Today, family ties with relatives in Wakayama are as binding as ever. For 20 years the two centers have been "sister cities" and frequently hold cultural, business, and friendship exchanges.

Return to First Avenue and continue south (toward the water) to a curved-front building that points to one of the darker periods of BC history. Once the Buddhist Church and Hall, the religious center of life for the Japanese, this 2-story building fell to disuse during the period of Japanese internment. The first building on this site was the *Star* hotel, which burned down in the 1918 fire; in 1946 the building was renovated into a 420-seat movie house, which closed in 1960. The building was vacant at press time, but in its time it has been put to a wide range of commercial uses, from a sausage factory to a flower shop.

Backtrack to Moncton Street, and turn west. Past the museum is the

Steveston Cannery Café (3711 Moncton St.; phone: 604-272-1222), one of the village's oldest buildings, with a flower-filled rowboat "docked" near the entrance. Built before 1900 as a cook house for the Lighthouse Cannery, it remained in that capacity for only 18 years, until fire destroyed the cannery. It was a private house until 1942, when a storefront was added and it became a radio repair shop. In 1984, it returned to its original function as an eatery. Stop here for good coffee and a slice of one of Judy's deep-dish pies. Cross Moncton Street and walk west to the brick Hepworth Building, the only structure on the south side of this street to escape the fire. From here the town doctor of the same name left for his house calls. Today it is home to well-stocked *Marty's Antiques Shop* (3580 Moncton St.; phone: 604-271-5637) and other shops and offices. Continue on Moncton Street to Third Avenue and turn right (north). On the corner is the old *Sockeye* hotel, now known as the *Steveston*. After extensive modernization all that remains of the original are two distinctive bay windows in the front of the building. The northern wing was added in the 1950s. This was also near the site in 1900 of the tent camp of the "Sockeye Fusiliers." Marking a dramatic moment in BC labor history, fishermen laid down their nets in a well-organized strike, demanding 25¢ per fish from the more than 30 canneries on the Lower Fraser River. The federal government answered by sending 160 armed men of the Duke of Connaught's Own Rifles to prevent riots, and the soldiers were sarcastically dubbed the "Sockeye Fusiliers" by the angry strikers. Full-scale violent outbreaks were avoided, though; the fishermen finally settled for 19¢ a fish and the soldiers broke camp.

Just north of the hotel (on Third Ave.) is a restored heritage building that was once Steveston's Municipal Hall and Courthouse. Behind this structure in a white concrete building with a flat roof, the Gulf of Georgia Cannery Society operates the *Gulf of Georgia Display Centre* (12138 Fourth Ave; phone: 604-272-5045; call for hours), 2 rooms of memorabilia and artifacts that date back to the first days of the fishing industry. At one time this building was the cannery office; the former manager's office boasts a vintage time clock. Stop by for a look at a Nootka dugout canoe, handmade nets, and a model of a period canning line. Now retrace your steps and follow Third Avenue to the harborfront to take a look at the former Gulf of Georgia Cannery, dubbed "monster cannery." Completed in 1894, it soon was the largest cannery in the province. Until 1946, salmon and herring was canned here, and for the next 33 years it was used by the Canadian Fishing Company (Canfisco) for herring products. The classic L-shape cannery with seine net loft to the west was declared a National Historic Site in 1978; today Parks Canada plans to open the old "monster" as a museum complex to commemorate the West Coast fishing industry. Opening is tentatively scheduled for next year, in time for its centennial. Across the harbor is a natural sandbar known locally as Shady Island (Steveston Island). Since 1954 it has only been accessible at low tide over the remnant of a rock causeway at its east end. Outside the harbor is the south arm of the Fraser River.

From here, go to *Dave's Fish and Chips* (3460 Moncton St; phone: 604-271-7555) for an inexpensive seafood lunch, or use the take-out window and carry your meal to a waterfront bench. Another good place for a seafood lunch is *Pelican Pete's* (3866 Bayview St.; phone: 604-275-8111) on the waterfront. Or, if you haven't the appetite for a full meal, pick up a cup of chowder at *Pajo's* (no phone; open summers only), which operates from a boat anchored at the dock. The fishing industry in this harbor has sustained the area for over 100 years, and today more than a thousand commercial boats tie up here (although they are not all berthed at the same time). In the winter there is cod, sole, prawns, and shrimp; in the spring, herring; and in the summer, salmon. From here you'll see freighters, tugs, Coast Guard and RCMP boats, and fishing boats galore.

For an even better overview of harbor life, an inexpensive 30-minute Cannery Channel Cruise is offered during the summer. (Times vary depending on weather and demand; call *Rainbow Charters* at 604-272-9187.) The tour aboard the 25-foot flat-bottom converted herring skiff leaves from the well-signed Fish Sales dock at the harbor. The narrated cruise notes the different types of vessels in the harbor and includes a history of the fishing industry here going back to the early 1880s, when sailing ships — not transcontinental trains — moved cargo. In those days, British sailing ships would come, via Africa and China, to stock up with salmon before their return trip to England. The boat travels close to Shady Island, where bald eagles, red tail hawks, and great blue herons abound. Sea lions can also be found in the harbor waters.

When you're ready to move on, walk west toward the park, circling the old Gulf of Georgia Cannery. At the south end of 6th Avenue, you will see a piece of an old steel bridge inside the dike. This is a remnant of the docking facilities of the *Motor Princess,* the old *CPR* ferry that ran between Steveston and Sidney on Vancouver Island from 1929 until the 1950s, when the terminal was moved to its current, much enlarged site at Tsawwassen. At the foot of 7th Avenue is the berth of the dredge MV *Fort Langley.* Now follow the curve into Garry Point Park. Coast Salish Indians camped here during the salmon runs in the 18th century. It received its current name in 1827 in honor of Nicholas Garry, a deputy governor of the Hudson's Bay Company who came here in search of a new fort site on the Fraser River. In 1899, the Scottish Canadian Cannery was built at the entrance to the slough where fishing boats still moor, so the area is still known as the "Scotch."

Walk north along the dike, which is part of a 12-mile trail system. Richmond, of which Steveston is a part, is the only community in Canada to be encircled by a protective wall of dikes. Look out upon the tall reeds and waving grasses. Look closer for blue herons, ducks of all types, and geese. The shimmering images of houses, on the other side of the dikes, reflected in the water, enhance the serene mood of this place. To return to the parking lot or pick up a return bus to downtown, retrace your route along the dike to Chatham Street and walk east to Second Avenue, where all the buses leave for downtown, or continue east to the parking lot.

INDEX

Index